LIFTING THE CHAINS

LIFTING THE CHAINS

THE BLACK FREEDOM STRUGGLE SINCE RECONSTRUCTION

WILLIAM H. CHAFE

OXFORD
UNIVERSITY PRESS

OXFORD
UNIVERSITY PRESS

Oxford University Press is a department of the University of Oxford. It furthers the University's objective of excellence in research, scholarship, and education by publishing worldwide. Oxford is a registered trade mark of Oxford University Press in the UK and certain other countries.

Published in the United States of America by Oxford University Press
198 Madison Avenue, New York, NY 10016, United States of America.

Library of Congress Cataloging-in-Publication Data
Names: Chafe, William H., 1942– author.
Title: Lifting the chains : the Black freedom struggle since Reconstruction/
William H. Chafe.
Other titles: Black freedom struggle since Reconstruction
Description: New York, NY : Oxford University Press, [2023] | Includes index.
Identifiers: LCCN 2023003794 (print) | LCCN 2023003795 (ebook) |
ISBN 9780197616451 (hardback) | ISBN 9780197616475 (epub)
Subjects: LCSH: African Americans—Civil rights—History. |
African Americans—Politics and government. | African Americans—Social conditions. |
Racism—United States—History. | United States—Race relations—History. |
African American soldiers—History.
Classification: LCC E185.61 .C49 2023 (print) | LCC E185.61 (ebook) |
DDC 973/.0496073—dc23/eng/20230127
LC record available at https://lccn.loc.gov/2023003794
LC ebook record available at https://lccn.loc.gov/2023003795

DOI: 10.1093/oso/9780197616451.001.0001

Printed by Sheridan Books, Inc., United States of America

For William E. Leuchtenburg, a brilliant historian, my mentor, and my dear friend for more than half a century.

Contents

Acknowledgements

This book could not have happened without the ongoing support of my colleagues in the history department of Duke University, and the historians of civil rights and Black history throughout the country. Most important for this work has been the scholarship of graduate students in the Duke Oral History Program.

My colleague Larry Goodwyn and I initiated the oral history program when we joined the Duke faculty in 1971, five months after completing graduate school. Both of us had been involved in civil rights during the 1960s, and both of us had used oral history interviews during our graduate student careers—Larry at the University of Texas, I at Columbia University. Amazingly, we were able to secure a $250,000 grant from the Rockefeller Foundation during our first year to provide graduate fellowships to white and Black students interested in interviewing activists in the civil rights movement to determine their motivation and their roles in the decision-making process of the movement.

Over the next four decades, we were able to raise millions of dollars more to support these graduate fellowships. Over four decades, we graduated thirty-eight PhDs, half Black, half white. Of these, twenty-eight published their dissertations on the movement, and sixteen won national book awards.

During this same period, I also interviewed numerous civil right activists for my own scholarship, including my book on the Greensboro sit-ins, which won the first Robert F. Kennedy Book Award in 1981.

Lifting the Chains could not have been written without the oral histories conducted by both our students and myself. I am also deeply grateful for the pathbreaking work of so many scholars who have written about race in America, especially my colleagues at Duke, William Darity, A. Kirsten Mullen, and Tim Tyson. I also deeply appreciate the comments of Tim Tyson and Thomas Lebien on an early version of the manuscript.

There has been no issue more central to American history than that of race, and racial inequality. This book could not have been written without our oral history program at Duke, and all the scholarship on race and civil rights history that has occurred in the last eight decades.

WILLIAM H. CHAFE

Introduction

This is a book about the long history of the Black freedom struggle in America—from the end of the Civil War until today. No American alive today is untouched by the story recounted here; all of us, whether we are aware of it or not, live with the consequences of this history.

When did my engagement with the Black freedom struggle begin? I grew up in a segregated white working-class neighborhood in Cambridge, Massachusetts. But I always went to schools that were racially diverse, because my white neighborhood was surrounded on one side by an all-Black community and on the other side by an Italian/Puerto Rican community. As students, we often played with each other after school—but we never went into each other's homes. Thus, from early childhood on, I became aware of, and was fascinated by, issues of racial difference.

Then as a teenager, I became part of a youth group at the Baptist church I attended four blocks from my house. The leader of our group was a man studying for the ministry who cared deeply about social issues. Every Sunday for four years, we talked about the Social Gospel, and what Jesus might do if faced with issues of racism and poverty.

That interest grew deeper when I went to Harvard as a commuter student in 1958. I took classes with sociology professors that focused on race. Then, when I started my history honors tutorial, I decided to write my senior thesis on W. E. B. Du Bois. I scoured his papers in New York, New Haven, and Cambridge, and became ever more fascinated by Du Bois's pivotal role in the emergence of the Black protest movement.

After a year at Union Theological Seminary in New York, I got a job teaching juniors and seniors at a progressive high school on the Upper West Side of Manhattan. Knowing of my interest in social justice, one of my colleagues—a physics teacher three times my age—said, "If you care so much about these issues, why don't you go down South with the civil rights movement?"

The next week, I got on a bus with fifty members of the Northern Student Movement and headed to Montgomery, Alabama, where our task was to lay the groundwork for the Selma to Montgomery march.

The next six days were the most important of my life. Our group was half Black, half white; half male, half female. We arrived late one evening at a Black Baptist church in Montgomery, where we slept on the floor. All night long, cars driven by Ku Klux Klan members drove around the church, beeping their horns. The next day we set out on our task—to recruit local residents to provide food for the marchers, and beds for them to sleep on. We worked in teams of two, usually integrated by race or gender. Our work went well, and we even thought about sitting in at local lunch counters—until we were told that SNCC, the Student Non-Violent Coordinating Committee, had no funds for lawyers to defend us if we were arrested.

Almost immediately, we sensed the tension that existed between the young people in SNCC and their older compatriots in the Southern Christian Leadership Conference (SCLC). SNCC people spoke with humorous contempt of "de Lawd," their nickname for Martin Luther King Jr. We also sensed their skepticism, and occasional hostility, toward Northerners. Long before Black Power became a slogan of SNCC and others in the movement, we saw its seeds growing in the response of the local movement people we were working with.

Four days later, we got on the bus and headed back to New York. Before we left, James Forman, executive secretary of SNCC, came on the bus to talk with us. This movement, he said, was the most radical and powerful since the Populist coalition of the 1890s, when poor white and poor Black farmers came together to try to overthrow the white ruling class in states like North Carolina, Alabama, and Kansas. It was a powerful message. And then we left.

For the next thirty-six hours, those of us on the bus talked non-stop. We reflected on what we had seen, heard, and learned. The conversations were intense. They concentrated on the divisions we had witnessed between SNCC and SCLC, but more importantly, on whether whites and Blacks could work together, and on what basis. We confronted the issue of whether "whitey" could fully understand the perspective of Blacks; whether whites, by virtue of their backgrounds, instinctively tried to assume authority and decision-making power within the movement. There was complete candor. But little anger.

When I got back to New York, I was appalled, reading the *New York Times* and the *New York Post*, to see how little newspaper columnists and reporters acknowledged or understood the divisions we had observed. The tensions between SNCC and SCLC were visceral—but this would only become evident nationally during the Meredith march in Mississippi, fifteen months later, when SNCC leader Stokely Carmichael proclaimed, "Black Power—Move on over Whitey or we'll move on over you."

In the meantime, I decided to go to graduate school in history. In the fall of 1965, I enrolled at Columbia University. As one indication of how much my trip to Montgomery had changed my life, I decided to write my master's thesis on the alliance of Blacks and whites in the Populist movement in Kansas. The choice was totally shaped by our discussion with James Forman on the bus in Montgomery. The thesis soon became my first published article. By then, as well, I had become convinced that the only way to understand social movements was to use oral histories to get at the source of grassroots activism. The SNCC experience had taught me that change happens from the bottom up, not the top down. Hence, my next article was on the sit-down strikes by automobile workers in Flint, Michigan, a strike that started the United Auto Workers, America's most progressive union.

Although initially I meant to write my dissertation on Black history, one of my classmates beat me to the topic I wanted to write on. So instead, I chose to write on women's history. I completed my dissertation—and first book—on the dramatic changes in women's experiences in twentieth-century America. It was the first of four books I would subsequently write on women's history.

But as I prepared to move to Duke University in the fall of 1971, I knew that I wanted my next major research project to be on civil rights history, with a focus on grassroots activism from the bottom up. Based on my Flint experience, I also knew that I wanted to rely on oral history, as well as written documents, in order to understand how and why Black protest movements evolved as they did. Within a few months, I decided to write about the Greensboro sit-ins, the student protests that launched the direct-action civil rights movement and within two months spread to fifty-four cities in nine different states. Using both documentary archives and oral histories, I was able to tell a story of how ordinary citizens—students, their teachers, their parents, and their ministers—had helped to transform race relations in America, from the bottom up. The most popular book on civil rights in the early 1970s was titled *John F. Kennedy and the Second Reconstruction*, but I knew that the movement came from below, not from the Oval Office, and that if I were to understand how it began, I had to go and interview those who lived in local neighborhoods and taught in local schools.

Consistent with this approach—indeed, central to it—my colleague Larry Goodwyn and I started the Duke Oral History project. As junior faculty six months out of graduate school, we raised $250,000 from the Rockefeller Foundation to recruit primarily Black graduate students at Duke to do community studies, using oral histories as a primary research tool. The goal of our students was to understand the history of grassroots activism throughout the South. Our program soon evolved into the Center for the Study of Civil Rights and Race Relations, where we invited SNCC veterans to come and write their books. Eventually, this evolved into the Duke Center for Documentary Studies. We raised millions of additional dollars from the Ford Foundation, the National Endowment for the Humanities, the Mellon Foundation, and the Lyndhurst Foundation, including a multi-year grant that allowed us to do 3,600 interviews with Black activists in twenty-two different communities in eleven different Southern states. Entitled "Behind the Veil"—a phrase first used by W. E. B. Du Bois in 1903—it uncovered the degree to which Blacks never gave up the struggle against racism, even during the height of Jim Crow segregation from 1900 to 1950.

Over four decades, we trained thirty-eight Ph.D. students, twenty-eight of whom published their dissertations as books on local civil rights histories. Sixteen of these won National Book Awards.

Eventually, the Center for Documentary Studies (CDS) made it possible for me, and others, to return to our original partnership with SNCC. Starting in 2013, CDS embarked on a new research endeavor with the SNCC Legacy Project focused on collecting oral histories and other materials from SNCC activists that would be available on a website open to everyone.

⋆ ⋆ ⋆

These interviews—as well as the work of our students in the courses we have taught over the past four decades—have created a growing awareness of how deep and long the Black struggle for freedom has been in our country. Moreover, it became increasingly clear that much of the historical literature on race in America has not dealt with the depth, the length, or the ongoing courage of a movement that continues to this day.

There are numerous themes in this volume. The first—and most important—is that despite the wishes of many whites to the contrary, the struggle for freedom has been carried out primarily by Black Americans, with only occasional assistance from whites. Yes, there were some alliances—between white Republicans and emancipated Blacks during Reconstruction; in the Virginia Readjuster movement of the 1880s; in the bi-racial Populist movement of the 1890s, especially in places like the Fusion movement in North Carolina; in some segments of the New Deal; and in segments of the civil rights struggle that emerged with new energy in the years after World War II. But overwhelmingly, Blacks—from the bottom up, in their churches, lodges, women's groups, schools, and colleges—carried forward the struggle for freedom and justice through their own institutions, their own families and alliances. On occasion, whites became supporters. But over 150 years, this has been overwhelmingly—and heroically—a Black struggle for freedom, with whites deserving only incidental credit for the reforms that were achieved.

Second, the Black struggle for freedom was led by both men and women, the older generation and the younger generation. The Greensboro Four could not have transformed the struggle as they did had it not been for people like Ella Baker, the NAACP field worker who started the local Greensboro youth NAACP chapter in 1943, and organized NAACP groups throughout the South; or the teachers at all-Black Dudley High, who taught their students about the historical resistance of *their* parents, and provided role models for citizens who refused to ride at the back of the bus, or sit in the balcony at local movie theaters.

Third, it was all-Black institutions—especially the churches, the lodges, the gangs in local communities, the neighborhood women's groups, the Black college clubs that gathered at local pool halls—that talked up the issues, examined different courses of action, and then put their lives on the line to make change happen.

Fourth, in most cases, whites responded only when they were forced to, and when it was in their self-interest to do so. Thus, Franklin Delano Roosevelt's executive order to enforce Fair Employment Practices in 1941 came only because he could not afford to face 50,000–100,000 Black protestors on the streets of Washington as he tried to mobilize support for American intervention in World War II. John F. Kennedy called Coretta Scott King when her husband was arrested and faced threats of serious personal violence against him because Kennedy desperately needed Black votes in the 1960 presidential election. He then introduced what became the 1964 Civil Rights Act only when Black demonstrators in Birmingham—and especially young children—placed their lives on the line against police dogs and fire hoses, and captured the nation's attention and rage.

Fifth, even as whites came to the conclusion that the civil rights acts of the 1960s had solved once and for all the problem of race discrimination, it was Blacks who carried forward the battle against the mass incarceration of people of color, and the persistence of economic impoverishment among African Americans.

Sixth—and in some ways most important—Blacks knew from the beginning that *true equality* required economic change as well as political and legal change. The right to eat in a desegregated restaurant was important. But it meant little unless and until Blacks had the resources to afford a decent meal. As long as Black Americans earned one third less than white Americans, owned far fewer homes, and owned houses were worth—on average—less that 20 percent of what white homes were worth, it would be impossible to talk about *true* racial equality in America.

Throughout, Black Americans faced the ongoing tension among those in power between politics on the one hand, and principle on the other. Nine times out of ten, they made a dent in the pervasive walls of white racism only when white politicians were forced to opt for principle.

In the end, the bottom line was what it had always been: it was Black Americans who bore the burden of carrying forward the struggle for racial equality and justice. Even if, on occasion, whites joined their ranks, Black Americans were the heroes who carried forward the struggle for freedom—now, as well as then.

Chapter 1

Present at the Creation, 1863–1877

It was 1863. Abraham Galloway—son of a white father and an enslaved mother—stood next to the Army recruiter, holding a gun to the soldier's head. He had escaped slavery in the hold of a ship four years earlier, fleeing to Canada, then became a master spy for the Union Army. Now, in the days after Abraham Lincoln issued the Emancipation Proclamation, Galloway had returned to North Carolina, becoming the leader of more than four thousand escaped slaves who had joined him in New Bern, North Carolina. We will join the Union Army, Galloway told the recruiter, but only on *our* terms. Galloway then laid down his demands: the right to vote, the right to serve on juries, the right to run for elected office, equal pay for Black and white soldiers, schools for their children, jobs for women, and care for their families. In retrospect, the demands seem revolutionary. But not so, given the roles that Blacks were playing in the war. Hence, the recruiter said yes. Within days, 10,000 Blacks had joined Galloway to enlist in the Union Army. Those soldiers—along with nearly 200,000 other Blacks who enlisted—proved pivotal to destroying the system of plantation slavery. Soon, they would inaugurate the quest to create a truly democratic America.[1]

It was as though the world were starting again. For nearly 250 years, slavery had provided the foundation for both politics and society. Slavery was a big business. It shaped the economy and life of the

South—and the North as well. The slave system was cruel and violent, with virtually all enslaved families forced to witness one or more of their relatives being sold to a distant planter. On a daily basis, field workers were harassed, and the wives and daughters of slave families were subjected to sexual assault at the hands of whites.

Not all whites in the South owned slaves. That was a privilege of wealth, which was never equally shared. But in the last third of the seventeenth century, rich whites had quelled protests against them by poor white farmers by appealing to a common denominator—their "whiteness." Rather than address the issue of economic inequality raised by less well-off white activists, white planters succeeded in persuading poor whites that they shared a common citizenship with aristocratic planters. They were people with the same skin color. This common denominator—their "whiteness"—became the pivotal point of division in society. Wealth did not count, nor class; being white was the primary descriptor. The color of one's skin overrode the profound divisions that separated poor whites from their more well-off brethren. Some poor whites even came to believe the myth that they lived in a world of equal rights—for white people. These same people may even have been convinced—or at least pretended to believe—that the enslaved descendants of Africa accepted their fate and appreciated the paternalism of their owners.

Behind this myth, of course, lay nightmare visions of slave uprisings, turning the image of docile slaves into bloodthirsty beasts bent on vengeance. Both images served to reinforce white supremacy.

Now, a civil war was underway that would destroy these illusions, exterminate the original sin of slavery, and make possible a new effort to realize the promise of freedom and democracy. Galloway and his regiment of Black soldiers stood at the forefront of this struggle. With a boldness difficult for any white person to imagine, Galloway and his brethren set out to claim their freedom. They hoped to create a brand-new world of democratic citizenship.[2]

If Galloway's assertiveness suggested the optimism of the immediate period leading to the end of the Civil War, Blacks soon learned how unpredictable their struggle for freedom would be. In 1865 and early 1866, reforms of every kind seemed possible. Just as Galloway had suggested, Black freedmen now looked to be treated as equal citizens, with the rights to vote, own land, send their children to school, and secure decent jobs. Most Northerners were convinced that, having surrendered in a state of abject helplessness, the white South would accept virtually any conditions the North imposed upon them, potentially including not only the right of Blacks to vote but also to occupy the plantation lands they had once worked as slaves, but now could own as independent farmers. The victors, after all, could impose on defeated Southerners whatever conditions they wished in order to achieve the goals for which they had sacrificed so much.

But then came President Andrew Johnson's arbitrary restoration of old-style Confederate rule in the defeated South. Rather than demand social justice and a new commitment to equal rights for Blacks, Johnson focused on reconciliation with the "old South." He undermined the determination of many Republicans to protect Black rights, and overruled their efforts to distribute land from masters to their former slaves. Johnson issued wholesale pardons to Confederate leaders and speedily readmitted former Confederate states to the union. Every governor he named to head the new state governments opposed Black suffrage. It was as if the 613,000 soldiers who had died for the cause of the Union had been lost for nothing, four years of torment wasted—simply to restore to power those who had been in control in the first place. "Never was so great an opportunity lost," Senator Charles Sumner of Massachusetts observed, "as our President has flung away." The Confederate power structure had been given the right to resume control, at least in substance. "The moment they lost their cause in the field," Republican Congressman Thaddeus Stevens commented, the Confederates "set about to gain in politics what they had failed to obtain by force of arms."[3]

Almost immediately, the Republican Congress revolted against Johnson, imposing a totally different regimen on the South, inaugurating what became known as Radical Reconstruction. A new set of possibilities came into being, setting up a conflict of values and policies that would besiege the nation in perpetuity. As historian David Blight has succinctly observed, the basic issue facing America after the Civil War became "how to make the logic of sectional reconciliation compatible with the logic of emancipation."[4]

In the end, national fatigue over the issue—and political opportunism—led to a pivotal decision. In the 1876 presidential election, Democrat Samuel Tilden won the popular vote against Republican candidate Rutherford B. Hayes. Notwithstanding the fact that slavery as a legal system had been confined to the South, the North too was deeply afflicted with racism. Even if many Northerners wanted to punish their enemy in the Civil War and showed some sympathy for Galloway and his supporters, their commitment to fundamental change in relations between the races was limited. It was now ten years since the war had ended. Hence, there was a willingness to consider a new path—one of compromise.

Thus, despite being the candidate of the party of emancipation, Republican presidential candidate Rutherford B. Hayes was willing to craft a deal that, in effect, sold out the hopes of Black people. Hayes's opponent, Samuel Tilden, had won the popular vote. But then Hayes proposed a deal: he would end Reconstruction and withdraw all federal troops from the South if three Southern states—Florida, South Carolina, and Louisiana—would cast their electoral votes for him rather than Tilden. The Republican Party abandoned Black Southerners in order to stay in power. The tension between political expediency and acting on principle reflected an ongoing pattern that would persist for well over a century. For most whites, expediency won out most of the time.

During the decades after emancipation, and beyond, Blacks never ceased their determination to be free. For most Blacks, principle—not expediency—prevailed. The circumstances might change. Every encounter with whites entailed a risk—how far to go, how direct to be in demanding change, how much to put on the line. But Blacks never gave up their determination to be free. Even as each of these moments posed an intimate challenge—one that often put life itself at risk—Black Americans never stopped pushing for change.

The first truth about the years between 1863 and 1900 is how fluid everything was: the social order that had once seemed immutable now was ripe for challenge. The hopes of African Americans for land, political equality, education, and self-fulfillment would soar to new heights, only to be followed by periods of plunging descent into near total oppression. During these four decades, the cycle of ups and downs occurred over and over. But amidst the volatility, one fact endured. Never monolithic, and embracing a wide spectrum of ideas and tactics, African Americans never gave up the struggle to advance the well-being of their families and communities.

To be sure, there were fundamental questions of direction. Was the goal of African Americans to achieve complete participation in a society shared with whites—what we now call integration—or was the primary goal to secure the freedom to pursue independent communities where Black people could create their own world—what we now call separatism? What mattered most? Land? Political rights? Security, for one's family and oneself? And how much did all of this depend on guarantees by the government, and equal relationships with white people? Yet even if the basic issues remained the same, the answers seemed to shift as rapidly as the times.

Confronting this shifting landscape of threat and hope, African Americans made what they could of the opportunities they had, building churches, schools, lodges, and towns. They worked tenaciously to protect and advance the opportunities of their children. They helped each other when trouble appeared, recognizing an allegiance to community based on the common history they shared. To be sure, Black hopes were undermined repeatedly, most dramatically when President Andrew Johnson failed to support racial equality in the South at a time when whites were ready to accept any change ordered from the White House. But the determination of Blacks to achieve this freedom never flagged. At no point did Black Americans cease to protest, or give up the struggle. And what progress was made was always first and foremost attributable to their tenacity, their commitment, and their willingness to bear the risks of demanding progress.

Everywhere they encountered the tenacious reality of white power. It assumed various forms—always economic exploitation, often physical brutality, psychological manipulation, or sheer terrorism. Yet within the framework of that dialectic between Black self-assertion and white power, the struggle to achieve equality persisted. The story would go on for more than a century. And at its roots, the subject matter was always whether it would be possible for the sons and daughters of Africa to become equal citizens in a society that had been founded on white supremacy.

The Beginning

Although, for their own psychic well-being, white plantation owners insisted that their slaves were content, a whole other world existed in the slave quarters and between slaves on different plantations. This was the world that W. E. B. Du Bois described in his 1903 book, *The Souls of Black Folk*, as "life behind the veil." After night fell on each plantation, when Blacks were no longer under the surveillance of whites, a separate existence flourished. Now, they occupied space they controlled. Families came together, singing, worshiping, dancing, talking, and politicking. News circulated about what had been heard at the master's table and carried from other plantations. Kinship networks sprang up between slave communities in adjacent areas, and slaves traveling to see family members on other plantations carried information back and forth about relatives, events unfolding in local communities, and what was taking place further afield. On weekends, many slaves worked for wages in nearby areas, providing access to still more information about what was transpiring in the world outside. The "other world" of the slave community offered numerous opportunities for developing separate institutions—like secret places of worship—and provided occasions for individual and group affirmation through cultural ritual, dance, and song. Women played a particularly important role in such communal development. The result was an enormous network of news spreading within the slave community about slave unrest, national and local moments of resistance, and prospects for change. As the grandmother of one twentieth-century Black farmer reported, Blacks "had to act [in front of whites] . . . just as though everything was all right," but behind the scenes another reality existed. Black perspectives, dreams, and aspirations were radically different from those the planter could see in front of him.[5]

It did not take long before this network quickly spread the word that a Civil War had begun. Booker T. Washington recalled his mother kneeling beside his bed "fervently praying that Lincoln and his armies might be successful." Slaves knew exactly where the Union lines were, and they looked to escape at the first opportunity to secure their freedom. One Tennessee planter wrote, "My Negroes [are] all at home, but working only as they see fit, doing little." In fact, he noted, they would prefer to "serve the federals." Even more threatening, the planter said, they seemed impatient to prepare "cotton lands for *themselves*," almost visibly anticipating the day when they could seize the land they had worked for their master and plow it for themselves. By rejecting the will of their owners, and forging new ties to their brethren, the slaves transformed their lives and forged a new sense of their distinctive identity. While control of their own lives might still legally reside with their masters, they were creating the foundation for practicing the politics of a freed people.[6]

With alacrity, African Americans bolted to join the Union Army as soon as they could. They did so with a political consciousness sharpened by their conversations "behind the veil" about the progress of the Union Army, and by a determination to uplift their entire community through becoming part of the common struggle. "I felt like a bird out of a cage [when I joined the Army]," one former slave in Georgia exulted. "Amen. Amen. Amen. I could hardly ask to feel any better than I did that day." Another Black soldier in New Orleans rejoiced in his ability to walk "fearlessly and boldly through the streets

. . . without being required to take off [my] cap at every step" in deference to whites. The experience of liberation transformed both behavior and self-perception. As one missionary observed, a slave had left the plantation still "cringing [and] dumpish," but within days of joining the Army he was "ready to look you in your face . . . wide awake and active."

Release from bondage was transformative. When a planter greeted one former slave with the paternal "howdy Uncle," the African American retorted, "[Now, you can] call me Mister." After President Abraham Lincoln took the decisive step on January 1, 1863, of issuing the Emancipation Proclamation—now letting the world know that this was a war about race and Black freedom, not just the reunion of a divided country—Blacks flooded into the Union Army. With almost 200,000 Black soldiers by 1864, half from the South, half from the North, Union troops were transformed into an Army of Liberation, part of what Steven Hahn has called the "largest slave rebellion in modern history."[7]

Quickly, African Americans who joined the Army became activists for equality. Protesting low wages and bad assignments, they insisted on the same pay as whites, and Congress responded, equalizing their wages in June 1864. Soon, they were demanding educational opportunities as well, turning their barracks into night schools where they learned reading and writing.

No one better personified the "new" Negro than North Carolina's Abraham Galloway. He and his community sought to put in place a new internal social structure, even as they prepared to do battle with Confederate troops. Blacks organized their own schools, created self-help groups, built churches, and laid the foundations for an autonomous Black political life. Addressing a large audience of Black supporters in New Bern, Galloway declared: "We want to be an educated people and an intelligent people. . . . If the Negro knows how to use the cartridge box, he knows how to use the ballot box." The same spirit infused Blacks everywhere. With pride, they exulted in their role in the Union Army's triumph. They constituted 10 percent of the 360,000 casualties on the Union side and helped to liberate numerous cities. They celebrated their victory publicly, with a band playing "Year of Jubilee" in Richmond. Black men and women danced through the streets singing, "Slavery chain done broke at last." The Union Army's commanding general, Ulysses S. Grant, wrote President Lincoln that Black soldiers were the most decisive factor in the Union Army's victory, an assertion that Lincoln soon adopted as his own.[8] Black Americans themselves had thus become a primary instrument of their own liberation.

Family, church, and education constituted the core priorities shaping Black activities. Once emancipation came, thousands of African American couples rushed to validate their family vows. In Granville County, North Carolina, 878 couples registered their unions, while in nearby Warren County, 150 couples took their vows in just two days. Churches became the first institutions totally controlled by Black people, with their own ministers and communities. However simple their physical structures, the Black church became the centerpiece of the community, a weekly reminder of how much people cared for each other, plotted together to advance their common interests, and sustained a sense of being part of a larger community, dedicated to collective advancement. From Bible school at nine thirty to morning worship at eleven, choir practice at noon, adult Bible school at four, and evening worship at eight thirty, this centerpiece of Black life brought joy, inspiration, and communal solidarity to each African American community in the South. As historian Hasan Jeffries observes about Lowndes County, Alabama, the places of worship might be no more than "simple clapboard in thin coats of white paint, with . . . roughly hewn wooden benches masquerading as pews, [but] these unpretentious buildings quickly emerged as the centerpieces of African-American social life." From children's Bible school in the morning to evening worship at eight thirty, the Black church served as the heart of the Black community.

It was the churches too that provided the meeting place for political groups, and they spawned the schools that represented the hope for the future of African American parents and children. "What a great thing larning is," one freed slave said. "White folks can do what they likes, for they know so much more'na we." Soldiers took advantage of the chance to learn to read and write. "A large portion of the regiment have been going to school during the winter months," a Black sergeant wrote from Virginia. "Surely this is a mighty and progressive age in which we live." In Richmond, Blacks created schools in warehouses and churches, with 1,000 pupils enrolled by April 1865, and 75 adults. In Georgia, Blacks built 123 day and evening schools. The appetite for education was insatiable. As one federal officer wrote, "A negro riding on a loaded wagon, or sitting on a hack waiting for a train, or by the cabin door, is often seen, book in hand, delving after the rudiments of knowledge. A group on the platform of a depot, after conning an old spelling book, resolves itself into a class."[9]

In the throes of celebrating emancipation, Lincoln became a new Moses and anything seemed possible. "There was to be no more Master and Mistress now," said one Richmond Black. "All was equal." Men insisted that their wives be called "Mrs." and that they no longer work in white folks' kitchens. In the South's cities, Black women often paraded with parasols, wearing brightly colored clothes and enjoying their newfound status as free and equal citizens. In response, whites complained of Black insolence, calling Black women "uppity." They raged at former servants, one of whom told her erstwhile mistress, "If she want any dinner she kin cook it herself."[10] Black troops occupied Southern cities, Black schools and churches grew like flowers in a garden, and a new day seemed in the offing.

In fact, the new day did appear, for a time. Eight years after the Supreme Court's *Dred Scott* decision in 1857, which declared that Blacks, slave or free, had no rights that a white person needed to respect, a Black lawyer was admitted to the bar of the Supreme Court; just a few months after draft riots in New York City had expressed deep anti-black sentiment, Manhattan organized a massive parade to honor Negro soldiers. In Illinois, Blacks were serving on juries; and Massachusetts passed a public accommodations law granting Blacks equal access to facilities such as restaurants and hotels. As freedmen's conventions met throughout the South in the summer and fall of 1865, there was a taste of a new Zion where past subjugation would be buried and a society of equality and self-determination created. Or so it seemed—at least at the beginning.[11]

Reconstruction—The Beginning of the Black Quest for Freedom

Those who marched out of slavery toward this new Zion held tenaciously to two basic dreams: political equality, embodied in the right to vote; and economic independence, symbolized by the ability to raise crops on land that they hoped to possess in their own right. These were two aspirations, separate but entwined. As they attained one, even partially, the other should advance as well. Or so they hoped.

Frederick Douglass, a former slave, a pioneering abolitionist, and most important, the greatest African American political leader of the nineteenth century, proclaimed the linkage between politics and freedom when he declared in May 1865, "Slavery is not abolished until the black man has the ballot." By the fall of that year, North Carolina's Abraham Galloway was meeting with more than a hundred other Black delegates in Raleigh to demand that Black Americans receive full rights of citizenship, public schools, a fair regulation of working hours, and abolition of all laws that permitted discrimination based on race. The South Carolina freedmen's convention in the fall of 1865 mirrored the sentiments of those in the state to their north: "We simply ask that we be recognized as *men*; that there be no obstructions placed in our way; that the same laws which govern *white men* shall govern over *black men*; that we have the right of trial by jury of our *peers*; that schools be established for the education of *colored* children as well as *white*; . . . that in short, we are dealt with as others are—in equity and justice."[12]

The military experience of Black soldiers provided the training ground for Black political self-assertion. The uniform of the Union Army licensed Black soldiers to see themselves as free—equal in every respect to their white compatriots, able, in the words of one observer, to walk "fearlessly and boldly through the streets . . . without being required to take off [their caps] at every [encounter with whites]." It was former soldiers, together with ministers, who took the lead in convening political meetings and drawing out the logic of the progression from emancipation to political equality. Just as the collective rush of slaves to join the Army built on the foundation of the "news networks" that had flourished on the plantations, so too the collective rush of former soldiers to freedmen's conventions in the fall and winter of 1865 built upon the battles they had won when they insisted on equal pay and fair treatment in the Army. The Wilmington, North Carolina, chapter of the national Equal Rights League demanded "all the social and political rights of white citizens"; and hundreds of freedmen attempted to vote in Norfolk, Virginia. Former slaves, having formed their own churches and built their own schools, now focused on the one political right that, more than any other, signified citizenship—the right to vote. And not surprisingly, the leaders in that effort came from the Black soldiers who helped transform Union forces into an army of liberation. Indeed, from their ranks came sixty-four of the Black legislators who would sit in state capitols over the next decade, three of the lieutenant governors, and four of the US Congressmen.[13]

But just as important as the vote—and some would say much more important—was the opportunity to own land. When the South Carolina Freedmen's convention articulated its goals, foremost among them was "that no impediments be placed in the way of our acquiring homesteads for ourselves and our people." It was not only "Master's niggers" who should be taken from him, said one Virginia freeman, but "Master's land too." If in fact there was to be a "new Zion," where former slaves could realize their wish to be fully free women and men, it would require the elimination of economic dependency and the removal of the power of whites to shape Black behavior by continuing to control their food and shelter. As W. E. B. Du Bois wrote almost four decades later, political freedom and economic independence were inextricably linked. It was difficult to imagine any people, white or Black, arriving at independent political judgments as long as they remained dependent on someone else for their family's survival. Thus, in the view of many, political autonomy depended upon economic empowerment.[14]

As the war drew to a close, the hope for such a linkage of political and economic democracy was almost palpable. As early as December 1861, the Port Royal Experiment operated on the principle that newly freed men and women should be granted land vacated by southern planters to engage in homesteading. When Congress enacted legislation establishing the Freedmen's Bureau in the spring of 1865, Republicans spoke specifically of the possibility of assigning land to every male freedman to cultivate. The Freedmen's Bureau reflected the determination of Republicans in Congress to guarantee that the federal government would implement the social and economic changes necessary to make freedom an existential reality, not just a hoped-for ideal. Thaddeus Stevens, the abolitionist Pennsylvania Republican who most eloquently articulated the changes that freedom might bring, envisioned a social revolution, achieved through seizing more than 400 million acres from the wealthiest 10 percent of Southern planters and reallocating it in 40-acre plots to former slaves. "The whole fabric of Southern society must be changed," he declared. "Without this [redistribution of land], this government can never be . . . a true republic. . . . How can republican institutions, free schools, free churches, free social intercourse, exist in a mingled community of nabobs and serfs? If this South is ever to be made a safe republic let her lands be cultivated by the . . . free labor of intelligent citizens."[15]

As if to prove that such a vision was not a utopian dream, the Freedmen's Bureau was authorized to divide some land that had already been confiscated into forty-acre plots to be owned, and farmed, by former slaves. When General William Tecumseh Sherman occupied the South, he issued Field Order 15, which delineated the Sea Islands and the Low Country of South Carolina for settlement by Blacks, with each family allocated forty acres, as well as a mule to pull the plow. Word soon spread among former slaves that the federal government was contemplating giving Black farmers at least 900,000 acres of land. More than 40,000 freedmen settled on these plots of land. "Gib us our own land and we can take care ourselves, but without land, de ole mass can hire us or starve us, as dey please," said one freedman.

For a brief moment, it seemed as though his hope—and Stevens's promise—would be redeemed. As part of its proposed plan for what would happen to the newly liberated slaves, the Freedmen's Bureau proposed that planter's land be seized from former slaveholders, and then be divided into 40-acre-and-a-mule plots that would be allocated to former slaves so that they could support themselves. Acting on their desire to become independent yeoman farmers, Blacks sought to control their own lives. They refused to work in gangs, as they had in the master's fields; they took to the road to find lost kin; and they refused to let women family members work in the fields as they had been forced to do on the plantations. The taste of freedom was tantalizingly close, even given the indifference of so many whites in the North to the condition of Blacks. With the Freedmen's Bureau plan for the distribution of planters' lands to former slaves, the prospect of joining the cause of political equality to that of economic independence seemed a real possibility.

But It Was Not to Be

Though for a brief few months some freedmen had reason to believe that their dream of independent Black homesteads might be realized, the immediate afterglow of war's end soon faded away. Notwithstanding Stevens's plan for "agrarian reform" and the Freedmen's Bureau's readiness to allocate small farms to former slaves in Tennessee, Port Royal, and the Carolina lowlands, the men who controlled power in Washington soon determined that confiscation of land from rich planters was *too* revolutionary. In 1866, a tug of war unfolded between those pressing to take advantage of new possibilities to create a genuine agrarian democracy, and those preferring to return to established patterns of stability, including respect for previously existing divisions of power and wealth in the South.

Ultimately, the issue came down to what the war had been about. It had started with the simple objective of restoring federal authority over a rebellious region. But with the passage of time, it took on the theme of giving new meaning to "equal rights for all." Would that goal lead to a social revolution, including racial equality in all matters, economic as well as political? Or was it only about control of political power? Was "waving the bloody shirt" enough to win Black votes for the Republican Party, or did the end of slavery mean something more—a new world of equal economic opportunity as well as political independence?

On the issue of land, those advocating maintenance of existing property distribution prevailed. Planters would retain control over their plantations. As a result, the government forced tens of thousands of freedmen to give up the forty acres and a mule that had been theirs; the fabric of faith that many Blacks had come to believe in was ripped asunder. "You ask us to forgive . . . the man who tied me to a tree and gave me 39 lashes," one former slave said. "That man I cannot well forgive . . . seeing as how he tries to keep me in a condition of helplessness [by taking back my land]." Instead of empowerment, freedmen were now left with "no land, no house, not so much as a place to lay our head." They now had to negotiate their livelihood with the same planter class that for a lifetime had controlled their prospects for independence, autonomy, and social mobility.[16]

It was in this context that the new economic paradigms of sharecropping and tenant-farming evolved. The South remained a one-crop culture, largely untouched by mechanization. Mules and humans remained the primary means of cultivating cotton, with former slaves dragging the plow through dusty fields, and striking a series of deals with planters. One option was to be a tenant farmer—to own the crop, then pay the landlord a rent when the crop was sold. The other option was to become a sharecropper—the freedman would plant and harvest the crop, but it was the landowner's to control, with the freedman getting only a predetermined share of the income. The advantage of these patterns was that the freedman and his family could still be "master of their own time." Gang labor would not exist. Women might be kept out of the fields. Some form of independence existed. And as long as prices remained stable or went up, some progress was possible.[17]

The "devil" in the system was the crop lien. The furnishing merchants, themselves under pressure from Northern banks, forced the farmers to pledge a portion of their crop in exchange for seed, supplies, and land. To secure the loan, merchants held a lien on the crop, and in practical terms, they controlled the terms of exchange. Merchants held unlimited power to set interest rates on the credit extended—often higher than 60 percent. The furnishing merchant (often the planter himself) tabulated each year's outcome. These merchants expected Black sharecroppers to accept the final figure, without question. Cheating was endemic, and if the sharecropper dared question the "boss," he could end up "six feet under." As a result, Black farmers sank ever deeper into debt. Once engaged in this kind of peonage, Black farmers found it all but impossible to extricate themselves. Every year was the same, one sharecropper's wife said. "After de last bale was sold . . . him come home wid de same sick smile and de same sad tale: 'As usual I settled up and it was naught is naught and figger is figger, all for de white man, and none for de nigger.'" The merchant/landowner ruled. If you stood up to him, you ran the risk of being brutalized, put in jail, or evicted. As one Black noted, "The white man did all the reckoning. The Negro did all the work." In Lowndes County, Alabama, landlords would set aside the contracts that federal agents had forced them to sign, withhold large portions of the monthly wage they were supposed to pay, and coerce workers into staying on the land. The situation might be better than slavery. But not by a lot.

One sharecropper aptly summed up the enduring reality of agricultural life: "Nigger got caught in the spokes of the wheel any way it rolled." There seemed no way out. You might escape by dead of night—but soon enough, you would become a tenant farmer for yet another oppressive white landlord.

The collapse of the dream for land redistribution by the late 1860s coincided with a violent white backlash against Reconstruction and Black citizenship. Threatened with the kind of total revolution envisioned by Thaddeus Stevens and the bold self-assertion of Black veterans and their wives, whites unleashed a wave of terrorism, intimidation, electoral fraud, and racial demagoguery. Southern states sent giants like Confederate vice president Alexander Stephens back to Washington as their congressional representatives, then moved forthrightly to enact a series of "Black codes" designed to legalize a new form of civil slavery. The codes denied freedmen the right to carry weapons, testify in court, or travel freely in the countryside without working papers. In the meantime, whites imposed an informal system of etiquette that kept Blacks "in their place," requiring that they enter white homes only through the back door, use deferential titles for whites, and refrain from the bold and colorful dress that conveyed, symbolically at least, a sense of entitlement and equality.

Organized in 1866, the Ku Klux Klan emerged as a murderous enforcer of racial domination, terrorizing any freedmen willing to act on the presumption of equality. Former masters received no punishment for shooting former slaves; race riots in Memphis and New Orleans left scores of Blacks dead, delivering the message that whites would not tolerate the independence envisioned by those who had once been their slaves. Everywhere, white authority delivered the same message: Blacks were inferior, whites were in control. As the historian John Hope Franklin observed about South Carolina: "Numerous fines were imposed for seditious speeches, insulting gestures or acts, absence from work, or possession of firearms." The message was clear to a North Carolina freedman who was beaten by a Klan member. "[He] told me . . . that whenever I met a white person, no matter who he was, whether he was poor or rich, I was to take off my hat."[18]

The myth of white supremacy not only survived emancipation but was reinforced with threatened and actual violence. In New Orleans white police and mob members killed more than two hundred Blacks who were marching to demand their rights. In Georgia, Klansmen brutally whipped fifty-two-year-old Abram Colby, a former slave who had been elected to Congress by newly enfranchised freedmen. In York County, South Carolina, the Klan lynched one local Black leader and burned the homes of countless others. Overall, more than two thousand Blacks were murdered in racial attacks. In North Carolina, when one young Black man was accused of expressing interest in a young white woman, four white men abducted him from his work. A week later, his neighbors found vultures surrounding his body hanging from the tree where he had been lynched.

In all these activities, white Southerners mobilized to defend their total control over Blacks at a time when, as never before, their presumptive power was coming under attack by freedmen. Race remained the fault line of the South. For nearly 250 years, it had functioned as the basis for defining a person's legal rights, occupational possibilities, economic power—even sexual independence—and political freedom. Now, that fault line had undergone a tectonic change—at least in theory—shifting dramatically the basis for defining political, economic, and personal power. Nothing could be more liberating, or threatening, to whites and Blacks. The world would either be turned upside down, or—if its previous state were to be retained—rebuilt and strengthened. Freedmen imagined a political Zion where equal rights existed both in the voting booths and—possibly—even in the distribution of land; powerful whites fought to retain all forms of their prior domination. Notwithstanding the energy, dynamism, idealism, and courage of the freedmen, whites still held local and regional power. Only if the federal government chose to cast its lot with those who placed their faith in the Emancipation Proclamation might the balance of white versus Black tip toward equality—which, to a degree terrifying to both sides, left the ultimate balance of power in Washington, DC.

As the contest for power and rights unfolded, the pendulum now swung once again to the freedmen, buttressed by their allies in the nation's capital. The rush of the white South to reclaim its prerogatives through Black Codes and terrorist organizations like the Ku Klux Klan tipped the balance in an already angry Congress toward ensuring that Southern rebels recognize, once and for all, who had actually won the war. Already deeply disturbed by President Andrew Johnson's swift recognition of former Confederate regimes, Republicans now took the occasion of enactment of the Black Codes and pervasive repression of southern Blacks to impose their own form of Reconstruction. In 1866 they passed a Civil Rights bill over Johnson's veto, stating clearly the rights of the newly emancipated freedmen to equal citizenship. Republicans then passed the Fourteenth Amendment to the Constitution, guaranteeing Blacks "equal protection" under the laws, and the Fifteenth Amendment, granting male freedmen the right to vote. Most strikingly, they imposed military rule on the South, dividing it into five military districts, and they refused to consider admitting any Southern states back into the union until those states had ratified the Fourteenth Amendment, disenfranchised former Confederate officers, and moved toward securing the rights of former slaves.[19]

On the surface at least, this was a bold and radical departure, a stunning effort to launch a new history of racial freedom and equality. In historian Eric Foner's words, "Alone among the nations that abolished slavery in the nineteenth century, the United States, within a few years of emancipation, clothed its former slaves with citizenship rights equal to those of whites." In a six-month period, the political terrain had experienced a seismic shift; from a total reassertion of white supremacy in the former Confederacy, there was now a return to the halcyon early days of emancipation. In 1867 the clock rolled back to the moment of Confederate surrender. No longer, perhaps, was there the prospect of agrarian reform or land redistribution; but here, at last, was a federal guarantee of the liberty most associated with freedom from servitude—the right to political participation on an equal basis with whites.[20]

Black Southerners seized the moment with the same tenacity that inspired them to escape to Union lines, join the Union Army by the tens of thousands, and educate themselves and their children at the earliest opportunity. Nearly 90 percent of eligible Black voters registered to cast ballots, and almost 80 percent of those went to the polls. In states like South Carolina and Louisiana, where Blacks represented a majority of the population, freedmen dominated the process leading to new constitutional conventions. Nearly two-thirds of the delegates to the South Carolina convention were Blacks, and when the first state legislature was chosen, 75 of 124 seats in the Assembly were held by freedmen, as well as 10 of 31 seats in the Senate. Throughout the South, more than one thousand Blacks were elected to state positions, including the offices of lieutenant governor, secretary of state, treasurer, and speaker of the House in South Carolina. Blacks often served as sheriffs and county clerks. In some major cities, such as Richmond, Raleigh, and Nashville, Blacks actually constituted a majority of those able to vote since Confederate leaders were disenfranchised; as a result, Blacks helped staff municipal police and fire departments. Freedmen also served a total of twenty-four terms in the US Congress from 1869 to 1879. Even in a place like Lowndes County, Alabama, where white supremacy seemed impregnable, more than four thousand Blacks registered to vote in 1867, arming themselves in order to protect their right to vote.[21]

With the Black-led Union League as an organizing base, Black Republicans forged coalitions with white Republicans, native Southerners whom their opponents dubbed "Scalawags" because they aligned themselves with the Union victors, and those dubbed "carpetbaggers"—Northerners who moved South to build coalitions with anti-Confederates. The constitutions they enacted reimagined state government: they provided for the first time for public education, more progressive tax policies, and a larger role for state governments in providing social welfare institutions like asylums for the mentally ill.[22]

Black pride and solidarity stood at the center of Black Southern political life. Every weekend Blacks flocked to meetings, often held at their own churches, to learn about the challenges before them and to develop strategies for carrying forward their new status. A federal official in Woodville, Mississippi, reported that Blacks insisted on having Saturdays off so that "they could attend public meetings of various kinds." In Waco, Texas, and Greensboro, Alabama, Blacks from the entire community left work once a week to attend a political rally and reinvigorate their will to fight on. More than just pursuing "integrationist" tactics, the historian Steven Hahn notes, Blacks "fashioned a range of political cultures [and] engaged in an array of political activities. . . . African Americans continually made and re-made their [own] politics . . . in complex relation to shifting events; they did not have their politics and political history made for them." Blacks embraced politics with a nuanced understanding of how pivotal were the stakes. As one Northern observer noted, "They were keen-eyed in their political vision, fully justifying the buoyant expectations of those who had conferred on them political privileges."[23]

Such sustained demonstrations of Black independence and political activism were a direct threat to Southern whites fearful of any diminution of their authority, and soon, the white South responded. The Ku Klux Klan experienced a region-wide revival in 1870–1871, intimidating Blacks who sought to vote, murdering those who violated social conventions of deference, and terrorizing community meetings. Although the federal government cracked down on the Klan in 1871, arresting hundreds, it was not clear that a subsequent revival of racist terror would provoke the same response. On more than one occasion, federal generals refrained from defending Blacks in the face of white violence, and it was never possible to predict the government's willingness to enforce the rights that allegedly had been guaranteed. Most disturbing was how unreliable were the political alliances that had secured the progress Blacks had made thus far in education, election to state legislatures, and employment by municipal agencies.

In their own political activities, Blacks had repeatedly demonstrated energy and activism. Black longshoremen went on strike in Charleston, Mobile, Savannah, and New Orleans to advance their rights; Black voters massed at the polls to prevent whites from attacking them in small groups; and with remarkable resilience, Black citizens stayed the course, waiting long hours to cast their ballots, and in defiance of fatigue, hardship, hunger, and threats of employers, defending their citizenship. But could they sustain this commitment if the politicians in Washington who served as their allies chose to betray them?[24]

Here, one of the critical issues was whether—as they had earlier assumed—Northern Republicans *needed* Black Southern votes to stay in power. But what if they did not? What if principle alone, not political self-interest, was necessary to sustain long-term Republican commitment to a racial revolution in the South—especially given the cost of maintaining troops there and the manifest determination of white Southerners to use whatever means necessary, including terrorism, to suppress Black autonomy? As support in the North for an ongoing federal presence in the South started to wane, the future of Reconstruction became ever more uncertain.

The Issue of Segregation

One of the issues that served as a barometer for this question was that of integration—would the two races go to the same schools, ride the same conveyances, attend the same churches?

From the beginning of their freedom, Blacks had repeatedly expressed the desire for an independent life—equal in its rights to the life lived by whites, but not necessarily one of integration with them. Just as in the slave quarters Blacks had created their own churches and communities, so now, they created a world with its own institutions, customs, and occasion for celebration. Black citizens filled their churches and gathering places, created their own lodges, held their own parades, and developed their own social life. In the new world that emancipation generated, affirmation of freedom did not necessarily mean occupying the space of whites. Rather, given the tensions that existed, one scholar has noted, it was natural that "blacks and whites withdrew into their own houses, churches and neighborhoods, watching each other warily."[25]

For whites, the heart of the integration issue was social equality—the fear that sitting side by side with Blacks, eating together, going to the same plays or entertainments, would eventually lead to other things. "If I sit side by side in the Senate, House or on the judicial bench with a colored man, how can I refuse to sit with him at the table?" one white official asked. "What will follow? . . . If we have social equality, we shall have intermarriage, and if we have intermarriage . . . we shall become a race of mulattoes. . . . We shall be ruled out from the family of white nations. So, it is a matter of life and death with the southern people to keep their blood pure." In a world where identities were ripe for redefinition, the fixation on "whiteness" testified to the insecurity of those who for so long had relied on their skin color for power and privilege. Of course, white men continued to promote illicit sexual relationships—often non-consensual—with Black women, even as they denounced the idea of "social equality." But from the beginning, whites purposely insisted that interracial sex would be the end result of racial equality.

Yet, Blacks did not seek intermarriage any more than whites did. As one Black carpenter noted, "What we want [is] to protect the virtues of our girls. That is the rights I want. I don't want no social equality with white people, and I don't want them to have none with me."[26] Notwithstanding the fervor with which whites raised the specter of Black men rushing to have sex with white women, scarcely an iota of evidence existed that Blacks even thought about such a possibility, whereas there is abundant evidence of white men forcing themselves on Black women.

Urban life further complicated the boundaries between Black and white. As tens of thousands of freedmen took to the road after Emancipation, more and more flocked to cities where jobs were more frequent and living conditions more open and free. The foundries of Birmingham and the waterfronts of Richmond, New Orleans, and Charleston beckoned to Black men with strong backs. Atlanta blossomed as a hub for commerce and transportation. So it was no surprise that the Black population of the South's ten largest cities doubled from 1865 to 1870. In Atlanta, Blacks grew from being 20 percent of the city to being 46 percent, in Richmond from 38 percent to 45 percent, Nashville from 23 percent to 38 percent, and Raleigh from 44 percent to 53 percent. Daily contacts in schools, at the market place, or on public conveyances like trolley cars crystallized the issue of the relationship between freedom and separation. Here on the streets of the urban South, Blacks and whites hammered out the new and evolving racial etiquette of the post-Emancipation era.[27]

Separation quickly became customary. Whites attended their public schools, Blacks theirs. Interestingly, although the expenditures per pupil always favored whites, at the beginning the gap was far less than it would later become—for example, $5.58 per white pupil in Montgomery, $3.47 for Blacks in the 1870s. Churches, lodges, and other voluntary associations were also segregated by choice. Shopping days were even separate, with Saturday afternoons set aside for Blacks. But in the instance of shopping days, acceptance of segregation by Blacks was less immediate. In particular, a younger generation saw little reason to desist from getting what they needed at a local department store just because of expected deference to white wishes. This was the same generation that insisted on being called "Mr." and "Mrs.," and resented being asked to step aside on a boardwalk so that a white person could pass. Typical was the response of one Black overheard by a white to say to his employer, "Well, I has no boss. I is my own darling boss."[28]

Public transportation, especially the new trolley cars, represented the most volatile test case of segregation and soon revealed who was actually boss. Practices varied. In Mobile, Alabama, there was a lattice-work separation between white and Black seating sections; in Richmond, Blacks were told to ride on the outside of cars; Nashville provided totally separate trolleys for Black and white. But for Blacks what mattered was whether or not they were *forced* to accept segregation. A Black minister in Richmond insisted that Blacks should *claim* the right to sit next to whites even if they did not exercise the right. Another Black in Nashville made the same point, declaring that no Black person should ride in a "colored" car "simply because it is set apart and labeled exclusively for Negroes."[29] The issue was one of individual rights. "We want public conveyances open to us according to the *fare* we pay, we want the privilege to go to hotels and theaters, operas and places of amusement. . . . We cannot go to the places *assigned* us . . . without the loss of self-respect" (italics added). Urban Blacks sought acknowledgment from whites that differences existed within *each* race, as well as between races, preserving the right of people, based on their education, income, or standing in the community, to be treated according to their individual situation.[30]

Although the rejection of segregation in principle was consistent with the affirmation of full citizenship rights, it did not preclude associating with one's own kind in most social settings. Clearly, Black Americans had demonstrated that they wanted to worship with each other, create their own lodges, and meet in their own political clubs. But that was different from accepting a white person's declaration that Blacks did not have the *right* to sit next to white people on the streetcar. And as a consequence, Blacks refused to leave a whites-only streetcar in Richmond, "sat in" on a streetcar in Charleston, and seized a series of trolley cars in New Orleans, driving them around the city. The issue was not whether one *wanted* to socialize with whites, but rather, whether one would accept a rule that proclaimed Blacks did not have the *right* to sit on the same streetcar. From the beginning, therefore, seating on public trolleys and buses came to symbolize the fundamental question of individual rights versus group treatment of *all* Blacks as inferior and separate, and *all* whites as superior.[31]

Community Building

As much as Blacks protested white efforts to deny them equal rights in public facilities, they devoted most of their efforts to strengthening the all-black institutions at the center of their lives. Of these, none was more important than the church. Throughout slavery, historian Lawrence Levine has pointed out, religious activities had created a necessary "free space" between slaves and their owners. Church services, shaped and conducted by Blacks, prevented physical slavery from becoming "spiritual slavery." Having sustained a sense of community and empowerment during captivity, the same churches provided the critical gathering places for newly freed Blacks to come together to develop their new life together. Sacred space not only allowed Blacks to testify collectively to their faith, but also provided the communal center where they could discuss their political options, plan Union League meetings, resolve disputes, and develop mechanisms for self-government and community justice. Places of spiritual renewal, churches also provided the training ground for community leadership. As W. E. B. Du Bois observed, "The church became the center of economic activity as well as amusement, education, and social intercourse." The original source of communal identity, churches quickly became the pivotal resource for communal advancement.[32]

Nowhere was the church more important than in becoming the birthplace for Black schools. If religious faith was the first passion around which newly emancipated African Americans came together, and politics the second, education was close behind. The church frequently proved central to all three. In Richmond, Nashville, and Montgomery, Methodist churches hosted the first schools. In just a few months, the number of students attending schools in Montgomery soared from 210 to 800. In Atlanta, the education day was divided into three sessions—the morning and early afternoon hours for children, later in the afternoon an adult school for married women, then in the evening a class for one hundred Black men.[33] Robert Moton, subsequently president of Tuskegee Institute, recalled his mother rushing the family through dinner so that the cabin could be prepared for adult night school. The intergenerational nature of the education process suggested the strengths inherited by freed people. "My grandmother always said that she was *Somebody* and she came from being *somebody*," observed one woman. "She had a feeling of pride in her background that gave her life meaning. Many people lost that pride because they didn't know their history," but schools helped teach both the history and its spiritual meaning. "Leaving learning to your children was better than leaving them a fortune," one Louisiana freedman said, "because if you left them even five hundred dollars, some man having more education than they had would come along and cheat them out of it all." In Lowndes County, Alabama, Blacks seized the opportunity for self-advancement, constructing the Calhoun School for 300 students. "By your education," the Calhoun principal said, "[you] fit yourselves . . . to lift up your own flesh and blood in your own climate and on your own soil." One white person, not necessarily sympathetic to the Black enterprise, commented that Black people "will deny themselves of any comfort to send their children to school." Blacks built hundreds of schools during this period, including, in Georgia alone, 123 day and evening schools, 90 percent of them funded entirely by Blacks.[34]

Learning proved contagious. By the end of 1865, more than a thousand volunteer teachers had gone South to teach over 200,000 Black pupils. With the new constitutions established under Reconstruction, systems of free, tax-supported schools became a publicly funded enterprise. Although Black schools might have been less well financed than white schools, they still provided a place where future leaders could thrive. The church also sponsored institutions of higher education that would create the next generation of teachers, ministers, and community leaders. Black Southerners and white philanthropists created the all-Black colleges Berea, Fisk, Tougaloo, Hampton, and Morehouse by the end of the 1860s. In 1869, largely because of these institutions, Blacks outnumbered whites for the first time among those teaching Black children in the public schools.[35]

Recognizing that schooling was inconsistent with submissiveness and servitude, many whites frowned on this Black drive for education. "The more education the Negro receives," said one white Georgia editor, "the more ungrateful he becomes for the blessings that made this education possible." Black teachers sometimes were dragged from their homes and beaten simply because they were "teaching niggers." Yet there was nothing that could stifle the recognition that only full mastery of numbers, ideas, and writing could prepare young Black people to fulfill the aspirations handed down to them by their elders.[36]

Nor was institution-building limited to churches, politics, schools, and colleges. Early on, voluntary associations of laborers, lodge members, and service organizations came together to build networks of mutual support. "Be up and active," said one Equal Suffrage meeting, "and everywhere let associations be formed having for their object the agitation, discussion and enforcement of your claims of equality before the law, and equal rights of suffrage." Central to this exhortation was the insistence that Blacks build their own institutions, and not focus on joining "with equally situated whites." The result was a proliferation of Black-centered structures—dance halls, communal laundries, billiard rooms, barber shops, and catering halls where cooks prepared fried fish and boiled ham, and neighbors gathered to eat the food and share the news of the day.[37]

Women were central to this community building. They created the catering centers, built neighborhood groups, and started voluntary associations for the uplift of the race. In Atlanta, it was the Daughters of Samaria, a woman's group that worked to help widows, orphans, and others in need; or Laundry Societies, where women workers, sharing common interests, could compare their experiences, and perhaps even choose to go on strike. Other times the focus was on politics. The Rising Daughters of Liberty Society came into existence to help support husbands and sons as they entered the political arena, the women standing guard while the men met to discuss the next election. One

Macon, Georgia, newspaper noted, "The Negro women, if possible, were [even] wilder than the men. They were seen everywhere, talking in an excited manner. . . . Some of them were almost furious, showing it to be part of their religion to keep their husbands and brothers straight in politics."[38]

Indeed, women were often on the front lines of standing up for Black rights. It was women maids and cooks who had to decide when to demand that their white employers call them "Mrs." and pay them a decent wage. Whites bitterly complained of the "sass" they received from their women employees. More than a few Black cooks recalled how they "got back" at the white bosses who denigrated them by spitting in the biscuits they baked or "peeing" in the coffee they brewed. But above all, the women came together to help each other, providing food when one of them fell on hard times, taking a shift doing laundry when "Sister Ann" fell sick—even though "Sister Ann" was not a blood relative.[39]

In the end, Blacks concentrated on institutions of mutual advancement. Particularly in a turbulent world where the good faith of white politicians proved tenuous at best, these provided a critical foundation for sustained communities. Throughout the years after liberation, Black optimism about gaining full equality had oscillated dramatically, depending on the attitude of the federal government. In the immediate aftermath of the Southern army's capitulation at Appomattox, hopes soared as political rights proliferated, mass mobilization occurred, and rumors of agrarian reform echoed throughout the South.

Dreams of "forty acres and a mule" soon faded, however, as Andrew Johnson welcomed the ruling class of the Old South back to power. Hope was reborn with the coming of Reconstruction, and the passage of the Fourteenth and Fifteenth Amendments. Political rights now seemed recognized by the foundational documents of the nation. Even if land redistribution were not to occur, there seemed reason to view the future as one of promise. Then came the upsurge of the Klan and a terrorist effort to eradicate the political freedoms that had been gained. One more time, the federal government intervened in 1871.

But these rhythms suggested the degree to which ultimate guarantees of security and political freedom rested upon a vacillating Washington.

Federal Betrayal

Now, the screw turned one more time. Whatever the hopes nourished by the Freedmen's Bureau, federal support slowly ebbed during the 1870s. This abandonment left Black men and women with barely a wisp of hope. Mandated segregation increased and violence against Blacks became more common, particularly meted out on those who had the temerity to challenge white political authority. In one Piedmont, South Carolina, county, five hundred masked men lynched eight Black prisoners in an act of political intimidation. As more and more Southern states gained readmission to the Union, the political prospects of a biracial coalition of white and Black Republicans diminished. A commensurate loss in Black office-holding and patronage soon followed. In Montgomery, when Radicals held power, half the police force was Black, but when Conservatives regained control in 1875, Black appointments ended. More and more, white Republicans ran their own slates of candidates, ignoring Blacks; and when a Black candidate was on the ballot, white Republicans proved tepid in their support. Most tellingly, President Ulysses S. Grant confessed in 1874 that the federal government was becoming "weary" of appeals from Blacks to come rescue them from the rising violence of whites seeking to destroy their rights. The Fifteenth Amendment, he concluded, "had done the Negro no good, and has been a hindrance to the South and by no means a political advantage to the North." The idea of the Republicans as the party of freedom and racial equality gave way to the Republicans as a party of railroads and banks.[40]

As Blacks had shown over and over again, they would never abandon their struggle. But as the 1870s unfolded, it became increasingly clear, as one Democrat said, how much influence whites still enjoyed over Blacks "as employer on the laborer, of the creditor on the debtor, of the rich on the poor, of the humane and charitable on the friendless."[41]

The end of immediate Black hopes for federal aid in their crusade for freedom came with the presidential election of 1876. Samuel Tilden, the Democratic candidate for president, outpolled his Republican rival, Rutherford B. Hayes. But Hayes would not admit defeat. Instead, he conducted behind-the-scenes deliberations with the electors from three Southern states that Tilden had won—Florida, Louisiana, and South Carolina. If those electors would cast their votes for him rather than Tilden, Hayes promised, he would withdraw all federal troops from the South, end Reconstruction, and return control of the South to supporters of white supremacy. By one electoral vote, Hayes became president, and the federal government betrayed its commitment to the rights of Black Americans. Within two months, federal troops had returned to their barracks. As one freedman noted, "The whole South had got [back] into the hands of the very men that held us as slaves." Those who had made possible the liberation of Black slaves had now retreated from the battlefield, leaving in place only a few of the stakes that had been planted on behalf of freedom and democracy in the preceding ten years.

Nevertheless, Blacks would not admit defeat. Hope remained. This was still a different world than the one that had existed fifteen years earlier—one informed by the collective determination of a people to seize, fight for, and defend their freedom. Building on the moral vision of the Black church in slavery, community institutions—from schools to churches to lodges to women's groups—committed to continuing to advance freedom, whatever the vagaries of the federal government. It was the end of the first decade of the Black struggle for freedom, but not the end of that struggle—not even the end of the beginning.[42]

Chapter 2

The Twilight Years, 1877–1898

Two stories, two different outcomes:

Sarah Petty was born into a comfortable, independent Black family in eastern North Carolina. She went to a private school established by the America Missionary Association, then to Scotia Seminary. She married a prominent Black minister who wore silk top hats. She rode in a carriage and shopped at all the best stores. She was an optimist about the future.

Anthony Crawford was a Black man with a good job and property who took pride in his well-being. When he stood up for himself with a merchant who belittled him, he was lynched. "His wealth," a local paper said, "emboldened him to assume an equality that whites will not tolerate. Because of his own reckless course . . . [his lynching] was inevitable and racially justifiable."[1]

★ ★ ★

With the withdrawal of federal troops in 1877, Southern white power now reigned supreme. Yet even in the face of resurgent white control, African Americans strove to hold on to their political rights, all the while persisting in their effort to strengthen their institutional and community life. The next two and a half decades—like the years that preceded them—would be contentious, confused, and often directionless. Still, hope persisted, even in the midst of confusion and worse. How to navigate such ambiguous terrain posed a huge challenge, complicated even more by variations that existed in different geographical areas. The heavily supervised and violent life in a lumber camp in the Everglades in Florida was not the same as the relative independence and freedom from white domination enjoyed by a Black funeral home director in downtown Atlanta. Whether one lived in an urban or rural area, in the Piedmont or in the Delta, significantly shaped one's daily choices. And always, wherever one was, a Black person confronting white racism had to recognize the risk being taken: How far could one go in expressing oneself, how much of a chance was there of being beaten, ostracized, or even killed?

But throughout the post-Reconstruction period, common objectives persisted: to build strong families, sustain community and faith through the church, continue to support the best education possible for one's children, keep a hand in politics wherever possible, and find a way to maintain a livelihood—all the while probing the system of white social control for whatever opportunities might exist to rekindle the drive for freedom.

The Community

Probably the most difficult task that existed during these years was that of being parents—how to teach children the steps necessary to survive in a hostile world controlled by whites. Mothers and fathers needed to implant a sense of self-worth, encourage the young to aspire to a better future; at the same time, parents had to give their children the inner strength to find a path between obsequious deference to white expectations, on the one hand, and violent rebellion, on the other. Acts of rebellion could easily lead to death. So Black young people had to learn how to gauge the right response, to fight back while staying alive. It was never easy.

In all of this, historical memory played a major role. For decades, African Americans had endured, resisted, and eventually triumphed over slavery. To keep this experience alive across generations was essential to sustaining the sense of connectedness between past and present. Black leaders vividly recalled those ancestors who had given their lives to defeat racist tyranny, testifying to the wisdom of Milan Kundera's observation that "the struggle of man against power is the struggle of memory against forgetting." Hence, a Black newspaper in the 1890s recalled, with celebration, efforts by Black soldiers more than thirty years earlier in the Battle of Fort Wagner: "The colored troops did not falter. They scale the breast-works, jump into the fiery hail. Three of them are actually standing on the parapet firing upon their white foes." Eulogies for those who had passed on helped make it possible to honor the faith, commitment, and service of those who had come before and who had delivered liberation.[2]

Like an anchor in a storm, Juneteenth—the annual celebration of Emancipation—provided a constant point of reference for the community at large. It re-created the sense of communal joy that accompanied the dawn of freedom, while reminding everyone of how far African Americans still had to go to redeem the promise of liberation. By honoring those who had come before, and forging anew a bond of community dedication to the values of equality and justice, such rituals provided an antidote to efforts by white Southerners to denigrate Black experience and identity. Even if keeping history alive could not thwart the immediate consequences of whites betraying Blacks in the Compromise of 1877, holding fast to the achievements of the past offered sustenance for the next era of resistance. By refusing to accept white definitions of their rights and opportunities, Blacks could continue their struggle for freedom and sustain the faith that change would someday come.[3]

Family memories, of course, provided the immediate framework for keeping a sense of intergenerational continuity alive. Blacks never ceased searching for long lost relatives. Escaped slave Mary Walker, for example, worked passionately to reunite with her children on the Cameron Plantation in North Carolina. So too did a Black man who rejoiced in finding a sister in Mississippi who had been separated from her kin for nearly sixty years. The family provided the focal point for transmitting the stories of grandparents to their grandchildren, and also served as the school in which mothers and fathers could teach their offspring the lessons they would need to learn in order to survive the brutalities of white racism, as well as persist in the struggle for justice.[4]

Although we do not have abundant first-person evidence of how these lessons were transmitted, the recollections of those living two generations later about how *they* responded to the same challenges can help illuminate the process by which connections to the past could be maintained. "My father told me," one man said, "that you pay for the space you occupy in life, that you gave back of the talents that had been given to you to make the world better. . . . I wasn't going to be denied, cause [you see] I'd been told I was just as good as anybody . . . [and so] I felt pretty good about myself." Instilling a sense of pride was critical. "You are my children," one mother said. "You look like you look because of your father and me, and you can do anything you want to do. . . . Don't ever be ashamed of how you look because of your color."[5]

But if that woman's children learned to have "high esteem," they and others also understood the indignities that their parents had to face as they struggled for independence. "When some things just really got out of hand," one son recalled, "[your parents] would sit down and talk to you and tell you, 'Now this is wrong. But the situation is that your father can't do anything about this [right now]. . . . This is just the way of life." And then they would try to provide a treat so that the children would feel better. "[They would] go out of their way to do something a little special. That is to keep you from being down."[6] However meager the resources or troubling the daily realities their parents faced, another son said, "they gave us some fundamental moral principles," and the "honor of having a mother and father [who] loved us." Running away might be easier, but the courage of staying to fight was itself a message of love. "What you talkin' 'bout did I love you girl," a Toni Morrison character says in her novel *Sula*. "I stayed *alive* for you." The message was clear. "Just stand up for what you believe," parents told one child. "Don't try to take advantage of anybody, but don't let anybody take advantage of you."[7]

If walking the thin line between deference to whites and defense of oneself was difficult, there were institutions available to help. One of the most notable was the church. The ethical bellwether of the community, it provided the gathering place where people could bring their daily problems, while offering a forum for reassurance that in God's time, a better day would come. One African American was asked, how did Blacks manage to survive white oppression? "Because we were taught different," he responded. "We were taught not to hate. . . . [Our parents would say] don't worry, the Lord will fix it. Vengeance is God." In the end He would settle all accounts. But if the church promised liberation in the future, it also offered leadership and guidance in the present. The Black preacher was the leader of the community, "a politician, an orator, a 'boss,' an intriguer, an idealist," W. E. B. Du Bois said.[8]

Weaving his message between an exhortation to seek justice and a recognition of the difficulties of the here and now, the Black minister played a role that mirrored that of parents—inspiring courage and pride, while also acknowledging the need to survive. It was a balancing act, not always carried out with success. Yet from the beginning, the church offered the sacred space—and the social space—within which Blacks could come together, bare their hearts, seek advice, get spiritual nourishment and political advice, and in the meantime create all the other groups, from the Ladies Aid to the Knights of Pythias, that helped give the community coherence and focus.

The family and the church both made education a top priority. Churches sponsored the first schools, the American Missionary Association provided the first teachers, and thereafter education and religion were inextricably connected, with preachers and teachers often being the same people, or at least coming from the same family. Parents taught their children to read and write if they were able, or tried to learn from them if they were not. Faced with the demands of white employers to shorten the school year in order to keep Black children in the fields, parents came together and raised the funds to keep the school open an additional month, providing the butter, eggs, vegetables, and meat to enable a teacher to stay. Often, parents moved to another location in order to find better schools for their children. In rural areas, one farmer said, "The landowner would not tolerate a tenant who put his children [in] school." Hence, the family moved to town, as one instinctively moves from a greater pain toward a lesser pain. Although often dilapidated and unheated, with students forced to use charred splinters from burned logs as pencils, the Black school represented, like the church, a pillar of the community around which endeavors to prepare for a better future might be built.[9]

Like everything else in the Black community, schools became a barometer of Black status in the white world. "The education of blacks had somehow to be reconciled with their political and economic subordination," historian Leon Litwack observes, "and in the eyes of many whites, the contradiction simply could not be successfully resolved." Most whites were committed to eradicating any distinctions that might exist among Blacks in status and opportunity. The doctor, preacher, and schoolteacher, in this view, should be subjugated in the same way that sharecroppers, tenant farmers, and domestic servants were kept down. As Henry Grady, editor of the Atlanta *Constitution*, wrote: "The supremacy of the white race of the South must be maintained forever, and the domination of the negro race resisted at all points . . . because the white race is the superior race. . . . This [truth] . . . has abided forever in the marrow of our bones, and shall run forever with the blood that feeds Anglo-Saxon hearts." Some whites, on the other hand, were prepared to acknowledge differences of class and station among Blacks, to accommodate the retention of certain rights, and to negotiate a quid pro quo that left some fluidity in the circumstances of African Americans as long as the basic structure of white control was not frontally assaulted.[10]

Politics and Economics

The world of politics highlighted the ambiguity of Black status in the post-Reconstruction era. Part of the Compromise of 1877 that resulted in federal troops leaving the South was the implicit understanding that Blacks could continue to go to the polls and receive Republican patronage from the federal government if they deferred to Bourbon Democrats in all affairs local and regional. White manipulation of the Black vote was also implicit in this agreement. Although South Carolina's Wade Hampton bespoke the larger compromise when he declared, "We will secure to every citizen, black as well as white, full and equal protection," in fact the vote was allowed only if it could be controlled. As the historian C. Vann Woodward has written, "The stuffing of ballot boxes, the use of boxes with false bottoms, . . . and the tampering of registration books were all highly developed arts." "The right of suffrage," the New Orleans *Republican* editorialized, "is fast becoming an article of merchandise and is placed upon the market with about the same eagerness that the fruit vendor betrays in the disposal of his fruit." For Blacks, the message was clear: vote against prevailing white power whenever possible. "We watches the white man," one elderly freedman said, "[to] find out which [way] he gwine vote. After we find out which way he gwine'r vote, den we votes 'zactly de other way; den we knows we's right." For white Democrats, on the other hand, the key was to make sure that the Black vote never challenged local white control.[11]

Within this larger context, significant differences existed from region to region. Overall the Republican Party remained a presence, sometimes competitive, though not dominant, in Virginia, North Carolina, Kentucky, West Virginia, Louisiana, and Mississippi. In the late 1870s and 1880s, Blacks played a particularly active role in cities like Nashville, Richmond, Raleigh, and Jackson, electing city council members and controlling significant patronage. Richmond's Black elected officials helped get streetlights and better roads in their community, as well as a Black night school. In Jacksonville, more than half the police were African American, and in Nashville, J. C. Napier, a skilled politician, helped hire Black teachers, open new Black schools, and develop a Black fire company. Napier, in particular, exemplified the nexus of Black associational life and political activism. An energetic participant in local churches and in various fraternal lodges, he demonstrated the synergistic interaction that generated strength in the larger community, and helped make politics work—at least on some occasions.[12]

On the other hand, Blacks continued to be dismayed at the ways in which whites subverted their rights. Despite the occasional J. C. Napier, most white Republicans sought to eliminate Black office-holding. Moreover, although Blacks turned out in force to vote for white Republican candidates—after all, this was the "party of Lincoln"—their commitment was not reciprocated if Blacks ran for office. When an African American ran for the state legislature in North Carolina in 1880, a Black newspaper observed with disgust, "There is no use disguising the fact [that] the Negro voters of Wake County have been sold out by their pretended white friends." More than a few Black leaders pondered why they should remain loyal to a party—the Republicans—that took for granted their vote while doing little to reward Black loyalty. "If the Democratic party proves a better friend to the Negro than the Republican party," one Nashville leader said in 1885, "the vote of the Negro will certainly divide and go with you, increasing as the friendly relation increases."

Self-interest was the key. Blacks might not have much to barter in the increasingly constricted arena of political participation, but they were willing to make the most of wholly new political alliances. As one Black said, "I offer my vote to the highest bidder, not for money but for the greatest measure of justice."[13]

Ultimately, politics and economic well-being were inextricably linked. As freedmen recognized from the beginning, the land you could farm, the job you could aspire to, and the living you could provide your family correlated directly with political independence and civic freedom. Although the federal government's retreat from the "forty acres and a mule" possibility had eviscerated the prospect that economic democracy might accompany political democracy, the struggle to advance economically remained, like politics itself, a primary focus of Black aspirations. The refusal to work in gangs, the insistence that women not be assigned to the fields, and the efforts by sharecroppers and tenant farmers to piece together enough money to buy even a small piece of land all testified to the determination of freedmen and freedwomen to exercise as much control over their labor as possible.

Nor was the narrative of Black economic life without tales of success. Charles and Lucille White scrimped and saved, hoarding their pennies from farming until they were able to buy twenty-seven acres of their own land in Texas. "It just set us on fire," White said. "We didn't seem to get half as tired, or if we did we didn't notice it. One day we was cleaning up a field [and] Lucille said, 'You know Charley, even the rocks look pretty.'" There were numerous other examples of families selling eggs, sewing dresses, raising pigs, or fixing tools to raise money and then proceeding to buy a "plantation" for themselves. Ned Cobb, the hero of Theodore Rosengarten's *All God's Dangers*, started by being hired out to plow fields, then rented land, eventually became a blacksmith, and in the end earned enough to buy and till his own farm.

In perhaps the most lyrical passage describing the progress that had occurred economically among some freedmen, W. E. B. Du Bois described the man who rose at dawn in his own home which a Black man had constructed, rode to work with colored neighbors, read a Black newspaper, patronized a Black insurance company, kept his money in a Black bank, attended Black musicales, and planned to be buried by a Black undertaker. As one indication that Du Bois was not fantasizing, the value of property owned by African Americans in Atlanta, Georgia, increased from $37,000 in 1869 to $855,000 in 1890. The progress that some Blacks were able to make in owning their own fields was evidenced by the fact that a majority of Black farmers in Warren County, North Carolina, held title to their land in the early 1900s. Indeed, by 1920, Blacks owned 925,000 farms in America.[14]

Yet the stories of success paled in contrast to the struggle for survival experienced by most African American farmers and laborers. While some could save enough to purchase a small plot of land, most became entrapped in the ever-deepening spiral of debt to the furnishing merchant or landlord. "Niggers plant the cotton, Niggers pick it out, White man pockets money, Niggers does without," went one song. "De big bee suck de blossom, De little bee make de honey, De black man makes de cotton and corn, and de white man totes de money," went another. If sharecropping had permitted the independence Black farmers originally envisioned, it might have served as a transition to more Black landownership. But with declining cotton prices and the growth of the crop lien system, sharecropping for most farmers became an unmitigated disaster, with the majority of Blacks, in the words of one historian, "enmeshed by [the turn of the century] in a system akin to peonage."[15]

Still, depending on their location and circumstances, African Americans fought back, uniting with each other in community efforts to find strength in solidarity. The historian Tera Hunter highlights this process in her description of how the washerwomen of Atlanta fought to secure a decent livelihood. Migrating to the city, they joined churches and clubs, formed neighborhood associations, and—via their networks of gossip and news—contrived methods to both resist and advance. As Hunter writes, "They fought for dignity and self-respect and won small gains, moments of reprieve, and symbolic political victories. But their lives involved more than struggle and pain. They found pleasure in their neighborhoods, families, churches, mutual aid organizations, dance halls, and vaudeville theaters." Having fled the plantation, they had journeyed to the big city in order to "'joy my freedom," as one woman told a federal official. With countless others, they wore their bright dresses and carried their parasols as they paraded their independence on holidays and weekends.

But come Monday they had to return to the workaday world where exploitation was rampant, and survival never certain.

For most of these women, the only job that was consistent with their skills and the opportunities available was to be a washerwoman. In Hunter's words, it was "the optimal choice for a black woman who wanted to create a life of her own." By taking laundry back to their own iron pots and heating irons, Black women avoided the captivity of domestic servitude within white households, and they secured at least a minimum of freedom to pursue their own lives; go on church outings; and spend time with each other gossiping, politicking, and sharing strategies for resistance. They helped each other when illnesses occurred, watched each other's children, provided food to each other when the pantry was bare. By virtue of their collective strength, they had established a minimum price per pound of laundry in 1877. They also had become more and more active politically, working with their men to challenge white political power, and trying to take over the white Republican Party in 1879.[16]

The women did their part two years later, declaring a strike against their employers unless their pay rate per dozen pounds of laundry was doubled. More than three thousand women joined the protest. They marched on the streets, held nightly church meetings, and reinforced each other's determination to stay strong. "The strike is causing quite an inconvenience among our citizens," the *Atlanta Constitution* observed after two weeks had passed. In the end, whites fought back by threatening to impose a new "business tax" on washerwomen that would more than eliminate any gain made by the increased wages they were demanding. Still, the women persisted, angrily denouncing the City Council for its deceitful tactics and earning the sobriquet "Washing Amazons." Ultimately, the strike failed, and the washerwomen resumed their tasks. Yet they were also resilient in their recognition of how coming together and acting as a united force provided the only weapon they had to find a better path forward.[17]

Women domestic workers in both Jackson and Galveston, and men in Nashville, Washington, Savannah, New Orleans, and Richmond launched similar strikes. Black longshoremen recognized the value of separate Black locals where they could nurture a social climate that was supportive and retain control over their own activities. Although few of the strikes were successful, Black workers persisted in their readiness to come together in a common cause, recognizing that acting as a collective association provided a measure of strength that could never come from acting alone.[18]

That solidarity among workers was easier in the cities, where 15 percent of Southern African Americans lived by 1890. Here, there were more opportunities for varied occupations. Approximately the same proportion of Blacks held skilled and semi-skilled jobs as did whites. Occasionally, there was even integration. Black and white carpenters in Atlanta labored on the same buildings together, and white and Black shoemakers and mechanics worked side by side. In rare instances, Blacks were even in charge, as at Shaw Institute in Raleigh—a Black school—where the Black master mason supervised two white subordinates. Both in politics and in labor, urban folkways offered a different set of opportunities and realities than rural life. Collective organization was easier, political mobilization more frequent, and opportunities for "acting out" more available.[19]

Resistance to white control took various forms—occasionally that of humor and song, sometimes individual acts of protest, in a few instances outright defiance. The blues were one way in which Blacks expressed their anger and retribution. "I asked that boss-man for to gimme my time," one song went; "Sez he, 'ole nigger, you're a day behin'; I asked him once, I asked him twaist; Ef I ask him again, I'll take his life." If the music did not lead directly to fighting back, it nevertheless offered catharsis in the present and cultivated defiance for the future.

Humor was yet another means of seeking—and vicariously experiencing—revenge. In *Black Boy*, his novel about Black life under white oppression, Richard Wright and his friends laughed about using poison gas from their breaking wind to get back at "Whitey."[20]

Time after time, individuals found the courage deep within to say no to white authority. One mother refused to leave her family on Christmas day to go cook for her white employer, making abundantly clear that her family counted for more in her life than obeying a white boss. Another woman resisted the sexual advances of a male employer. "If a black man done that to a white woman," she told him, "You'd be the first to . . . find a limb to hang him to. So if you would hang the black man about doing it, you think I'm going to let you do it to me?" In cities, mothers would refuse to patronize stores where they were insulted, and defended their children when they were beaten by white store owners, as occurred in a Black neighborhood of Greensboro, North Carolina.[21]

The most explicit forms of resistance occurred in these urban areas, where the collective strength of the Black community would rise up in protest. When a young man in Atlanta was arrested in 1881 for allegedly pushing a white woman off a sidewalk, the police brutally beat him—until a Black mob gathered, threatened the police, and the mother of the beaten man pulled out a revolver and pointed it at a policeman's head. Whole areas of New Orleans were off-limits to police lest they come under attack. As one white observer noted, "The moment that a negro steals, or robs, or commits some other crime, his person seems to become sacred in the eyes of his race, and he is harbored protected, defended and deified. . . . The leading negroes drum up a mass meeting and proceed to pass a string of senseless but sympathetic resolutions, after a series of harangues that would be a discredit to the Zulus." But the result was clear. "What would you do if sent to Decatur St." one police joke went. "Answer: Blow your [whistle] and run like the devil." These were the areas where Black life reigned supreme, populated by Black businesses, dance halls, singing, new forms of music, and a community where white people dared not intrude—places like Decatur Street in New Orleans, Auburn Avenue in Atlanta, and the Hayti section of Durham.[22]

The all-Black towns that sprang up in the South, dedicated to running their own affairs and being free of white interference, offered similar refuge. Renova, Mississippi, had its own public schools and elected officials. So did Mound Bayou, where locals could sell and buy cotton on their own at Black-owned cotton gins, manufacture "white lightning" at their own liquor stills, and run their own social life, including ostracizing those who broke with prevailing norms. "Black folks in Mound Bayou have always said what they want to say," one local resident declared. "We were the boss. We were in charge. Yeah, we were the majority owners," Blacks owning their own banks, stores, and funeral homes. From Oklahoma to North Carolina, such all-Black towns represented an oasis, cut off from white interference, that permitted Black Southerners to live a life largely free from white surveillance.[23]

That impulse for autonomy also fueled the campaigns of the 1870s and early 1880s for Blacks to emigrate to Liberia, or to move within the United States to Kansas. Henry Adams, a former slave, joined with Martin Delany and Bishop Henry McNeil Turner to urge Black Americans to journey to Liberia, where they could once and for all be free of white people. Others, like Benjamin "Pap" Singleton, urged a similar course of flight to Kansas, where they could create towns where "a black marshall carries the billy [club], a black postmaster passes out the mail, a black ticket agent sells the ticket, and the white man's waiting room is in the rear." Although only twenty thousand Blacks followed these emigration patterns, there was a period when whites felt that the unbridled "exodus" of Blacks was beyond control, generating the fear, in historian Edward Ayers's words, that "the white-columned porticos of [old plantations] . . . [would be left] mouldering in decay."[24]

Significantly, resistance to enforced segregation focused less on the existence of separate facilities than on the exclusion of African Americans from places reserved for whites. Most historians now recognize the degree to which segregation existed throughout the post–Civil War era—North as well as South. It did not suddenly appear in the 1890s, as C. Vann Woodward argued in the early 1960s. Yet the pre-1890s segregation occurred in a context of some ambiguity.

Notwithstanding enactment of the 1875 Civil Rights Act, which prohibited segregation, separate facilities were the norm in schools, prisons, theaters, and restaurants. (The US Supreme Court struck down the 1875 law only eight years later.) Blacks preferred that their children go to Black schools and that they be taught by Black teachers who truly cared about them. Of far more importance was the quality of those facilities—how close they came in resources and excellence to those provided to whites. It was the condition of the building, books, and facilities of the all-Black school, not its existence as a racially separate entity, that prompted concern.[25]

But when it came to streetcars and railroads, Blacks repeatedly resisted the idea that they should be forced to accept second-class treatment, or be denied access to a first-class ticket, simply because of their race. Whites, in turn, tended to see the issue as symbolically significant, infused with a political message that the white race should rule. Thus when a Black woman in New Orleans protested being assigned to a separate section on the streetcar, the driver—playing to his white audience—declared, "No back talk, now that's what I'm here [for]—to tell niggers their places." And when a well-dressed Black man refused to give up his first-class seat on the railroad and move to the dirty smoking car set aside for Blacks, white passengers beat him up, stomping his silk hat. The Black activist Mary Church Terrell noted that "self-respecting colored people would not go into the coach set apart for them." When her father produced first-class tickets, the conductor ceased trying to force Terrell and her father into the "colored" car.

Blacks regularly sued to protest such treatment. Ida Wells did so, unsuccessfully, when forced to sit in a filthy Jim Crow car in Tennessee. But others won their cases. In two court decisions in the 1880s, courts ruled in support of Black plaintiffs who had been removed from first-class cars, one judge declaring that railroads forfeited their right to have separate cars for Blacks "when the money of the white man purchases luxurious accommodations amid elegant company and the same amount of money purchases for the black man inferior quarters."

In these cases, as in others, judges ruled that citizens were entitled to what they could pay for. No Black citizen should ride in a separate car "simply because it is set apart and labeled 'exclusively for negroes,'" a Nashville Black attorney argued. "We want public conveyances open to us according to the fare we pay. . . . We cannot go to the [segregated] places assigned us . . . without loss of self-respect."[26]

This, in turn, suggested the degree to which the courts, as well as laypeople, saw the question of racial segregation as intimately tangled up with issues of class, and individual differences of status. If a Black person had risen to the middle or upper class, secured a decent education, purchased a home, and possessed the resources to travel in first-class accommodations, that individual punctured the stereotype implicit in segregation that every Black person was inferior and deserved only second-class treatment. Yet if individual differences in achievement and status were the basis for assigning social space, whites and Blacks alike—if they were poor and ill-educated—would receive lesser treatment, while whites and Blacks alike—if they were well-off—would be treated according to their social station. Race—and hence white supremacy—would lose the paramount and all-encompassing significance that whites insisted it have.

It was largely for that reason that wealthy Blacks of superior achievement challenged the entire foundation of white supremacy. Yet the irony was that many of those same Blacks understood the need to downplay their success lest they be subject to violent reprisals. As one former governor of North Carolina said, "The negro who gets very prosperous is to be pitied, for straightway, he is in a situation where danger confronts him. Let him own a fine farm . . . and dare to ride in a carriage, and if I were an insurance agent, I would not make out a policy on his life. In plain English, to get above his *ordained* situation in life is, generally speaking, to invite assassination [italics added]."[27]

The contradictions were enormous—and everywhere. Growing up in America meant striving to get ahead, yet for Black citizens the act of fulfilling the American dream could bring disaster. As one Black commented, "A Negro did not always feel as safe in a neat cottage with attractive surroundings as he did in a tumbling-down shack." An African American teacher told about a Black man "building a nice house, but the whites advised him not to paint it" if he cared for his personal safety. Ned Cobb encountered the same reality as he moved from plowing someone else's fields to harvesting his own. "Soon as I got to where I . . . was makin' something of myself, then they commenced runnin' at me. . . . They didn't like to see a nigger with too much; they didn't like it one bit." And when Cobb eventually bought a horse and buggy, his white neighbor looked at it "in a way that made it clear he didn't like to see no nigger have an outfit like that." It was such experiences that led W. E. B. Du Bois to observe that white Southerners would much prefer having five hundred Black vagrants to a group of college graduates, "not that they fear Negro crime less, but that they fear Negro ambition and success more." Faced with a choice between being surrounded by poor Black sharecroppers and rich Black professionals, whites would always opt for the former.[28]

The problem with African American prosperity was that it challenged the myth of white superiority. "We are, on the one hand," a British writer noted, "to suppose the negro ambitious, progressive and prosperous, and on the other hand, to imagine him humbly acquiescent in his status as a social pariah." To a foreign observer, the conundrum made no sense. To a white Southerner, on the other hand, the presumption of white superiority and Black inferiority anchored a way of life. As a certain number of Black Southerners began to prosper, white people felt more compelled to hold all Black people down and paint them with the broad brush of innate racial inferiority. After touring the South, one Northern traveler commented on how "the colored race in the South has divided into two classes—one moving upward, the other down. The former class are acquiring property and consideration; the latter are in danger of being swept from the earth." The habits of the rich and poor differed, as often did their skin color, with lighter skinned Blacks being more frequent among the prosperous. Different too were their churches, social patterns, and club life. "Few modern groups," Du Bois observed, "show a greater internal differentiation of social conditions than the Negro American. . . . The forward movement of a social group is not the compact march of an army, where the distance covered is practically the same for all, but is rather the straggling of a crowd, where some of them hasten [and] some linger."[29]

Yet that was precisely the point—difference. Black middle-class citizens went to cultured dance performances and concerts, not juke joints; and having "made it," more and more of them insisted on being treated according to their station. A recently appointed Black college president journeying to his new home in Louisiana saw no reason to move to the dirty "colored" smoking car because a white woman getting on the train needed a seat. Nor did proper Black ladies and gentlemen see any reason why their first-class tickets were worth any less that those of white patrons who had bought the same class of service. As one South Carolina newspaper observed, "Property ownership [and status] . . . make the Negro more assertive [and more independent]." The problem was that "the cracker can't stand it."

Except that it was not just the "cracker." Whites of the middle and upper classes had made their own decision. Henry Grady might argue that "one drop" of Black blood ensured permanent inferiority. The Black writer George Washington Cable, on the other hand, believed that education, culture, and class should be the dividing line. Yet as time passed, historian Grace Hale has noted, notions of "racial essentialism [grew] to counter black success." For growing numbers of whites, segregation became the sine qua non of white racial superiority, with the "division of the world into absolute blackness and whiteness . . . the central metaphor of [a] new [southern] culture."[30]

Thus while significant tensions still existed, and important differences remained in the actual treatment of Blacks on streetcars and railroads from Louisiana to Georgia to North Carolina, a growing tendency emerged to eliminate the distinctions among white individuals and Black individuals, and to make skin color the sole basis for allocating power, station, and rights in the social order. Blacks continued to protest, occasionally with success. Courts still recognized the power of the purse as a criterion for treatment in public facilities, in addition to the color of one's skin. But in the years after federal troops withdrew from Dixie, the idea that Blacks might retain some rights based on their individual achievements rapidly disappeared. Race became the sole variable determining one's status, and an ever tighter system of social controls—really a series of concentric circles of social control—increasingly limited the possibilities available to African Americans.

White Instruments of Control

The first circle of control—and the ultimate threat—was physical violence by whites toward Blacks. A Savannah Black newspaper commented on the frequency with which "prosperous and industrious" Negroes were killed. In truth, no Black could feel safe. "In those days," said one Black man, "it was 'kill a mule, buy another. Kill a nigger, hire another. They had to have a license to kill anything but a nigger. We was always in season."[31]

Nor was there any predicting when terror would strike. "Back in those days," another Black man said, "to kill a Negro . . . was like killing a chicken. . . . The whites would say, 'Niggers jest supposed to die, ain't no damn good anyway—so jest go on an' kill 'em." When Richard Wright was growing up, he asked his mother why Blacks did not fight back. She replied: "[Because] the white men have guns and the black men don't." Worst of all, the very capriciousness of violence made its power overwhelming. "Indeed," Wright wrote in *Black Boy*, "the white brutality that I had *not* seen was a more effective control of my behavior than that which I knew. . . . As long as it remained something terrible and yet remote, something whose horror and blood might descend upon me at any moment, I was compelled to give my entire imagination over to it, an act which blocked the springs of thought and feeling in me." Nor did violence necessarily have to involve lynching. Repeatedly, Black young people of a later generation talked about white school buses careening down a road where they were *walking* to school, then speeding up "to hit [puddles] as hard as [they] can, . . . try[ing] to wet us down and put our eyes out." Assessing the sheer ubiquity of white terror, historian Leon Litwack concluded, "The extent and quality of violence unleashed on black men and women in the name of enforcing black deference . . . cannot be avoided or minimized."[32]

Yet violence was only the outermost circle of social control. Equally pernicious were the ways whites used economic power, the law, and psychological intimidation to curb Black freedom. The economic circle of control appeared every time a Black farmer brought his crop to market and encountered a white merchant who calculated the value of the crop, then compared it to the farmer's indebtedness, and concluded that the Black farmer had not only failed to make a profit, but instead—by the white man's estimation—had fallen deeper into debt. Blacks could be common laborers, domestic servants, or sharecroppers; or they could preach and teach and perhaps even practice medicine in the Black community; but never could they compete for the same jobs or opportunities as whites. Whites would rather pay Blacks starvation wages than recognize their dignity with a living income. "I, who stole nothing," Richard Wright notes, "who wanted to look them in the face, who wanted to talk and act like a man, inspired fear in them. . . . [But] Southern whites [preferred that] Negroes who stole work for them . . . [placing] a premium upon black deceit; they encouraged irresponsibility, and their rewards were bestowed upon us as blacks in the degree that we could make them feel safe and superior."[33]

Such treatment blended seamlessly with the psychological intimidation whites deployed. It started in childhood. Black children and white children might play together, almost as equals "when you're small," one Black man said, "but now, quick as he gets a little age on him, he wants you to call him Mister." As a young adolescent, Richard Wright performed household chores for a white family. Part of his wages were in food. But as the white family ate bacon and eggs, he was served week-old bread with moldy molasses. When his employer, a woman, asked why he was still going to school, Wright responded, "I want to be a writer." "Who put that idea into your crazy nigger head," she replied. At every turn, Blacks were cut down, their manhood and womanhood denigrated, the humanity they shared in common with whites dismissed with a racist wave of the hand. And when Blacks persisted, the government and the law could be used against them. Whites created separate registration books for Black voters, separate voting lines, with fewer poll workers to serve the Black voters, and, overnight, new rules and regulations to help disenfranchise Black voters.[34]

While many Blacks continued to fight back in whatever way they could, it often was necessary, simply in order to survive, for many others to dissemble, play roles, and appease white people whose power over them was growing increasingly tight. "Had to act . . . just as though everything was all right," Ned Cobb remembered. "Had to do whatever the white man directed 'em to do, couldn't voice their heart's desire." At a given moment in growing up—usually just before adolescence—the consciousness dawned that one had to suppress real emotions and substitute those that whites wished to see. "We kep our places," one Black said of growing up in the 1880s. "We always remembered dere wuz a difference. We didn't furgit we wuz black." The bottom line was summed up by Benjamin Mays, the man who would become president of Morehouse College, one of Black America's proudest institutions of higher education. "In this perilous world," Mays noted, "if a black boy wanted to live a halfway normal life and die a natural death he had to learn early the art of how to get along with white folks."[35]

One way to "get along with white folks" was to dissemble. In order to placate white expectations—and survive—Blacks adopted a "grinning deference, acquiescence by inflections, gesture and demeanor." But often the result was a form of schizophrenia. A famous blues song evoked the duality: "Got one mind for white folks to see, 'Nother for what I know is me; He don't know, he don't know my mind, When he see me laughing, Just laughing to keep from crying." The African American author Zora Neale Hurston dug even deeper. "[White man] can read my writing," she said, "but he 'sho can't read my mind. I'll put this play toy in his hand, and he will seize it and go away. Then I'll say my say and sing my song." When Richard Wright's friend Griggs chastised him for his risky behavior—"You're black and you don't act a damn bit like it"—Wright responded, "Oh Christ, I can't be a slave." But then Griggs delivered the lesson. "You've got to eat. . . . When you are in front of white people, think before you act, think before you speak." This was Black people's "darky act," as novelist Ralph Ellison called it, "the mask that grins and lies," in writer Paul Lawrence Dunbar's phrase. But behind the mask lay a different person, seeking a better life for children and family even while bobbing and weaving to pacify white people's need to feel complacent about the state of racial affairs—two selves, moving back and forth, one to deceive white people, the other holding on to oneself. This was the "double consciousness" that W. E. B. Du Bois wrote about so powerfully, two selves in one body, struggling to find a way forward while retaining one's integrity and self-esteem.[36]

Nothing better crystallized the sickness of white supremacy than the circles of control white people relied on to enforce their dominance, and the charade of deference some Blacks adopted as the price of staying alive. It was a pathology whites depended on, as they confused, in Ralph Ellison's words, "slave and ex-slave masks with [real] black selves." Blacks understood the pathology well, reflecting it in the lyrics of their songs and the insights of their humor. Most whites, on the other hand, embraced the lie of Blacks dissembling literally—"an absurdity never more evident," Ellison wrote, "than in their ante- and post-bellum assertions that they alone understood 'their Negroes.'"[37]

The period from 1877 through 1890 exemplified all this confusion, highlighting the risks and dangers present in any given moment. For some Black Southerners, it was a time of continued political self-assertion and rising prosperity; for others, it became an era of dismaying poverty, shattered dreams, and a resignation to white oppression that brought forth the "mask" of role playing as a means of buying time for the next phase of struggle. But the motif of the era was ambiguity. The world was full of chaos; nothing seemed predictable. In the kaleidoscope of race relations in a South that no longer had federal troops, but had not yet institutionalized unqualified white supremacy, one fundamental question remained: How would "the state" resolve the ongoing quest of Black Americans for full political and economic rights, and the insistence of powerful whites that such a quest be forever obliterated?

The Dawn of Jim Crow: 1890–1900

In both the 1880s and the 1890s, Black activists, with the support of some poor white farmers, repeatedly threatened to upend the racial status quo and inaugurate a new era of grassroots democratic reform in the South. It began with the Readjuster Movement in Virginia in the 1880s, then moved on to a coalition between the Southern Farmers Alliance and the Colored Farmers Alliance in several Southern states in the 1890s. The movement for a totally new kind of politics culminated with the Fusion movement in North Carolina between 1894 and 1898—an alliance of Populists and Republicans that came as close as anything since the height of Reconstruction to realizing the goal of a true economic democracy built on equal rights for both whites and Blacks. Still, even as hope burgeoned, white supremacists, using draconian methods, fought viciously to suppress these activist voices, and not only retain, but strengthen immeasurably, the iron rule of white supremacy.

That outcome was by no means preordained. And what remains tantalizingly compelling is the alternative agenda that Blacks and their white allies in the South helped bring to fruition, even if only temporarily. Indeed, if the experience of North Carolina is any indicator, the vision of a true biracial democracy was never closer than in

1898—until the very moment that it was snatched away and snuffed out amidst murder and mayhem.[38]

Placing shared economic interest ahead of racial division constituted the heart of all three efforts to dismantle the white power structure. In Virginia, the reformers were called "Readjusters." Made up of white and Black Republicans and—crucially—a group of Democrats and Independents, they won electoral power in 1879 and instituted dramatic political change for the four years they held power. Electing two US senators, six of ten Congressmen, and a governor, the Readjusters openly embraced the principle of equal rights for Blacks. In the words of the *New York Post*, "They are fighting caste. They assert that they represent the dignity of labor [and] . . . they champion the rights of man against the privileges of an aristocracy."

Consistent with that perspective, the Readjusters increased public monies for Black and white schools, raised taxes on railroads, lowered them on average citizens, and aggressively pursued popular control of government. As Governor William Mahone declared in his inaugural address, "Today, Virginia . . . [offers] all the blessings of free citizenship, of absolute freedom in politics and religion [to its citizens]. . . . The laws of Virginia guarantee equal protection and privilege to every citizen." Explicitly burying the color line in politics, the Readjusters appointed Blacks as postmasters, justices, police officers, and teachers. "Under the Readjusters," one Black woman said, "for the first time black men feel like men." And although the Readjuster movement in Virginia eventually fell victim to a revived charge that what Blacks really were seeking was "social equality"—mixed schools, the *Richmond Dispatch* argued, led to mixed marriages—the movement clearly suggested a powerful alternative to white supremacist politics.[39]

Potentially even more powerful was the emergence of agrarian radicalism in the Farmers' Alliances movements that spread like wildfire across the South in the mid- to late 1880s. Growing out of the Greenbacker movement and the Agricultural Wheel of Arkansas—social movements committed to more fluid currency and to agricultural reform—the white Southern Farmers' Alliance recruited organizers in each county. These organizers, in turn, convened weekly rallies at local churches and homesteads. There, poor farmers gathered to hear Alliance speakers dissect the horrors of the existing system of peonage and advocate instead taking over state governments. They also demanded that the federal government buy farmers' crops, then store them in federal warehouses until market prices rose and the time was ripe to sell. Under this program, there would no longer need to be loans from furnishing merchants, or the debilitating impact of creeping indebtedness. The alliance program called instead for the federal government to issue more money (the Greenbacker link), open public lands to homesteaders, and introduce a graduated income tax—all as a means of undermining the crop lien system and control of agriculture by rich planters and bankers. Using a phalanx of "lecture/organizers" and movement newspapers, the Alliance generated massive excitement in local communities, imparted a new sense of empowerment to farmers fed up with perpetual indebtedness, and offered a political platform that reached out to labor (the Alliance called for recognition of unions and workers' rights) and other disenfranchised groups who were fighting the status quo. By the end of the decade, the Southern Alliance claimed almost a million members.

So too did the Colored Farmers Alliance. Choosing to organize separately, the Colored Alliance adopted many of the same organizing tactics as its white counterpart. Meeting in Black churches, using organizers in each county to visit farmers and mobilize grassroots support, the Colored Farmers Alliance had recruited up to a million members by the late 1880s. Most important, although the Colored Farmers Alliance remained distinct from the white Southern Alliance, the two groups functioned in ways that made them a mirror image of each other. Moreover, each group engaged in repeated efforts at building bridges between the two.[40]

Perhaps most important, the two Alliances seemed ready to join forces to overthrow the existing economic oligarchy. "There is no reason," the charismatic Southern Farmers Alliance leader Tom Watson declared in the 1890s, "why the black man should not understand that the law that hurts me, as a farmer, hurts him as a farmer." Self-interest, Watson argued, should prevail over racial tensions. "The accident of color," he declared, "can make no difference in the interests of farmers, croppers and laborers." Watson ordered his own devoted followers to protect a Black man threatened with lynching. While both the Colored Alliance and the Southern Farmer's Alliance continued to defend having separate organizations, more and more they met together at the same places, and endorsed the same political platforms and candidates. When national figures came to town, white and colored farmers alike shared the honor of escorting them. It was not as explicit a commitment to biracialism as occurred with the Readjusters, but given the numbers involved, and the overall power of the collective movement, the Alliance threat to the white supremacist politics of racial division came as close to piercing the heart of the system of white supremacy politics as at any time since Reconstruction.[41]

Precisely for that reason, beginning in 1890, those who constituted the ruling class of the South sought systematically to disenfranchise Black voters. Led by bankers, rich white planters, furnishing merchants, and the up-and-coming manufacturing class, the political elite sought to remove *all* Black participants from the political system. In effect, they were repeating the effort of their eighteenth-century forebears who insisted that race—the fact of being white—totally trumped class, the importance of economic differences between rich and poor. Thus, the campaign to eliminate the vote for Blacks had two purposes: first, to destroy the possibility of a class-based biracial coalition of poor whites and Blacks directed against rich whites; and second, to crush the one symbol of freedom—the ballot—that more than any other signified to Black Americans their emancipation from slavery.

After Congress proved unwilling in 1890 to enact the Lodge Bill, which would have sanctioned federal intervention on behalf of Black voting rights, powerful Southern Democrats felt free to proceed. One tack was to impose a poll tax—a critical instrument of disenfranchisement that had already worked well in Montgomery, Nashville, and Atlanta. But Mississippi took the lead in straightforwardly defying the federal government and implementing statewide disenfranchisement of Blacks.[42]

Mississippi moved forward because it remained one of the places where Black political insurgency continued to be a viable presence. Blacks demanded more offices, refused to pay their taxes unless allowed to vote, initiated discussions with Democrats about fusion tickets, applied for more and more federal civil service positions, and—in convention—demanded federal intervention "to break up lawlessness and ballot-box stuffing." In three out of seven Mississippi congressional districts, Republicans mounted a serious challenge to Democrats.[43]

In the face of such ongoing turmoil, the Democrats called a constitutional convention that would put a permanent halt to independent Black political power, and the prospect of any biracial coalitions based on economic self-interest that might challenge white rule. As if to demonstrate the potential of such coalitions and the degree to which traditional white rule was threatened, the Democratic call for a convention barely passed. Moreover, once it was in session, close divisions occurred between predominantly white and predominantly Black counties over educational or property requirements for the right to vote. Yet in the end, the "Mississippi Plan" passed: a poll tax and a residency requirement were imposed, prospective voters were required to pass a literacy test, and the secret ballot was introduced, which essentially made it impossible for those who were functionally illiterate to vote. Reluctantly, Isaiah Montgomery, the one Black delegate to the convention, went along with the education and property criteria, believing that at the very least, one-third of the existing Black electorate would still be able to vote.

In reality, few if any Blacks were able to qualify—and as subsequent history would prove, most poor whites were eventually also disenfranchised on similar grounds, ensuring that politics would remain for decades the domain of well-off white people. Louisiana, Florida, and Tennessee enacted similar provisions. In Louisiana 100 percent of white males and 95.2 percent of Black males were registered in 1897. One year later, the number was 46.6 percent of white males, and 9.5 percent of Black males. In Mississippi, after the disenfranchisement laws, Black registration fell by 96 percent, the number of Blacks who could vote plummeting from 190,000 to 8,000. Asked about the passage of laws denying Blacks the vote, Virginia senator Carter Glass announced: "Discrimination! Why that is precisely what we propose . . . with a view to [eliminate] every Negro voter who can be gotten rid of." The first phase of Black disenfranchisement had begun, inaugurating a decade that would see a rapid hardening of attitudes toward racial separation and an extraordinary resurgence of Black political strength before the final, total suppression of Black rights occurred.[44]

The one issue on which courts had upheld the right of individual Blacks—the ability to ride in first-class accommodations—now also came under attack. In earlier state court decisions, segregation ordinances regarding railroad cars had been struck down on the grounds that everyone had the right to ride in the category of seat they could afford. Black resistance had focused less on separate institutions than on the legal mandate that *all* Blacks be consigned to inferior facilities. The issue was raised once again in Louisiana in 1890, with Black and white legislators joining together to reject a Jim Crow railroad bill. But shortly thereafter, whites defected from their Black allies and wrote the segregation rule into law. A Black man named Homer Plessy—who was actually seven-eighths white—soon tested the law, seeking arrest in order to challenge the courts once more to determine whether the ability to pay—an issue of class—overrode the color of one's skin, even if the person might otherwise pass for white. While the case made its way through the appeals process, most other Southern states, with the notable exceptions of North Carolina, South Carolina, and Virginia, enacted similar statutes.[45]

It was a time when the entire country seemed increasingly racist. Chinese immigration had been banned in 1892; a new eugenics movement was thriving; and the nation's newspapers were trumpeting the notion of America having a "manifest destiny" where it could proceed to impose its rule on "heathens" in foreign countries. Moreover, at last some Black leaders seemed, on the surface at least, ready to accommodate the new trend. In 1895 Booker T. Washington, the president of Tuskegee Institute, told the assembled white throngs at the Atlanta Exposition that Blacks should be prepared to embrace the work of farming and industrial labor; forgo the struggle for equality with whites in higher education, politics, and the professions; and, in "all things purely social," accept the reality that whites and Blacks could be as separate as the fingers on a hand.[46]

It was in this context that the Supreme Court heard the *Plessy v. Ferguson* case in 1896. "Segregation," it decreed in an 8 to 1 decision, was "in the nature of things." Whatever the Fourteenth Amendment required, the equal protection clause did not envision "enforced commingling of the races." Each locality enjoyed the right to establish the rules and regulations it chose regarding race and public accommodations, and if one race felt itself "inferior to the other socially," that was the problem of the people of that race: "The Constitution of the United States cannot put them on the same plane." Class—or the individual rights of a Negro citizen to buy a first-class ticket—mattered not at all. Race determined everything.

Justice John Harlan, in a ringing dissent, spoke for the ages in recognizing the consequences of such reasoning. "The destinies of the two races in this country are indissolubly linked together," he wrote, "and the interests of both require that the common government of all shall not permit the seeds of race hate to be planted under the sanction of the law." Yet by its ruling, the Court had undermined "the beneficent purposes" of the Fourteenth Amendment, sowed the seed of race hatred, and concluded, on behalf of the government of the United States, that "colored citizens are so inferior and degraded that they cannot be allowed to sit in public coaches occupied by white citizens."[47]

The highest court of the land had now blessed the essentialism of race as the ultimate determinant of an individual citizen's rights. Not only had the Court eviscerated the Fourteenth Amendment, cutting the heart out of the meaning of "equal protection" before the law, it also had forced Black Americans into a legal and political box from which they would not be able to extricate themselves for nearly sixty years. From *Plessy* forward, Blacks would have to use as the framework for seeking change a premise that segregation was part of the basic law of the land, and only its unequal implementation could be challenged as a denial of equal citizenship rights. In short, *Plessy*—by presuming the constitutionality of segregation—created an almost impossible legal dilemma for those who wished to challenge that assumption.

How strange, then, that at the same time Booker T. Washington was delivering his speech in Atlanta and the Supreme Court was hearing the arguments in *Plessy*, Blacks in North Carolina were bringing to fruition the fondest hopes that Black Americans had entertained in the aftermath of Emancipation and Reconstruction—a biracial democracy that celebrated the achievements of both races and was committed to biracial politics. Ever since Abraham Galloway, North Carolina had spawned strong Black leaders like Bishop J. W. Hood and George White. Although ups and downs characterized the North Carolina experience, Blacks boasted a consistent record of office holding. Moreover, as individuals, they repeatedly disproved the notion that all Black people should be poor, submissive, and deferential. Middle-class and professional Blacks rode in fine carriages, built quality homes, and displayed the lifestyle appropriate to their station.

New Bern was one site where Blacks thrived. More than 25 percent of its Black residents were already free in 1860. Edward Dudley, whose mother had taught him to read and write, became one of the first Black legislators, and went on to serve as justice of the peace in New Bern from 1880 to 1884. The local Democratic paper reflected the degree to which this might be a different kind of city. "Drawing the color line is wrong in principle," the paper editorialized in 1886. "Why seek to array one race against another? The negroes are citizens, and have the right of suffrage."[48]

The story of Blacks in North Carolina offered more encouragement than despair. Sarah Dudley, the daughter of Edward, went to

Normal School in New Bern, where she was trained to be a teacher by other African American teachers. She then went to Scotia Seminary, one of the post-secondary schools founded by Northern missionaries. Subsequently, she married a prominent minister, Charles Petty. They and their neighbors lived in fine homes, with pianos and servants and lace curtains. The Pettys opposed segregation, calling it "class" legislation. They deeply regretted the "Mississippi Plan" of 1890, but they saw such actions as temporary setbacks. In their own state, Black doctors were being trained at a new medical school at Shaw University, friends of theirs held significant political power, and the future still looked bright.[49]

The Pettys believed in the "Best Man" approach to political and social dilemmas. Parallel to what W. E. B. Du Bois would later call his faith in the "talented tenth" of both races to solve America's racial dilemma, the Best Man approach presumed that talented African Americans would pursue higher education, be civically active, marry well into stable families, and above all, work with their white peers to resolve community problems. What this amounted to, in effect, was a faith that by accepting the rules of the larger society and putting their own benchmarks of accomplishment on the wall, they would advance the opportunities available to talented Black people, and in conjunction with their white peers of the same class, achieve a life of greater freedom and accomplishment.[50]

As evidence to support the Best Man theory, Blacks had successfully defended their citizenship status in New Bern. They worked as post office clerks, were elected to the City Council, and taught in the schools. They also stood up for themselves, as reflected in the story of Jim Harris and Laura Lomax, a couple who were insulted by a white man whom Harris (and some of his friends) then beat up, and eventually brought to court on charges of assaulting Laura Lomax (she was the daughter of a Black bishop). Such displays of self-defense and self-assertion suggested a readiness on the part of at least some Blacks—and some whites—to play by the same rules. The Best Men in the Black community would control and discipline the rowdy behavior of poor Blacks, just as, it was hoped, the Best Men in the white community would restrain the anti-social and racist behavior of poor whites. The key assumption here, of course, was that the Best White Men would play the part assigned them under the overall Best Man paradigm.[51]

Two problems led ultimately to the unraveling of the Best Man approach. First, it was not at all clear that whites were willing to grant special privilege to Blacks who *were* middle class. The courts might agree, as they did in the 1880s, that if you had the money to buy a first-class ticket, you could get first-class treatment. Yet no consensus existed to that effect, and it was more blind faith than evidence of things seen, that well-off whites would choose not to indulge their own racism, which was equal to if not greater than that ascribed to poor whites. It might be true *that some* of the history of Black/white relations in Wilmington gave the Pettys and others reason to believe that the Best Whites could be trusted. But it was still, in most respects, a leap of faith.

Second, given the turbulence of racial politics in the South, the effort of *some* North Carolina Blacks and whites to pursue an interracial movement to unseat the white political and economic oligarchy would inevitably end up challenging directly the rule of the Best White Men. How they would respond was in no way predictable.

Still, a new Fusion movement crested in North Carolina in 1894. It joined together a biracial coalition of Black Republicans and white Populists. For the first time since 1876, Democrats failed to control the legislature. Two years later, the Fusionist candidate for governor won, with banners proclaiming "The Chains of Servitude Are Broken." A political revolution seemed in the offing, whites working side by side with Blacks on city councils, school boards, police forces—even the state legislature and the US Congress.[52]

During the period of Fusion rule in North Carolina, Black Americans exercised more political power than at any time since Emancipation. Election procedures were reformed to facilitate more Black voting; the legislature increased taxes on railroads and bolstered support for schools. Home rule was restored so that local communities with a substantial Black presence were able to recruit Black citizens to join law enforcement forces and court offices. Hundreds of African Americans received government appointments. In New Bern the postmaster was Black, as were four of the sheriff's deputies. When a white woman bartender broke the law, she was arrested by a Black officer and brought before a Black magistrate. Confrontations between white and Black women highlighted both the new assertiveness of Black women, and the explosive tensions latent when issues of gender and class intersected. In Wilmington, a Black woman obstructed the path of a white woman, and when whites tried to move her aside, she stabbed the white woman with her umbrella, a Black man urging her on, "That's right, damn it, give it to her." In the words of historian Glenda Gilmore, North Carolina had embarked upon a "daring experiment" which, if successful, would pose a stark alternative to the world of Jim Crow being imposed elsewhere.[53]

But powerful white Democrats in North Carolina, like their counterparts in Mississippi and Louisiana, were intent on not letting that happen. The real parallel to the Best Black Man turned out not to be the Best White Man—the Black man's peer in gentility, tolerance, and statesmanship—but what Gilmore has called instead the "New White Men." Many were in fact the "best" white men. They shared the same upper-class origins as former planters. Others were upwardly mobile members of the new middle class. They were journalists like Josephus Daniels, editor of the *Raleigh News and Observer* and distinguished lawyers and writers such as Charles Aycock and Thomas Dixon. Far from wishing to share their class status with talented Blacks, they were intent on regaining control of power, eliminating the complexity of biracial politics, and re-creating a simple, bifurcated world in which all Blacks were treated one way, and all whites another. Repeatedly, Aycock and Daniels circulated the blasphemous doctrine that all Black men were out to rape white women.

Stories like those coming out of Wilmington and New Bern of Black women challenging white women with their umbrellas led to a sharp response: the New White Men must galvanize the white community around the issue of protecting white womanhood, not only from "sassy" Black women who challenged their status, but more importantly, from brutal Black men who, by the definition of these New White Men, sought to take sexual advantage of white women. As Glenda Gilmore notes, "By emphasizing sexuality, the Democrats placed race over class and spun a yarn in which white women of all classes highly prized their chastity and black men of all classes barely controlled their sexuality."[54]

These were, of course, some of the issues on which the Best Black Men hoped to make common cause with their white allies. Blacks of the upper class denounced aberrant behavior by lower class Blacks, including in areas of sexuality. Here, they sought to play the "class card." "There are at least two grades of society into which each of our races may be classified," the pastor of Sarah Petty's church said in response to charges that all Blacks were responsible for a case of rape, "and as a better remedy than lynching, I suggest . . . a combination of sentiment and purpose between the best elements of both races."

But the New White Men were not ready to accept such terms of distinction. Their own political aspirations depended on white solidarity on issues of race, not subtle distinctions based on education, achievement, and wealth. From their perspective, the "social equality" issue was the defining one of the day—a natural path to victory—and they would permit nothing to dilute their brazen appeal to white solidarity.[55]

In calculated fashion, these New White Men linked reports of sexual assault to Fusion rule. The state's leading newspaper, edited by Josephus Daniels, inflamed white readers by publishing exaggerated stories of Black insolence toward whites, and harped on every episode of reported rape. White Democrats created "White Government Leagues" to drive home the vengeful message of white racism. "Rise, ye sons of Carolina!" a Government League song went, "Proud Caucasians one and all; Be not Deaf to Love's appealing—Hear your wives and daughters call, See their blanched and anxious faces, Note their frail but lovely forms, Rise, defend their spotless virtue, With your strong and manly arms." Every episode of racial conflict was played up, each using the vulnerability of white womanhood as the crucible for galvanizing white rage against Blacks.[56]

Negro leaders retorted that individuals, not racial groups, were responsible for violations of a person's sexuality. Class status proved more predictable than a person's race as a source of aberrant behavior. Thus Alexander Manly, the proud and courageous editor of Wilmington's Black newspaper, declared that "the morals of the poor white are on a par with their colored neighbors of like conditions"—to wit, the lower classes in *both* races were the problem. Carrying the argument still further, Manly wrote that, in a similar fashion, white women were not "any more particular in the matter of clandestine meetings with colored men, than are the white men with colored women."

But *there* was the rub. Manly was arguing that "loose" women and "loose" men of both races were equally disposed to cross the race line in their sexual liaisons—hence the issue was not white purity contrasted to Black lasciviousness, but a case of individual behavior tied to class origins. White men, Manly implied, had simply been careless in protecting their women.[57]

That view was "vile and villainous," declared Josephus Daniels. White newspapers throughout the state reprinted Manly's editorial, and Daniels's paper itself circulated a record 300,000 copies. "If it does not make every decent man's blood boil," one paper editorialized, "then the manhood is gone, and with it Anglo-Saxon loyalty to the pure and noble white women of our land." The White Government Leagues mobilized around the forthcoming elections in 1898, asking supporters to join together in destroying the Black threat to white sovereignty. "We hope the white men will read again and again that brutal attack [by Manly]," another editorial said, "and swear upon the altar of their country to wipe out negro rule for all time in the noble old commonwealth." Leading the statewide crusade was Charles Aycock, Democratic candidate for governor: "I come to you today on behalf of the goddess of Democracy, the white womanhood of the state, and I appeal to you to come to their relief. Will you come to their rescue? Will you?" Citing eight recent incidents of rape in North Carolina, Aycock insisted that the crimes were all products of Fusion rule.[58]

In Wilmington, these events fused into an explosive cauldron, the energies of race hatred focusing on the city, not only where Alexander Manly published his paper, but where Black political self-assertion had reached new heights. By 1897, half of the city's aldermen were Black. The governor had appointed dozens of Blacks to political positions. Manly's editorial response to those whites who accused all Black men of having rapist instincts created a situation that was anathema to conservative whites in the city—men who not only seized on the rhetoric of white essentialism, but also were prepared to zero in on local Black activists.

At the head of the white vigilante movement was Alfred Waddell, a Democratic leader in the city. One group of white vigilantes targeted the demands of Black women for equal treatment on streetcars, vowing to put an end to rising crime and to "negro women parad[ing] the streets and insulting men and ladies." Together with Red Shirt companies formed by whites, Waddell set out to mobilize whites to intimidate Black voters, and to purge the city of even the possibility of Blacks going to the ballot box. The day before the election in 1898, Waddell exhorted his white townsmen: "You are Anglo-Saxons," he declared. "You are armed and prepared, and you will do your duty." If the Black man tried to vote, Waddell declared, "kill him, shoot him down in his tracks," choking the [Cape] Fear River "with bodies if necessary." Other "new white men"—and poor whites—rallied to Waddell's banner. A cousin—a woman—provided reinforcement for his plea from the perspective of white women. "It has reached the point," she said, "when bloodletting is needed for the health of the commonwealth." Quoting the Bible, she pointed out: "Solomon says, 'There is a time to kill.' That time seems to have come . . . and don't stop short of a complete clearing of the decks."[59]

It seemed as if the entire white community was listening. Shortly after election day, hundreds of whites joined a rampage through the streets, led by a prominent white organizer, Hugh McCrae. Armed with two cannons and a rapid-firing gun, they terrorized the Black community, seized city hall, burned down Manly's newspaper office, and in accordance with Waddell's exhortations, filled the Cape Fear River with Black bodies. Scores were killed, while hundreds of other Blacks escaped to the woods and eventually left Wilmington. With Waddell now occupying the sheriff's office, Aycock was elected to the governorship, and Black officeholders were driven from their posts. It was as if in one day the whole world had turned upside down. The optimism of Sarah Petty had been crushed, the courage and fortitude of Alexander Manly smashed to pieces. No longer could the Black community have any faith in the Best Man approach. Whites of all classes, triggered by the rhetoric of people like Aycock and the *News and Observer's* Josephus Daniels, had taken to the streets to re-establish the rule of white supremacy, once and for all. The radical hopes of Fusionists for a biracial democracy had been quashed—by the "best" white men.[60]

The next year, the newly elected Democratic regime in Raleigh officially moved to disenfranchise Blacks with a literacy test and poll tax. When Congressman George White, the last African American officeholder, asked federal officials in Washington for help, he was turned away. After his term of office ended, he sought exile in New Jersey. "They manage us like oxen," he said. "I cannot live in North Carolina and be a man." As if to demonstrate how complete a disaster had occurred, when two Black federal officials sought to attend a Republican convention in North Carolina, they were booed from the hall, the delegates singing, "Morning, night or noon, It's better to be a white man than a coon, coon, coon." Just two years earlier, the Black vision of political equality had seemed finally within reach, at least in one state. Now, that dream had exploded in the face of the determination by whites—upper-class whites with power, the "best white men"—to make the essentialism of race the sole basis for dividing power, resources, and human rights. It was, one Black leader declared, like the "shock of an earthquake," realigning the very foundations on which one lived.[61]

Reflections

With the *Plessy v. Ferguson* decision in 1896 and the Wilmington race riot in 1898, the struggle by African Americans for full recognition of their rights had encountered barriers that would take decades to overcome. Blacks had always supported institutions in their own community—churches, schools, lodges, women's associations—created by and for members of the Black race. As long as they could build those institutions, they would strengthen their own community, using their home base as a departure point from which to engage in ongoing efforts to compete with whites, as well as function together with them in a multiracial society. Thus Black Americans had not opposed separation per se. What they did oppose was state-imposed segregation that denied the race as a whole the right to equal treatment under the law; hence, the long years of protest against being denied first-class railroad tickets, or the individual right to choose how and where to spend one's money. Differences existed within the white community and within the Black community, Black leaders argued, and these individual differences should be the basis for social relationships and behavioral norms.

The US Supreme Court had rejected the argument of individual rights and equal protection before the law, opting instead for a race-based exclusion that insisted that all whites were superior and all Blacks inferior. The fact that it was the Supreme Court that decided this—and by an 8 to 1 vote—meant that the fundamental law of the land now contradicted the spirit and substance of the Fourteenth Amendment. Just as important, *Plessy* now meant that Blacks had to carry on their fight for freedom inside a box that already, by definition, constrained their freedom. They might argue that a separate facility was not, in fact, equal, and thus violated the "separate but equal" standard established by the Court. But they had to argue within a framework which declared that segregation by race was fully compatible with the US Constitution.

Even worse, the Wilmington killings signaled the intention of prominent and powerful white people to use terrorism to keep Black people from asserting their rights. Violence had always constituted the most extreme of tools by which whites could exercise control over Blacks. Lynchings, burnings, beatings—all these were commonplace in the years after Emancipation—made the willingness of the federal government to step in and protect Black citizens essential to the continuation of the Black struggle for freedom. Now, vigilante violence increased. On average, three Black people per week were lynched in the United States from 1890 to 1917.

But what made the Wilmington race riot most frightening was the state sanction of the violence. It had been promoted by the "best white men" of the state; moreover, as soon as it accomplished its goals, they followed up on it by systematically disenfranchising Blacks. Nor did they have the decency to even be embarrassed by what they were doing, either in North Carolina or in the other states that followed North Carolina's lead in embracing Jim Crow and Black disenfranchisement. "Discrimination! Why that is precisely what we propose," Carter Glass of Virginia proclaimed, as the Virginia constitutional convention prepared its own disenfranchisement measures. And he was echoed by a Louisiana delegate to that state's constitutional convention: "Doesn't it stop the black man from voting," he asked, "and isn't that what we came here for?" When a skeptic asked whether or not Christ himself could register to vote under Alabama's "understanding" clause, a politician said, with a verbal wink, "[Well] that would depend entirely on which way he was going to vote."[62]

It was now clear that the state sanctioned the denial of fundamental human rights. Before it had been individual factions within the state that did that. The situation was fluid, with accommodations between whites and Blacks occurring even after 1877; and occasional breakthroughs took place in the direction of freedom and equality, as manifested by the Readjusters in Virginia, the Farmer's Alliances in the late 1880s, and the Fusion movement in North Carolina. But now whites with power determined to suppress all Black rights. As Senator Furnifold Simmons of North Carolina said: "Governor Aycock . . . and I decided that the Democratic Party must go forward educationally, industrially and morally, but in order to do that . . . the negro *can never come back into politics again*" (italics added). No more equivocation. The state would impose a denial of rights as a condition of birth, and it would not shy away from using violence to reinforce that result. To be born Black was to be denied the fundamental rights of political freedom and citizenship allegedly guaranteed to every American.[63]

Throughout the three and a half decades since Emancipation, Black Americans in the South had used every instrument at their command to advance their own freedom, claim the right to decent jobs and a homestead, secure the benefits of an education for their children, and fight for political justice and recognition. While their struggle had been unwavering, their progress was more akin to climbing peaks and descending into valleys than a straight journey forward. The initial freedom struggles of Blacks had brought joy, anticipation, and some victories, only to have these cut back by a president who sought to restore antebellum white leaders to their prior positions. Then, with the dawn of Reconstruction came a resurrection of Black political hopes and achievements. If forty acres and a mule no longer seemed in the offing, the right to vote, to negotiate one's own labor contract, and to share in the benefits of democratic self-rule appeared guaranteed by the Fourteenth and Fifteenth Amendments, and the presence of federal troops. Then, with the Republican betrayal of 1877 came a new setback—the withdrawal of federal forces, and the restoration of white Democratic rule.

Even then, amidst the vicious social controls put in place by whites, Black self-assertion continued, with promises—sometimes realized—of biracial coalitions coming into being. Nowhere did such promises seem more exhilarating than in North Carolina. Then, with the

Wilmington race riot and the Supreme Court decision in *Plessy*, the veil descended once again. The government of the United States now was formally committed to the doctrine of segregation, and the assorted states of the Confederacy explicitly conspired to deny Black Americans their basic rights of citizenship.

It was like having to start all over again, on a new stage. But this time, the stage was defined by opposition—not potential support—from politicians in Washington, and by the recognition that whites with power in the South would frame every issue according to the essentialism of race.

In the end, African Americans would not set aside their struggle for freedom in America. A people sold into slavery would not give up their quest for emancipation and collective advancement, even when their "owners" broke up families and brutalized them. But now, a new set of conditions existed, defined by race, built on segregation, and premised on Blacks' inability to exercise fundamental citizenship rights. Now, the struggle would be harder, take more fortitude, and involve more imagination.

Yet hope still persisted, reflected in the words of the Black poet Langston Hughes: "I, too, Sing America. I am the darker brother, They send me to eat in the kitchen, When company comes, But I laugh, And eat well, And grow strong. Tomorrow, I'll sit at the table. When company comes, Nobody'll dare say to me, 'Eat in the kitchen' then. Besides they'll see how beautiful I am, And be ashamed, — I, too, am America."

Chapter 3

Family, Church, and Community

As Black Americans faced ever tightening efforts to limit their freedom and autonomy in the years after Reconstruction, they relied more and more on their own institutions, both as a source of strength and as a base from which to take on the wider world. In response to the concentric circles of social control that whites used to confine them, Blacks developed their own concentric circles of resistance and opportunity. These were, first, family, church, and community; second, education and work; and third, politics and resistance. No matter how oppressive whites were in their insistence on total domination, Black Americans never ceased to fight back. They retained control of their own responses, never giving up their own agency and power to resist. Even without any outside help, they always battled for their freedom, in the process laying the foundation for a frontal attack on the white oppressors who tried to keep them in bondage.

The historian Rayford Logan has written that the years between 1898 and the New Deal constituted the "nadir" of the African American experience. The number of Blacks who were lynched soared; white-organized race riots decimated Black communities; and political rights were trampled upon, as if the very idea that Blacks were citizens represented a fantasy.

African Americans struggled to find a road that might lead them out of the wilderness. Some rallied to the message of accommodation with white rule, preached by Tuskegee president Booker T. Washington. Others followed the commitment to protest, spearheaded by W. E. B. Du Bois. Harvard's first Black Ph.D., a founder of the Niagara Movement in 1905, then the National Association for the Advancement of Colored People (NAACP) in 1909, Du Bois spearheaded the political and legal struggle to advance racial equality.

But most Black Americans conducted their daily lives in the muddy middle ground between accommodation and protest. The risks were everywhere, individually, communally, generationally. Confronting the threat of physical violence, discriminatory laws, and economic repression, Blacks somehow found the strength to fight back, sometimes in group meetings where they discussed avenues of protest, or in self-help gatherings where they reinforced each other's strength and resilience. Most devoted themselves to finding a decent job with which to support themselves and their families. Many continued to pursue an education with which to increase the opportunities available to the next generation.

All of these choices rested ultimately on the solidarity of the Black community. No community is a monolith, of course, and divisions existed among African Americans based on color, class, ideology, region, and religion. But to a remarkable degree, Black Americans sustained their will to survive—and to prevail—by pulling together as one. It all began with the family, which nurtured a sense of togetherness and mutual responsibility; the family's moral compass was rooted in the church, where spiritual faith and political awareness were honed during religious services which were the highlight of each week; and both church and family provided anchors where people recognized that they would rise or fall together, not alone. One of the greatest assets, if not *the* greatest, was the broad awareness throughout the Black community that you could help yourself only by helping others. In the decades that constituted the "nadir" of African American history, these institutions—and values—made the difference between abject defeat and a determination to find a better way, no matter how powerful and cruel the obstacles placed in their path.[1]

The Family

No institution was more central to the quest for Black autonomy than the family. Ever since the first slave ship arrived, African Americans had been denied the right to celebrate their love and commitment through marriage. The searing pain of forced separations marked all enslaved families. So it was no surprise that as soon as slavery ended, Black Southerners rushed to record their marriages, search for kin, and protect their children from exploitation at the hands of whites. Initially, Blacks enlisted the Freedmen's Bureau to help find long-lost relatives. Mary Walker, for example, an escaped slave then in Massachusetts, made contact with General Oliver Howard (known as the "Christian general" for his strong faith, and a leader of the Freedmen's Bureau) to ask that he tell her two children where she was, and arrange for a reunion. Using the grapevine of African American kin networks, former slaves sent messages across county and state lines to reach out to children and grandchildren long ago ripped from their families by the cruelty of former masters who had given little thought to selling off brothers, sisters, and children to planters in faraway states.[2]

Children became the focal point for newly empowered Black families to assert their independence and autonomy. Putting their faith in the future over short-term economic needs, families insisted that their children not go to the fields but instead attend the newly opened schools, often staffed by Northern religious whites and recently trained Black teachers. When North Carolina freedmen convened in Raleigh in 1866, they called out the blasphemy of white farmers that sought to force Black children into labor without the consent of their parents. "Our children," the delegates protested, "are ruthlessly taken from us and bound out without our consent." Insisting that such practices end immediately, the freedmen demonstrated by their order of priorities just how fundamental family integrity was to all their hopes for the future.

No task called for more wisdom, strength, and sensitivity than teaching African American children how to survive in a racist, hostile world where danger lurked behind each encounter with white people. On the one hand, parents needed to convey the intricacies of the racial etiquette of segregation, training their children to avoid circumstances where any action they took might suggest a challenge to white domination and consequently call retribution down upon them. Thus when Anne Pointer, a granddaughter of slaves, wanted to protest the abominable living conditions that a white landlord imposed on her family in Tuskegee, "My father [ruled] 'no,'" she said, "and we would listen to him, 'easy way is the safest way home, just walk around it, don't get in their way.'" Once jailed for bootlegging, her father knew the cost of ending up on the wrong side of white authority.

But prudence was not acquiescence. Even as her father counseled patience, Pointer's parents urged the children to go to school, improve themselves, and become independent. "My mother was proud," Pointer recalled. "We could not tell people that we didn't have anything." Rather, the family should revel in their achievements. "[We] stayed out front at school, at church, and everywhere else," she noted. "All six children had abilities other children couldn't touch," including excelling at math and in athletics.[3]

Growing up in northern Louisiana in the 1910s, W. C. Tims also learned the twin lessons of self-respect and compliance with the segregationist social order. The lessons were complex and multilayered, their mastery conveyed through both "overt expressions" and "the language of signs and expressions." From a young age, Tims understood that he must not "act in a way that would . . . make white persons feel that you didn't know they were white." He absorbed early on the importance of stepping off the sidewalk if a white person approached, and of always letting white people get served right away at the store no matter when they entered the store's premises, or how many Black people were already there awaiting help. Yet simultaneously, Tims developed a sense of efficacy and pride. His parents expected him to stand up for himself, even to defend himself against white boys—at least up to an age when such behavior would become dangerous.[4]

Growing up in Virginia in the early twentieth century, Bernice Burnett had the same experience. "My father often said," she recalled, "'You're as good as anybody else.'" The result was that she never had low self-esteem. In Virginia, Olivia Cherry was taught the same lesson. When Cherry was a child in the 1920s, her mother "told us that we were somebody and we should never feel inferior or act inferior." This instruction included the use of language itself. Cherry's mother was insistent. "She wouldn't allow us to say 'can't.'" As a result, when Cherry encountered discrimination, she felt angry, "but it did not make me feel inferior. It did not stop me from . . . trying to make things better. . . . I always knew that I was somebody, and that God made me this color because that's the way he wanted me." Generations of young people intuited, learned, and internalized the mixed messages necessary for survival: be careful, avoid inflaming white anger, but stand up for yourself wherever possible, because you are worthwhile and loved. W. C. Tims even came to understand that the very forced nature of Black deference generated its own form of suppressed resentment, confirming the degree to which, underneath the surface, the entire community seethed in anger. To an astonishing degree, a majority of that community channeled its anger and resentment toward their own advancement.

Someday, sometime, Tims believed, that anger would be unleashed, and "one day it [will] be better." Generations later, when things did become better and Blacks could attend previously all-white institutions of higher education, those pioneers attributed their achievement to their forebears. "We grew up in protective Black communities," one Black woman college student recalled, "with incredible history [and people] who demonstrated by example the dignity that our ancestors had been able to call on . . . to convince themselves that they were real people and they were good people."[5]

One reason that Black Americans so keenly appreciated the importance of family solidarity was the frequency with which parents, grandparents, and other kin told stories of how life used to be. Susan Weatherby, growing up in eastern North Carolina at the turn of the twentieth century, learned early on, as a child, about the sufferings of slave women. She heard tales of Black women being sexually abused by plantation owners, of members of her own family who were denied the right to marry or were forced to see their children sold off to distant sites—all a reminder of how critical it was for African American families to now hold together, help each other, and never give in to despair. Anne Pointer had similar memories. On Sunday evenings, she recalled, family members would gather to "talk about the old times and the work they did and the hard time that they had." Her father, she said, regularly related stories of his ancestors' experiences in slavery, including accounts of how his mother had been raped by white landowners. Slavery was all they talked about, she remembered. All of this by way of exhorting children to stay in school, act responsibly, and continue to move the family forward. "Make something of yourself," Pointer's parents and kin enjoined, "be my dream." If the previous generation could not read or write, the next generation would. Standing atop the shoulders of those who came before them, the new generation would make something different of their lives. By repeating these stories of struggle in the past, parents underscored the degree to which the family was the foundation of community well-being and the vehicle for pushing forward.[6]

As perhaps the ultimate expression of family celebration, regular family reunions brought together extended kin networks for weekend-long gatherings. Amidst singing, hugging, feasting, and laughing together, families caught up with each other's news, learned of new births and recent deaths, rekindled family bonds, and chatted about individual stories of trials and achievements. Celestyne Porter, from the Chesapeake Bay area of Virginia, recalled vividly how such gatherings reaffirmed a sense of community. "The older people, my grandparents and all, had family reunions [where] . . . everybody comes back, as near as possible, for that . . . all-day meeting and dinner on the ground." For Porter, as for everyone who attended such events, the reunion served as a source of strength, where the singing of spirituals, and discussions of freedom, justice, and a better day to come all delivered a message of hope.[7]

In fundamental ways, these family reunions spoke to a much larger reality: rather than being composed of isolated nuclear families such as those that dominated the suburbs of the 1950s, the Black family at the turn of the twentieth century represented an extended kin network. Anthropologist Carol Stack captured this distinctive feature of Black America in her book *All Our Kin*, in which she described the manner in which individual Black families merged into larger community groupings of friends and family. It was not just one's own mother and father who taught Black children how to navigate America's social and economic restraints. Friends and neighbors frequently stepped in to help as well, acting as surrogate parents to assure the safety and well-being of the young. The family extended into the community, which collectively passed on communal values.

"The entire black community was . . . a family," one person recalled. "People would always call your mother or your parents if you were not doing what you were supposed to be doing. The teachers would spank you and call your parent and you would get spanked again. People were looking out for each other because no one in the *white* community at that time . . . cared much about black youth." The survival of the next generation demanded it.[7]

Through such networks, children learned to avoid the humiliations of racism and how to function within segregated spaces while maintaining their feelings of self-worth. "Parents taught us about segregation and how to navigate the system," a young woman recalled. "Our parents were teaching us what to do in society." Parental authority extended beyond the house to cover all the children in a neighborhood or local community, as if the entire neighborhood was full of "mamas and fathers." "Everybody was family," one resident of a Kentucky coal mining town recalled, a circumstance that by widespread custom granted all adults the right to intervene if they observed children misbehaving. "The broad perspective," David Matthews of North

Carolina noted, "was that the community observed the actions of the children and if they were out of line then any citizen in that community would be willing and ready to call you back in place."[8]

It was through such family and kin networks that the etiquette of racial segregation was transmitted from generation to generation. In some areas, Blacks and whites were so thoroughly separated that Blacks rarely encountered whites. But in most places, interaction was the norm. At cotton gins, country stores, Black-owned juke joints, private homes, and rural plantations, interracial mingling might be encouraged, albeit under highly prescribed terms. Within the tobacco markets of Durham, North Carolina, for example, Black and white farmers sold their wares together, and spent long hours in the same place—though usually in separate groups—waiting between auctions. In rural communities, Black and white children often played together in their early years, and on occasion, adults interacted as well. "The white men and the colored men would go to the courthouse," Virginian Celestyne Porter noted, "and they'd drink their beer, their booze [and] . . . then they would walk on home." Often, she continued, "If Miss Annie didn't have all the flour she needed, she'd send over . . . to get some. If Mama didn't have all that she needed, she'd borrow from Miss Annie. . . . We forgot about who was colored and who was white." Except that she was "Miss Annie," and they were "Uncle Wilbur" and "Aunt Sue." "We used to have a joke," Porter said, that "white folks would rather be kin to you than to call you Mr. and Mrs."[9]

But there was always the looming threat of arbitrary white retaliation. Black children learned early the importance of signs indicating "colored" or "white" drinking fountains; and while the absurdity of such labeling represented an ongoing source of ridicule—what, after all, was "white" about water?—parents and aunts and uncles made sure that children never violated the signs lest they be humiliated by white store employees. Just as painful were the psychic costs, as when a childhood playmate with whom a youngster had shared long afternoons fishing and swimming suddenly decided that henceforth he should be called "Mister." Or when future scholar and nationally known activist Pauli Murray, walking in Durham to her all-Black school with its peeling paint and broken toilets, passed whites going in the other direction to their brick school with its landscaped grounds and impressively equipped playground. "We never had fights," Murray observed of her daily journey. "It was worse than that. They passed me as if I weren't there!"[10]

Navigating this world of mixed signals and contradictory experiences would have tested the most talented diplomat. Yet the Black family provided the training ground that enabled Black children to survive and prevail. With shrewdness, subtlety, and a marvelous faith in the power of storytelling, parents and grandparents taught their children where to bend, how to feint, and what to say, all the while instilling in their offspring a sense of self-esteem, confidence, and hope for the future. The family—extended as well as local—provided the economic, psychological, and emotional foundation from which African Americans throughout the South sought to sustain their fight for freedom. "The generation of elders around you . . . were uncanny [in the way they prepared you for the day] when doors started to open," one activist noted. "It was in . . . the way you were nurtured and counseled and trained." Explicitly understood was the purpose and the goal. "You do it for your mother, your father, your people, your community, your church. This is your duty." Young African Americans were being groomed "to take our places as the next generation of black leaders."[11]

The Church

If the family represented the emotional anchor for African Americans in their quest for a better life, the church provided the vessel for carrying that quest forward. In its spiritual dimension, coming together in the Lord's place offered sacred space to pursue the higher power of redemption and to find a message of meaning in one's daily struggle for survival. But the church also offered a political space where aspirations could be shared, new initiatives undertaken, hopes rekindled, and an agenda developed for carrying forward the historic pursuit of true freedom and justice. The center of the community, the church provided a safe space for people to be themselves and say whatever they wished, with no fear of white surveillance. It also was a social space where insurgencies could be born, laughter shared, joy celebrated, and pain ameliorated by community participation.

To observant witnesses, the role assumed by the church came as no surprise. As W. E. B. Du Bois observed in 1903, "The Negro Church is the only social institution of the Negroes which started in the African forest and survived slavery; under the leadership of the priest or medicine man, afterward of the Christian pastor, the Church preserved in itself the remnants of African tribal life and became after emancipation the center of Negro social life." In Du Bois's view, church congregations were "the real units of race life," serving as the crucibles within which Black Americans forged their sense of communal identity and their collective determination to survive—and prevail. The question was how the church could devise ways to do this under the conditions imposed by pervasive segregation. How to pursue uplift in the face of economic powerlessness? Citizenship in the face of disenfranchisement? Education when "the sight of the Veil . . . hung between us and Opportunity"? Resistance in the face of lynch law? Somehow, African Americans found a way, and through its robust refusal to surrender the search for a higher and better life, the church instilled purpose and vision, and even took small steps forward when all around there seemed no reason to believe in the possibility of a better day.[12]

In part, the church performed this mission by becoming the vehicle for celebrating the community's most powerful memories. Each Emancipation Day, it was the church where the people gathered to remember what slavery had been like, to hear the words of the Great Emancipator, and to tote up the balance sheet on what had been achieved, what had been lost, and how much still remained to be done.

Emancipation Sunday was almost literally a time for communion, joining the sacred history of the Lord's sacrifice with the pilgrimage to freedom of the lost Israelites fleeing from Egypt's pharaohs. Lincoln was a new Moses, but the people had not yet reached the Promised Land. Where better to meld these messages than in the center of Black community life—its spiritual as well as its political temple.

Likewise, the Black church provided the meeting place to highlight communal events of the Black community—a week-long "big meeting" or revival, for example, family reunions, and homecoming Sundays. Each community had its own traditions, but in most, the idea of a "fifth Sunday" meeting of several church congregations together was commonplace. One church would host a special revival, the specific location shifting from month to month. Congregants worshipped (usually for three to four hours at a time), raised monies by special collections, then dined together with the host church, which provided the fried chicken, gravy, biscuits, and hushpuppies. It was an all-day event that not only brought sinners home to Christ, but provided a broader community the opportunity to celebrate ties with relatives who might have moved away, or to indulge in local political gossip about whose landlord had cheated which tenant farmer, and what the community might do to fight back. Like a protective bubble, "fifth Sunday" meetings offered free social space in which people could say what they wished, "let go" of their daily worries, and receive an infusion of purpose and joy that could be drawn upon for days and weeks to come.[13]

In this manner, the scholar Albert Raboteau reminds us, the church offered African Americans multiple ways to extend their faith and fight back against Jim Crow. The church, Raboteau writes, was a source of economic cooperation where people could arrange to share equipment and "an arena for political activity, a sponsor of education, and a refuge in a hostile white world." Churches opened and staffed Sabbath schools to supplement the daily public schools, and furnish additional literacy instruction in evenings and on weekends. These Sabbath schools also sowed seeds of support for universal public schooling, which, Du Bois points out, was fundamentally a Black contribution to the post-Emancipation South. (Whites had not initiated public school systems before the Civil War.) Churches also spawned countless voluntary associations—the Prince Hall Masons, Oddfellows, Good Samaritans, Independent Order of St. Luke, and United Order of Tents—that promoted self-help, charitable activities, and women's service clubs throughout the South. Partnerships between lodges and churches, as in Richmond, Virginia, also created the first African American insurance companies and banks, fostering a group economy "within the veil" that bolstered Black self-sufficiency and countered white racism. Churchgoers were the foot soldiers who helped create countless women's clubs and social welfare groups, the National Association of Colored Women, and in the early twentieth century, local chapters of the newly formed NAACP. The gospel of liberation that they imbibed in their local congregations deeply informed the strategies of Black pride, self-help, and solidarity.[14]

Nowhere was this synergy of church and community development better highlighted than in Durham, North Carolina. Primarily a tobacco market and manufacturing city, Durham also steadily attracted a vibrant and energetic entrepreneurial class. Effectively using their relationships to the Washington Duke family of tobacco fame—white entrepreneurs—a cadre of Black men from White Rock Baptist Church, St. Joseph's AME, and the Royal Knights of King David chartered the insurance and banking businesses that gave Black Durham its reputation. Promoted as the "company with a 'Soul and a Service,'" the North Carolina Mutual Insurance Company funded and helped support additional Black enterprises so that by 1925, Durham was anointed the "Capital of the Black Middle Class." Cogently defining the church as the bridge linking Black enterprise and community social uplift, one Black minister observed that "the influence of the pulpit [in making this happen] can hardly be overestimated."[15]

Perhaps most important, the church helped shape the Black community's response to events that defined future possibilities of freedom and equality. It was one thing for an individual or his family to stand up and protest a racial injustice. It was another for the church as the collective voice of the community to do so. The church spoke for the race as a whole, providing both power and legitimacy to otherwise isolated citizens who might or might not be able to find the strength to express themselves. After the Wilmington race riot of 1898, and subsequent legislation by the North Carolina General Assembly to disenfranchise Black citizens, it was Bishop James W. Hood of the AME Zion church who led a convention of Black citizens in Raleigh in 1900 to issue "An Address to the White People of North Carolina," demanding a repeal of those actions. The protest might be ignored—as it was, in this instance—but there remained the community's pride in having fought back, and the reinforcement of knowing you could trust the most honored leaders of the community to lead the way, however great the risk.

Sometimes, ministers took a gentler, more diplomatic approach. One church leader affirmed his faith in "God and humanity," declaring that "I do not believe that the white people of North Carolina have repudiated the spirit of Christ." But whether a church was militantly defiant or instead appealed to a common faith in Christianity, African American religious leaders empowered Black people as a community, encouraging their congregations to close ranks, and overcoming fear, to persist in the struggle for freedom. To be sure, standing up for the race would have taken place among some individuals regardless. But the church, with its sacred social and political space, offered room for a collective statement of will that went far beyond what any single individual could attempt.[16]

Not surprisingly, the church fulfilled its other role of providing support to people in pain, even as it sustained a voice of protest. During Wilmington's bloody race riot, scores of Black people died and hundreds were exiled and scattered over the countryside. But in response, the Black churchwomen of Wilmington—representing more than a dozen congregations—mobilized to offer help for the poor and the sick. Love and Charity Lodge raised money for medical care. It also sought to rebuild its hall, which had housed Alexander

Manly's newspaper, the *Daily Record*, and had been burned down in the riot. Women from church groups worked for temperance (more than one thousand people attended their rally in 1912), built a new library at St. Stephen's AME Church, opened a YWCA, and raised funds to construct a new industrial high school. When World War I broke out, Black women in Wilmington created their own Red Cross unit. They also crusaded for women's suffrage and were pivotal members of the group that formed the Wilmington NAACP—a group that declared its purpose to be that "men and women may know how to qualify and then exercise all the rights and privileges of citizenship." Even during a period of dramatic political oppression, African American church groups, and particularly women, continued to lift and climb, preparing the ground for the day when greater political activism could once more emerge.[17]

The church also provided benchmarks in a person's life—events or honors that warranted pride, awarded status, and conferred a sense that there was another world, beyond that of white-controlled patronage, where a person could find fulfillment and gratification. Since everyone went to church, such special moments were witnessed by a whole community. "My people were always highly religious," factory worker Tolbert Chism said about his childhood in Fargo, Arkansas. "We went to church every Sunday," and most often the day was long, starting with a three-hour service in the morning, a celebratory meal in the early afternoon, and another service at night. The church was *the* social life of the community, as well as the source of its spiritual well-being. But the very fact that everyone attended gave extra importance to those moments of ritual significance. "Always, baptizing was big," Anthony Farmer of Danville, Virginia, recalled. After the baptism, "they would have the service and give you what is called the right hand of fellowship which is communion. And everybody would come around and shake your hand and wish you well." Even simpler, more mundane activities could take on the power of self-affirmation. William Davis, a laborer from Indianola, Mississippi, remembered especially the "hymns. . . . Seems like they were just belting them out, louder and everything." In this context, his neighbor Annette Clayborn noted, baptizing was especially memorable. "That was a very special time for us. . . . That's a coming out thing for the individual that is involved in the baptizing." Like baptisms, marriage, or having one's first child, those moments that a person would remember forever became communally shared and acknowledged at the church.[18]

Responsibilities within the congregation also provided a source of prestige and leadership status within the community. Women earned local fame, whether by the quality of their singing, being elected chair of the hospitality committee, or their role in orchestrating congregational responses to the preacher with repeated "Amens" uttered from the pews. Men, in turn, aspired to be chosen as church elders. Even if they could not read, and in the "white world" were denied the respect of being paid a decent wage or called "Mr.," in the church the same people became deacons—highly respected figures who occupied a status barely less than that of the preacher himself. The person who was a poorly paid janitor by day became venerated by the entire Black community given his role as a deacon in God's holy sanctuary.

There was something about going to church that made the whole experience one of affirmation and joy. Ida Belle of South Carolina, who worked as a maid, talked about the happiness she achieved by going to a congregation where everyone accepted you for who you were. "Church was much different," she said. "People were loving. [You wore] what you had, if it's a gingham dress or homespun dress, you were good and clean. You would wash it and starch it and you'd go on to church. . . . You went to church and love was there." Theresa Lyons, a clerical worker in Durham, echoed that experience. "For a long time I had a terrible inferiority complex," she said, "because I had come up so poor." But at her Baptist church she found hope "because the people were warm. . . . [The] preaching, gospel singing, praying, testifying . . . would give me hope, something that I could live from this week to that week." Indeed, Cleaster Michell of Brinkley, Arkansas, said, the church "was the lifeline of the community. . . . [People] never had telephones, a lot of them couldn't write . . . but they would gather up on a Sunday. That's when they prayed together, they visit together, they talk, they caught up on everything that was going on. . . . That was a glorious time."[19]

For young people growing up, the church was also the focal point of their social life, especially the ability to meet members of the opposite sex. As already discussed, baptism represented a critical rite of passage, bestowing pride, dignity, and status on the young. But the all-day church activities on Sunday also provided a wonderful opportunity to establish personal ties with other teenagers, to share gossip, to make contact with the opposite sex. As Leamon Dillahunt noted, boys participated actively in church affairs not only because their parents insisted that they do so, but "[be]cause the girls would be at the church."

The same was true for the young women. Wilhemina Baldwin remembers how the Sunday school and social affairs around the church service taught her "how to get along with the boys." Some churches had special activities for the young. At Cleaster Mitchell's church in Arkansas there was a youth band. "A lot of them would stay out under the shade trees there, and they would sit and talk and everything, and then we would go in later and have this Bible class, and we played with all the other children." The church became *the* place where African American life happened, including courtship. As Manuel Crockett recalled, he became a Baptist for one reason and one reason only: "to marry [my] wife Myrtle."[20]

The church complemented the family as a foundational source of Black community life. Literally as well as metaphorically, it was a manifestation of congregation, helping to secure one's sense of self, provide a shelter amid life's storms, and create the reality of a larger body, spiritual as well as social and political, that provided belief that a better day was a'coming. "The preaching, gospel singing, praying, testifying . . . would give me hope," Theresa Lyons said. By people coming together to share pain as well as joy, Cleaster Mitchell observed, "they was [*sic*] really sharing in all kinds of ways with each other." Religion provided resiliency of spirit and a determination to persist. "We were taught not to hate," Mitchell noted, but also nurtured to be strong, secure in the faith that standing up for truth and justice was the Lord's way.[21]

In this manner, religion provided not only the backbone of the community, but the will—and faith—to struggle forward. Faced with the daily brutalities and denigration of Jim Crow, the belief that God "hath made of one blood all nations" offered the promise that one day, things would be different. Even in the face of the most horrific expression of white supremacy, religious faith offered an alternative to hatred. Susan Weathersbee, a former sharecropper, a widow, and a mother, shed tears when a son of a friend was lynched for defending his mother in front of a storekeeper ("Cause he, like his ma, . . . didn't take nothing off'n nobody"). But in spite of her pain, she clung to the faith of her religion. "I know how to treat people," she said. "I don't care what race they is, I know how to treat them, how to love them. And if I can do anything for you to help you, I will." Ultimately, Cleaster Mitchell said, the church offered the promise that, notwithstanding the trials of the present, "the Lord will fix it. Vengeance is God."

It was a complicated message, this Christian Gospel. Combining the strength that came from community solidarity with the message of protest, forgiveness, and reconciliation embodied in Jesus, the African American church accomplished a nearly impossible goal: it offered solace in the face of tribulation, the will to fight back, and the faith that there existed a higher purpose—a world in which there was neither Jew nor Gentile, slave nor master, that someday, somehow, would become a reality.[22]

Helping One Another—the Larger Community

If nothing else, the centrality of family and church to the Black community generated a set of values that focused on the good of the whole rather than the personal advancement of an isolated individual. Naturally, there were selfish members of the community—criminals, hustlers, those who cheated on friends and family for the purpose of self-aggrandizement. As Zora Neale Hurston noted, "The Negro race was not one band of heavenly love. There was stress and strain inside as well as out. Being black was not enough. It took more than a community of skin color to make your love come down on you." Yet more than most people, Black Americans grew up with a different ethos. Memories—constantly re-invoked by family and civil commemorations—vividly recalled the estrangement of enslavement. The weekly practice of church services—as universal a weekly practice as existed in any subset of Americans anywhere—reinforced the mandate of a communal moral imperative, the faith in redemption through suffering, the belief in an all-encompassing love that made the experience of Black Americans akin to that of the Israelites, persisting through apparently insuperable obstacles to continue their journey as a "chosen" people to reach the promised land.[23]

Perhaps because of this ethos, African Americans embraced the example of the Good Samaritan. Understanding in the depth of their being the experience of hard times, they knew the importance of reaching out to help those most in need of assistance. On a Sunday morning, Celestyne Porter's grandmother would put the children into a surrey driven by a mule and set out to town. When a neighbor asked, "Where are you going?" Porter would respond: "I'm going to see the sick and afflicted, the poor and the needy, and [those] cast down on account of trouble." That message seemed contagious in many Black communities, especially when things got worse rather than better. "If you had sickness," Anne Pointer declared, "it was everybody's sickness. . . . Neighbors always lent a helping hand, even to the hobos who came through." Pointer remembered one night when her father heard someone chopping wood out in the family woodpile. "And papa would take a lantern and he'd go out into the yard and find a hobo [who said], 'hey friend, nobody to hurt you, I'm just cutting up some wood if you all would give me a meal.'" Her mother then fed the man, and "they'd fix him a pallet [to sleep]—and that happened all the time."[24]

Reaching out to others, offering help when it was needed became the expectation—not the exception—in the Black community. Booker Federick, growing up in the Arkansas Delta in the early twentieth century, noted the tradition of cooperation in the community. "If we would be fortunate to get through [farming our land]," he noted, "and you wasn't [*sic*] through when we got through, we'd just take our hoe and go on over there without asking any questions. That's the way we'd help one another then." And in case anyone believed that the ethic of mutual help was without political purpose, Federick noted that when the cooperative venture involved helping a tenant farmer, "then we'd start putting some full ears on top" to deceive the farmer who owned the farm, then putting less full ears on the bottom. Such cooperation extended to helping when a mistreated tenant ended up "slipping his family off the plantation." Members of the Black community would provide cover so the family could escape.[25]

Women in the church often spearheaded outreach activities. Celestyne Porter recalled with pride the activism of her women's community. "During the age of separate and unequal," she said, "we developed, all of us developed, a society totally on our own." African Americans might have to sit in the back of the bus under segregation laws, but "you knew that you had your churches, your own school, your own—everything." The women joined various clubs and played "every kind of role you could think of." They raised monies for a new operating table at the Black hospital, read to children on Sundays, helped new mothers out with their washing and cleaning chores, and used their church connections to provide a support network for the community as a whole. Dora Dennis recalled the community vision of her Episcopal church. "Anybody—you didn't have to belong to the church—anybody that needed help, our church would help them." The minister started "what they called the sale room, [with] clothes . . . and shoes that the children could wear" when they came to school with "no coats and sweater." And if the family did not have money to pay for the clothes, "[we] would give them to them so the children could go to school and church."[26]

This ethos of mutual help extended everywhere. In virtually every Southern community, Black families shared surplus goods raised in gardens and from livestock. If a family milk cow dried up before calving, for example, neighbors would send over extra milk and butter to help out. Reciprocity was the norm. If you helped others, they would help you. In rural Clarendon County, South Carolina, a farmer died, leaving his family in desperate straits. In response, a community of day laborers worked the acres of land, helping the family to survive.

Offering solace and aid when a neighbor died represented a benchmark of such communal support. Lillian Fenner of Halifax County in North Carolina remembered her family's involvement in protective and cooperative associations. "My daddy was a member of the . . . Knights of Gideon and . . . when somebody would pass in the family, [the lodge] would always give . . . a certain portion of money to help them. Then they would fix food and carry it to the house. . . . Wont [*sic*] no insurance or nothing, [just a world where] different ones would pitch in and help."[27] "We knew everybody who went to every church," another woman recalled, "so there was [literally] the community neighborhood. Because of that, the commitment of the teacher, the church, the community and the home was so connected that you couldn't fail."

Sometimes, community members would intervene to preserve the moral tone and well-being of the community. When an African American woman in Price Davis's neighborhood in Charlotte hosted a series of white men in her home, presumably for sexual activities, Davis's father talked to the woman, saying that she was setting a bad example; and when the behavior continued, Davis and his friends took to puncturing the tires of the white visitors' cars, breaking windows in the woman's home, and running the interlopers out of the neighborhood. Herbert Cappie, from rural Louisiana, recalled the same kind of episode. A local white bus driver "would stop his bus and . . . go into this woman's home and . . . spend considerable time in there. It was obvious to everybody what was going on—until a bunch of men in the neighborhood got together and . . . caught the man and . . . beat the hell out of him."[28]

Perhaps most impressive were those occasions when Black members of the community offered aid and assistance to those escaping from whites who were intent on violence. Fleeing a white mob in Alabama, Walter Cavers hopped a train northward. He jumped off in Charlotte in mid-winter and nearly froze to death from exposure until local Blacks discovered him near death. They put him to bed and nursed him back to health. Responding further, the local Sunday school gave him $13, "saw to it that I got food, [and helped me to recover]. I didn't know nobody," Cavers remembered, "and I've been here ever since."

James Hall in Warren County, Georgia, told a similar story. When his father narrowly escaped being murdered in 1920 after a dispute over payment for a cotton crop, Hall's aunt drove his father to safety; then a group of neighbors from the aunt's church provided protection, enabling him to resume making a livelihood. Stories of local churches or kin networks providing protection from mob rule were legion.[29]

In all these ways, African American communities extended the collective values of the family and church into caring for the community as a whole. The experience of slavery had heightened a collective awareness of how much every person's fate was tied to that of every other person. Families learned the practice of placing the well-being of the whole ahead of the individual. The church, rooted in the gospel of Jesus and the exodus of the Israelites from captivity, championed the same sense of mutual responsibility and caring. Together, family and church grounded the larger community's determination to watch out for the good of the whole, and building and sustaining the institutions necessary to promote the collective well-being of all African Americans.

Reflections

The world "behind the veil" was one of limits and boundaries. Abandoned by the federal government, with discrimination enshrined by the Supreme Court in its *Plessy* decision, and with the constant threat of violence, vividly captured in the Wilmington race riot of 1898, Black Americans in the South confronted a starkly constricted and oppressive world. Where they could go, how they would get there, what their attitude should be toward whites they met along the way, and what jobs, property, and education they could aspire to were spelled out by Jim Crow law and the racism of white supremacy. Jim Crow was intentionally cruel, oppressive, and anti-human. From beginning to end, the overriding purpose of Jim Crow was to crush the human spirit, stifle all impulses to freedom, and deny the basic instinct of God's creatures to move forward and create a better life for their families and children. It was an unspeakable assault on human dignity, from the young whites Pauli Murray passed on her way to school who refused even to acknowledge her presence, to the sheriff who dragged a middle-aged Black woman down the street because she did not move quickly enough to get out of the way of a white man about to pass her on the sidewalk.

Yet if Jim Crow set forth intentionally to suppress all instincts for self-determination and human dignity, it held no sway on life "behind the veil." The world of segregation might tightly circumscribe any and every step toward freedom by Black Americans seeking to penetrate the larger society. But it could not destroy the will and determination of African Americans to build their own families, institutions, and community life.

To the contrary—segregation gave African American communities a degree of independence, albeit within the constraints of Jim Crow, to sustain the determination of African Americans to "lift and climb," as the motto of Black women's clubs proclaimed. Black inventiveness emerged to address the needs created by racial separation. Families were drawn closer together to protect each other and work collectively, not just for the opportunity to survive, but to strive for collective advancement—through mutual sacrifice, whether the goal was to buy a piece of land, send children to school, or engage—together with the larger community—in ventures for greater fulfillment.

Most often, the church was the birthplace for such efforts. The centerpiece for the entire community, it offered the spiritual solace and the assurance that the daily struggle for survival held inherent meaning. It also offered a democratic social space, free of white surveillance, where every person could speak their mind, and people could develop strategies for improving community life and fighting back. Out of the churches came the myriad lodges and women's clubs that sprouted throughout the Jim Crow South. Out of the churches also came the networks that made possible the development of Black businesses—grocers, barber shops, beauty parlors, and pool halls, as well as banks and insurance companies.

Through all of these activist institutions, a community of mutual support evolved. People helped each other. Children helped parents with cooking and tending babies; neighbors offered their labor and equipment to the tenant farmer next door who was having trouble harvesting his crop; church members provided food and shelter to those seeking to escape white pursuers; burial societies eased the burden of grieving relatives; and mutual benefit societies helped bridge a family's need for immediate food and clothing in the midst of a financial crisis. These institutions formed the basis for a community whose strength rested on the ethos of mutual care and responsibility. It would never be an easy life. But by hanging together, members of the Black community were "like a family," helping each other make it through hard times.

During Jim Crow, survival itself was a form of defiance. Getting married, having children, going to school—all these represented defiance. Given nothing and left utterly on their own, African Americans turned to each other, most often through the church, to not only survive but to start to lay the groundwork for resistance and confrontation.

With precious little help from any other source, they turned to each other and embraced a Christian ethos of community help.

The foundation of family, church, and community would lift Black Americans out of repression and into the full promise of racial justice. These institutions might not in themselves have been sufficient to create freedom and equality. But surely, they constituted the strengths without which the struggle for freedom would never have had a chance.

Chapter 4

Education and Work

Black life in the age of Jim Crow embodied a constant tension. On the one side were institutions such as the church and family that offered a sense of security, and a "home base" from which to deal with the world outside. On the other side were all the obstacles African Americans faced as soon as they left their home base. How to earn a living? How to advance the life chances of one's children? What paths to pursue in seeking to defend the rights of African Americans to equal protection before the law, the opportunity to have political representation, the chance to receive equal wages?

For African Americans, daily life was a constant journey back and forth between these two realities, one of relative safety, the other of shifting and uncertain risks. With their fellow congregants in Sunday worship, Southern Blacks could feel in control. This was *their* church, *their* spiritual home. Among family and their immediate communities, Black people shaped their own destiny, defining the values they would impart to their children, teaching the behaviors and aspirations that would dictate the future of the next generation. But once they left the protective enclosure that constituted life "behind the veil," it was a different story. Either directly or indirectly, white people became the dominant reality. White power generated a series of expectations and practices that required extraordinary sensitivity on the part of Blacks to detect and negotiate—how to walk the tightrope that would protect the well-being of one's community and family, and simultaneously create the possibility for advancement to a different and better way of life.

Whenever they ventured past family, church, and community, Blacks were not in control. Instead, they needed constantly to seek a middle ground that would permit progress toward their collective goals, yet avoid alienating those whites who governed their fate.

No two areas of life exemplified the tortuous path of this negotiation better than education and work.

Education

Frederick Douglass anticipated the explosive stakes involved in Blacks seeking an education when he wrote about his first encounter with learning. While still a slave, Douglass was taught how to read by the wife of his owner. Then her husband discovered what she was doing. "At once," Douglass wrote, "[he] forbade her to instruct me further." "It was unsafe to teach a slave to read," the slave owner said. "A nigger should know nothing but to obey his master." He all but admitted that education would spell the demise of slavery. "If you teach [a] nigger how to read there would be no keeping him. It would forever unfit him to be a slave. He would at once become unmanageable. . . . [Learning] would make him discontented and unhappy."[1]

That experience highlighted all the underlying risks—and possibilities—of pursuing an education. To Douglass, his master's words "stirred up sentiments within that lay slumbering." They also "called into existence an entirely new train of thought" that he had never grappled with before. It now became clear to Douglass that withholding knowledge from Blacks provided the underpinning for "the white man's power to enslave the black man." Immediately, he realized as well that acquiring knowledge "was a grand achievement." If withholding it ensured the perpetual captivity of the slave, then securing it opened the door to advancement. "From that moment," Douglass wrote, "I understood the pathway from slavery to freedom. .

. . The argument . . . against my learning to read only served to inspire me with a desire and determination to learn."[2]

Black Americans understood from the beginning the power of Douglass's observations. From Emancipation Day forward, they flocked to Sabbath schools in churches to learn to read and write. Missionaries reported from the Sea Islands off Georgia that children and adults came at all times of the day to practice the alphabet and begin to write. Reading circles multiplied in communities across the South. Children went to class during the day, adults at night. "We want to be an educated people and an intelligent people," Abraham Galloway told his fellow freedmen in New Bern, North Carolina, in 1865.[3]

Families set the norms that made education the first priority for their children. William Childs of Wilmington, North Carolina, grew up in a household where education and religion, hand in hand, defined the good life. His father, a railroad cook and preacher, insisted that he and all his brothers and sisters seize the opportunity to go to school. "His thing was that he wanted us to be in church . . . and in school . . . and in the library," Childs said. "He had this thing about reading, . . . principally the Bible." Every child in the family finished high school, three completed college, and two earned master's degrees. Childs himself became a teacher.[4]

Often, extended families offered assistance in securing education that was not available in a local community. In her hometown, Celestyne Porter noted, "school didn't go any farther than 5th grade so [our mother] started farming us out to everywhere else we could get an education." With the help of relatives, Celestyne Porter went to Norfolk with her older sister, who finished high school there and entered the Presbyterian-run Norfolk Mission College. Porter herself went to a high school where her aunt "taught us all about blacks," and each year invited Carter G. Woodson, a college professor and founder of the *Journal of Negro History*, to come and talk about African American history. Eventually, Porter went on to Hampton Institute, where—like so many of her peers—she put herself through college by working as a housekeeper, before she took her first job as a schoolteacher for $2.00 a day. But she was proud of what she had accomplished. "I had beginners," she recalled, "first grade to eighth grade. . . . But all my students were reading when I left there in May."[5]

Ann Pointer told a similar story. "Mama wanted us to go to school," she told an interviewer. "She wanted us to be good." Like Porter, Pointer worked to put herself through school, earning $4.00 a week cleaning for white people. But she persisted. Eventually she went to Tuskegee Institute, where she once again earned the money for her tuition by working. Once she had graduated, she started teaching school, then went on to be a practical nurse. Continuing her quest, she ultimately entered a commercial college, where she acquired the skills to start her own business.[6]

The teachers in these Black schools were pivotal figures. They showed their dedication every day, one student recalled, by always being "supportive and encouraging." Another student remembered that "every teacher I had cared about us and what we would become." Growing up in Durham, North Carolina, Minnie Forte noted that the teachers in her high school visited the home of every student before the school year began. The teachers in Durham, she said, "would help you gain and rise to whatever level you wanted to go," telling the students that they came from a "long history of achievements . . . against a lot of adversity." In another more rural location, a student recalled how the teachers "met us as we walked into school," took the students to museums and concerts on weekends, and spurred them on to become the best that they could be."[7]

In addition, throughout the South—sometimes with help from white philanthropists and sometimes with money raised in their own communities—Black Americans created institutions that served as a magnet for aspiring young people. Church denominations helped start colleges like Shaw and Livingstone in North Carolina, and Scotia Seminary for young women—the school that Sarah Petty of New Bern attended, and where, by the end of the 1890s, more than 1,800 young women had gotten an education. In the 1880s, Cornelia Bowen founded Mt. Meigs in Alabama, and Lucy Laney started Hains Normal Institute in Augusta, Georgia—both of which trained hundreds of young students. In South Carolina, Emma J. Wilson started Maysville Institute, accepting from local residents whatever they could offer in the way of help, including chickens, eggs, and nickels and dimes. After three years of community mobilization, she succeeded, and Maysville received its accreditation in 1896.

These Black-run institutions inspired and educated generations of future leaders. Mary McLeod Bethune, later a prominent Black official in the National Youth Administration under Franklin Roosevelt's New Deal, had her start at Maysville Institute near the turn of the century. "The whole world opened up to me when I learned to read," she said. "[And] as soon as I understood something, I rushed back and taught it to the others at home." Bethune exemplified the ways that Black institutions formed a network of mutual support, as well as providing a model for future growth. Bethune went to Scotia Seminary after Mayfield, then secured a teaching position at Hains Normal Institute, and finally in 1904 journeyed to Daytona Beach in Florida, where she founded the Bethune-Cookman College and became a leader among Black women reformers prior to her move to Washington in the 1930s.[8]

Clearly, significant differences separated the experience of young people growing up in cities from those born in far-flung rural counties where sharecropping consumed the energies of entire families. Suzie Weatherbee, for example, grew up in the Black belt area of eastern North Carolina. Her grandfather was a deacon in the church and ruled the extended family with an iron fist. The desire to provide the young with an education and the compelling need to bring in the crop and survive were in constant tension. As a result, Suzie attended school only through the third grade. "I loved school and went as often as I could," she later recalled, but to make ends meet the family depended on her labor in the fields. As a consequence she sharecropped into her late sixties.[9]

City dwellers had considerably more options. This was especially true for young girls. Among other things, they could earn money after school by working in white households. From Ann Pointer in the early 1900s to Anne Moody in the 1950s, working in the white community to clean bedrooms and feed children provided two contradictory results. On the one hand, it reminded young Black women on a daily basis of the injustice that infused white treatment of Blacks, from the moldy food served them for breakfast to the insistence on deference and submissiveness. On the other hand, it helped make possible staying in school and perhaps finding some way to advance in the future. Going to a Black school, Theresa Lyons remembered, carried the explicit promise that "there was a better world" out there. And even if the city schools Blacks attended were decrepit by comparison with those that whites attended—Pauli Murray noted that her Black school sat on a dirt road near a dump, with peeling paint and leaky toilets, while whites attended a brick structure on a paved street with a well-equipped playground—those schools still offered a stepping stone to a different, more fulfilling future.[10]

At the same time, for Blacks the act of seeking an education inherently involved confronting white power and racism, with all the horrific implications that Frederick Douglass had spelled out more than half a century earlier. For African Americans even to raise the prospect of book learning was to encroach on territory previously restricted only to whites. The very experience of entering the classroom presumed an ability—and a right—to use one's brain to challenge, even disprove, the myth of white superiority. By definition, education led to mobility, the ability to move into areas previously off limits. Once the basic tools of knowledge were mastered, anything was possible—becoming a doctor, a lawyer, a politician, a statesman, a scientist. Traversing such a road also automatically entailed the prospect of competition where people of equal skill might strive for the same goals and earn the same rewards. In short, education opened the door to a world where race no longer could serve as the sole determinant of one's life chances. As the scholar James Anderson has noted,

Black educational institutions were shaped by the community's need to be able to compete with whites, engage in politics, and contribute to the fight for equal rights. More to the point, educational opportunity for Blacks assaulted the entire architecture of white power and ideology—precisely the argument that Frederick Douglass had recognized so succinctly in his autobiographical narrative a century and a half earlier.[11]

The pursuit of education required Blacks to exercise consummate diplomacy. Whites had to be fooled into believing that schooling for Blacks in no way threatened white hegemony. To accomplish this historical sleight of hand, Blacks employed arguments that began with the assumption that Black education would reinforce—not undermine—the agenda of white superiority and Black submission. To state otherwise would unleash the same vitriol captured in the words of Douglass's slave master: "Learning would spoil the best nigger in the world." Instead, whites had to be persuaded that learning would create a more submissive, helpful, and pliant servant, someone who would "know his place" even better after going to school than beforehand.[12]

Whites had to be convinced that Black education was an aid to, not an enemy of, white supremacy. At the same time, Black young people had to be taught that the intellectual weapons they were learning could ultimately be used to dismantle white power. It was an exercise in diplomacy that required consummate skill, guile, and nuance. It was inherently risky. Any step that crossed the boundary between deference and assertiveness risked brutal reprisal. How then to successfully navigate a terrain with flashing red lights at every turn?

The first step forward depended upon soliciting white Northern philanthropic support for Black education. But this had to be done in a manner that would neither alienate the potential benefactor nor alarm native white Southerners. The strategy chosen was remarkable for its sophisticated ingenuity: Blacks would seek support from Northern foundations for schools that would support "industrial" education—skills that could be employed to make Blacks better servants, more skilled artisans, more effective carpenters and bricklayers. In this context, industrial education would constitute an asset that supported the goals of white businesses and plantation owners. Instead of making Blacks "uppity," the lessons they would be taught would "improve" Black character, help African Americans to shed characteristics like irresponsibility, unreliability, idleness, and ineptitude, and replace them with dutiful hard work, dedication to completion of a task, and skillful competence. In effect, industrial education, as presented to Northern philanthropists, amounted to behavior modification that would instill in the Black populace new skills complementary to white goals, not subversive of them. Yet—and this was *the* paradox—industrial education also provided an indispensable foundation for movement upward, in jobs, skills, and social status.

With this approach, Southern Blacks and their allies in the North were successful in securing substantial aid from Northern benefactors. Starting with the Peabody Education Fund, established in 1867 by Boston banker George Peabody, Northern funding quickly extended to the John F. Slater Fund for the Education of Freedmen, founded in 1887 to provide support for "industrial and normal" schools. Furthering the same aims were the General Education Board created by the John D. Rockefeller Foundation, the Julian Rosenwald Fund, and the Anne T. Jeanes Fund, each named for their benefactor. All were dedicated to supporting schools that would institute respectful behavior, teach high standards of hygiene, spread morality, and train Black workers to fit perfectly the needs articulated by the white Southern elite. The strategy worked, at least to establish a beachhead for Black education, but it required that Blacks be willing to move forward inch by inch, not yard by yard. Northerners felt as though they were doing a good thing and helping those least able to help themselves. Black Southerners, in turn, viewed the conditions of the support they received as a price they must pay in order to advance, even if at a pace slower than they might prefer. Although it was less than what they might desire, it was nevertheless a first step.[13]

Perhaps most important, white Southerners were persuaded that such minimal educational reforms were consistent with maintaining the hegemony they had long enjoyed. They too were walking a tightrope. Notwithstanding the withdrawal of federal troops in 1877 and the institution of Jim Crow after 1896, there remained a fear that Northern sensibilities might be aroused were whites to completely deny Blacks any educational opportunities in the South. Thus education reformer Charles D. McIver worried that opposition to public education for Blacks in North Carolina might "arouse hostility among people outside the state" and reactivate a desire to intervene. On the other side of the equation, white leaders, such as North Carolina's superintendent of public instruction, were concerned that if nothing was done for Black education, "most of the wisest and most self-respecting negroes will leave the state." Thus the combination of some Northern-supported schools, Black acceptance of a focus on industrial education, and a minimal amount of state support for segregated Black institutions seemed to be a viable compromise to whites.[14]

Still, there were limits to what they would sanction. Control was paramount. When Durham's James E. Shepard founded the National Religious Training School and Chautauqua for the Colored Race in the 1890s, he sought to advance both a university-style education and a typical training school for imparting industrial skills. Modeled on the prestigious Northfield Academy in Massachusetts, Shepard's goal for his school was to "awaken . . . dormant energies and turn them into channels of usefulness and service." On the surface, such aspirations sounded similar to those of other normal and industrial schools. But members of the General Education Board believed that Shepard wanted too much. His was "largely [a] one man enterprise," the Board ruled, and Shepard wished to have "a perfectly free hand." Repeatedly, therefore, the board rejected Shepard's appeal for funds. Shepard only succeeded in securing state funding for his school—subsequently called the North Carolina College for Negroes—when he agreed to make it conform completely to the accommodationist norms of those schools that encouraged acceptance of the racial status quo.[15]

The tensions in this delicate ballet were crystallized in the opposite philosophies about education adopted by Booker T. Washington from Tuskegee Institute, and W. E. B. Du Bois, a Harvard Ph.D. Their conflict—between "accommodationism" and "protest"—quickly became iconic, taking on symbolic importance not just about what kind of schooling made the most sense for Black Americans, but also about the larger issue of what stance Blacks should adopt toward whites, and ultimately how they should pursue their own freedom. Washington, born a slave, grew up in a world defined by white power. His ability to move forward, economically and educationally, depended on cultivating, not alienating, white sources of power. Beginning with his experience as a student at Hampton Institute, he internalized brilliantly the tactic of advancing his own interests—and those of his people—by massaging the egos of his white benefactors.

Through this approach, Washington exemplified the degree to which he had become a master practitioner of Jim Crow diplomacy. He would follow, in his own way, a course that advanced the well-being of Black Americans. But his efforts would be framed in terms that Southern whites could accept because they avoided any direct challenge to white supremacy. Washington ascended to power in the Black community by taking control of Tuskegee Institute—*the* exemplar of industrial education—and creating the Tuskegee machine, a network of African American newspapers, colleges, and civic institutions, which he ruled with an iron hand, and which served as the gateway to status in the African American South.[16]

Washington's arc of triumph culminated in two historic moments, each a manifestation of the political dynamics Washington practiced to perfection. The first came in Washington's appearance at the Atlanta Exposition in 1895. The most prominent Black speaker at the Exposition—a tribute to the fame he had already achieved—Washington chose to use the occasion to mollify powerful whites who were concerned about stirrings in the Black community toward greater equality with whites, including social equality. In all things social, Washington told the assembled throngs, Blacks and whites should remain as separate as the fingers on a hand. Yet in all things economic, they should be as one, working toward a collective good that would benefit all. Within the politics of white supremacy, Washington had struck exactly the right note, with consummate skill advancing both his own agenda for racial progress while appeasing the always latent anxiety of whites. As a consequence, he soon had even more money for his beloved Tuskegee Institute.[17]

The second moment came when Theodore Roosevelt, the newly elected president of the United States, invited Washington to dine with him at the White House. Not since Frederick Douglass conversed with Abraham Lincoln in the Oval Office had an African American received such recognition. It was an occasion unprecedented for its time—an age when Jim Crow had been blessed by the Supreme Court and written into law by state legislatures throughout the old Confederacy. Here, the country was witnessing how Jim Crow diplomacy played out on the national political stage. In return for paying homage to white supremacist values, Washington was given the imprimatur of President Roosevelt's approval. That meant two things: first, that Washington could continue to seek advancement for his people by pursuing the course of gradualism; and second, that the president of the United States had given his personal endorsement to those Black Americans, like Washington, who refused to challenge directly the presumptions of white racism.

Washington was also pursuing simultaneously a series of private actions designed to subvert Jim Crow. He provided large sums of money to legal groups whose goal was to challenge the entire Jim Crow system. But the two public moments—in Atlanta and at the White House—represented rituals of conformity that celebrated and affirmed a modus operandi in Black/white relations that, within a Southern context, provided the only means for Blacks to move forward.[18]

W. E. B. Du Bois came from a different place, literally as well as figuratively. Born in 1868 in the Berkshire Mountains of Massachusetts, he grew up going to school and playing with white children. Race became the central experience of his life for the first time when he sought to exchange calling cards with a young classmate. Du Bois's card was refused, and as he later wrote, "the veil descended." Forever thereafter, he became acutely aware of his "two-ness"—he was both a Negro and an American, struggling with how to reconcile the two. Unlike Washington, however, Du Bois never adapted to or accepted that duality. Rather than using the assumptions of white racism as the departure point from which to deal with white people, Du Bois always fought back. Never would he sacrifice the belief that he was as good as any white person. Nor would he ever cease to be surprised, offended, and outraged when whites treated him with condescension and bias. Hence his disbelief when as a Fisk student, he was invited to dinner by the white school superintendent who had just offered him a teaching job in Tennessee—only to have Du Bois eat in the kitchen, by himself, while the superintendent ate in the dining room. And his exultation, when as a Ph.D. student at Harvard studying in the summer in Heidelberg, Germany, walking the "philosopher's path"—a winding trek in the hills overlooking the city—he celebrated the joy of being truly free.[19]

In order to make his Heidelberg experience one that every Black American could share, Du Bois devoted himself to studying Negro America, not with the intention of accepting what had been, but with the goal of using that knowledge to challenge frontally the entire structure of white racism. Based on his own experience at Fisk and at Harvard, Du Bois rejected the stigma of inferiority that was attached, in his view, to the idea that Blacks could benefit only from "industrial education." Instead, he insisted that Blacks receive a *full academic education*, with the goal that a cadre of Black leaders would be created—a "talented tenth"—who would carry forward a direct assault on Jim Crow and the inferiority it forced upon his people, as well as collaborate with a "talented tenth" of white intellectuals committed to the same goals.

To carry forward that mission, Du Bois confronted directly Booker T. Washington's philosophy of accommodationism. In his 1903 book,

The Souls of Black Folk, Du Bois asserted that it was fundamentally wrong to accept a worldview based on the assumption of Black inferiority. Instead, he declared, Blacks must assert forthrightly their civil rights, attack Jim Crow, and use every weapon at their command to achieve the equality under the law guaranteed them in the US Constitution. To that end, he helped create the Niagara Movement in 1905, and then four years later became a founder of the National Association for the Advancement of Colored People (NAACP). From that point forward, the NAACP would forcefully carry the banner of direct protest, refuse to adopt the rhetoric or behavior of accommodationism, and insist on nothing less than full equality under the law.[20]

The issue of education thus subsumed far larger questions of politics, resistance, and Black autonomy. Unlike the church and the family, education automatically entailed contact with whites. More importantly, it raised implicitly and explicitly the question of what Blacks could aspire to. The curriculum offered by their schools spoke worlds about the assumptions that their parents and their employers held about their potential as African Americans. As embodied in the Du Bois/Washington dialogue, Black decisions on politics were inextricably connected to choices about how to engage the issue of schools.[21]

In the early twentieth century, Southern Black Americans clearly demonstrated their determination to advance themselves through learning. With limited assistance from Southern whites, they had created a separate Black education system. People helped each other. Extended families provided educational homes where none existed in one's place of birth. A cadre of teachers—Black and white—were trained. Farmers found the resources to keep schools open an extra month so their children would not be sent back to the fields. Northern philanthropists provided the wherewithal for a variety of higher education institutions to grow. Networks of support developed across county and state lines. It was never easy, or without risks. And forward progress all too often depended on a process of deception and dissembling—one that eventually exposed fault lines of profound conflict between those willing to go along in order to advance incrementally, and those adamantly opposed to anything but full equality. Yet it was a dynamic that fed a movement which, even in the face of brutal repression and racist legislation, persisted in seeking the day when the life of the mind could lead the effort to undermine and destroy Jim Crow. It might take deception and flattery toward white power brokers to keep Black high schools open an extra month, but ultimately, these high schools provided the foundation for the Black Freedom Movement.

Work

As with education, the task of making a living almost always involved interacting with white people. Whites usually occupied the role of immediate boss: the owner of a plantation, the mistress of the household where Blacks served as maids or cooks, the foreman at a tobacco factory, the chief of a mine crew or an assembly line. Even in schools, authority ultimately rested with a white superintendent or the gifts officer of a Northern foundation. Life "behind the veil" certainly created some situations where autonomy reigned. Black ministers, lawyers, and doctors had no white supervisors to report to. A Black funeral director, pharmacist, or operator of a "juke joint" dealt only with Black customers. Nevertheless, where money was the final source of control, and where whites controlled almost all banks and municipal coffers, the threat of intervention from above was never fully absent.[22]

For most of the period until World War I, toiling in the agricultural fields remained the primary occupation for most Black men and for many Black women and children. Each year, Black sharecroppers and tenant farmers struggled to make a crop and come out even. But it was like pushing a huge rock up a hill, only to have the rock plunge back downward when the time came to settle up with the white boss. Booker Federick recalled his experience with his early twentieth-century white boss in Alabama: the white owner, Federick said, might sell all the cotton a sharecropper had produced. "But if he got 22 cents a pound for [it], he would settle with you on 13 and 14 cents a pound." As often as not, the owner advanced Blacks credit for their food and supplies, only to charge exorbitant interest—as much as 60 percent—when the bill came due.

The entire family suffered the consequences of this crop lien system. They tried to send the children to school, but as Booker Federick found out, the school year ordinarily lasted a maximum of forty-five days for each growing season. Even if tenant farmers "had the learning," Federick noted, "they didn't have no rights [and] that's what throwed them [back to] . . . just about the same shape I was in myself." The choices were minimal. To challenge the system directly was to risk one's life. "It was unfair," Federick said, "[but] we didn't know anything to do about it but try to make another crop with [the owner] or move to another plantation."[23]

Almost always, whole families were involved in trying to make a living. Often, three generations—grandparents, parents, and children—would help plant and harvest a crop. Suzy Weatherbee's family pooled their labor and tried to relieve her elderly mother of the most arduous farm chores. Girls as young as nine or ten would take over cleaning homes, minding the younger children in white family homes and preparing meals, while boys would go to the fields to help. Sometimes, the collective effort made it possible to put some money aside and over the years accumulate enough to buy a piece of land, a mule, or even a tractor. But the difference between moving forward and being stuck in permanent poverty was often razor thin. Moreover, as Federick noted, even if Blacks sold their own crops, "they still didn't get a fair price for it."[24]

One tactic was to move. Migration from one area to another became a common economic instrument for survival, when sinking deeper into debt with an existing landlord seemed the only other option. Indeed, many families traveled as units, like the migrant farm workers of post–World War II America, seeking somehow to make a living while moving from one locale to another. In the sugar cane fields of rural Louisiana, similar arrangements prevailed. Family work crews came together in extended kinship networks under the supervision of one leader who operated as straw boss for the community and negotiated wages, transportation, and living accommodations.

The same thing happened in turpentine camps. By the turn of the century, turpentine extraction had become one of the most lucrative businesses in Alabama, Georgia, and Florida. Whole family units moved together as opportunities arose. But it was a life of hand to mouth, with little possibility of earning a stake that could lead to bigger or better opportunities. Turpentine workers sang this tune, with banjo accompaniment, to express their bitterness at the options they faced:

> Niggers get de turpentine
> Niggers empty it out,
> White man pockets the money,
> Nigger does without.

With the passage of time, thousands of Black families—tormented by the agricultural depression of the 1890s—picked up their belongings and moved to the cities of the South.[25]

Urban life might be no fairer than living on the farm, but by the very nature of city existence, opportunities proliferated. Port cities such as Charleston, Savannah, New Orleans, and Galveston attracted significant numbers of Black longshoremen. While segregation operated as stringently on the docks as on farms, the difference was that strength existed in numbers. Soon, longshoremen organized into unions. On occasion they launched successful strikes, and they built associations that vied for influence in municipal politics, sometimes even in alliance with whites. Ultimately, Black dockworkers acknowledged the ultimate source of their bosses' power—the gun. But they also refused to give up their determination to be paid the wages owed them:

> Captain got an owl head [pistol] jus' like mine,
> Beat me pullin' de trigger but I don't mind dyin.'
> I don' mind workin' from sun to sun,
> But I want my pay when my payday come.[26]

If it was not always possible to secure the full pay they deserved, Black longshoremen nevertheless stood by each other. For example, the African American longshoreman's union in Pensacola, Florida, established a tradition of shutting down the docks whenever a comrade died. Union members believed that each brother's passing should be marked with solemnity and honor, thereby asserting their humanity against their employers. When Pensacola's shipping bosses objected to the stoppage of work on these occasions, the union fired back, refusing to sacrifice their commitment to each other for the sake of adding profits to their bosses' wallets.[27]

Frequently, cities also generated a culture that supported Black entrepreneurship. Sometimes these were all-Black cities, like Mound Bayou in Mississippi or Biscoe in rural Arkansas. There, a mini-Black-professional class existed. An African American school superintendent presided over a cadre of Black teachers. A Black doctor ministered to the health needs of the community. A Black constable secured public safety, a Black minister tended to the spiritual needs of the people, and a Black postmaster presided over the delivery of mail. Just outside Tulsa, Oklahoma, another such community flourished in the early twentieth century. One of its leaders was a Black lawyer named Buck Colbert Franklin, who practiced both in his hometown and in Tulsa, and who instilled in his young family a determination to succeed no matter what the odds. The preeminent African American historian of the twentieth century, John Hope Franklin, was his son.[28]

Nowhere did the potential of urban Black communities prosper as much as in Durham, North Carolina. Its tobacco factories and textile mills attracted hordes of in-migrants from surrounding rural areas, white and Black. While the whites secured the best jobs in the growing tobacco and textile industries, Black men and women also secured positions. Most often, they were jobs as common laborers, the unhealthiest and most difficult of all positions available in the factories. In textile mills, whites alone could work the machines. The very few Blacks who were employed all did outside work, hauling supplies, dealing with barrels of dye. Blacks did work inside of tobacco factories, but in totally segregated areas, performing the dirtiest jobs.

But whether in tobacco or textiles, these jobs were different from the strict agricultural work and field labor of the recent past. Together with other opportunities generated by the bustling Black neighborhood called "Hayti," they helped give Black Durham an electricity and feel of promise rare for African Americans in the early twentieth-century South.

It was a place not only where poor Blacks found a new range of potential jobs, but also where an aspiring middle class could plant roots and grow. Once again, accommodating whites was an essential part of the process, but on occasion, at least, they played a more positive role. Some members of the local white elite encouraged rather than suppressed Black ambitions. The Watts and Duke families, prestigious, wealthy, and in large part responsible for Durham's new prominence, chose to invest in Black enterprises that could then grow their own strong base in the community and play a major role in generating a new class of Black leaders. The North Carolina Mutual Insurance Company became the first of these giants, followed by Mechanics and Farmers Bank, helping Durham to earn the sobriquet "capital of the black middle class."[29]

Durham developed a remarkably diverse group of Black entrepreneurs. John Merrick owned a barbershop that helped serve an elite white clientele. But Merrick and his shop also served as the hub for a network of Black business enterprises that not only earned the continued support of the white Durham elite, but also created a level of Black civic leadership remarkable for its time. York Garrett came from one of the families that eventually proved a cornerstone for that civic leadership. Garrett had been able to take advantage of "industrial education" typified by Tuskegee Institute. He had attended Elizabeth City Normal School. He then joined the army and became a company clerk—one of the most influential jobs a Black person could hold in the armed services. He was in charge of 250 Black soldiers. After leaving the army, Garrett went back to school, secured a doctorate in pharmacy, and set up his own business in Hayti. Soon he became a pillar of the Black community, a leader in the White Rock Baptist Church (one of the most prominent religious centers in the community), and a model civic leader. Key to his success was the fact that, notwithstanding the passive support of the white elite that John Merrick had cultivated, men like Garrett were their own bosses.[30]

Durham represented just one example—along with places like Atlanta and Tulsa—of a place where "Jim Crow diplomacy" resulted in greater freedom for middle-class Blacks. Selected by the white elite, these Blacks had more autonomy, greater freedom, and substantially enhanced resources that enabled them to assert greater control over their own lives, and those of their fellow Black citizens. But the underlying reality was that the Black elite occupied that position only because the white elite created and sanctioned their position.

Reflections

In that sense, Durham was the outlier that proved the rule. No one would ever describe the early twentieth century as a period of ascendancy for the civic, educational, and economic chances of Black Americans. The measures of oppression produced by Jim Crow were incalculable. It was almost impossible for a sharecropper or tenant farmer to support a family or stay out of debt. The manipulation of profits by plantation owners was rampant. Danger lurked behind every contact with a white person. As much as Black families struggled to build decent schools, teach their children to aspire to a better life, and create a foundation for moving forward, they encountered at every turn white resistance to any change. The central dynamic of Southern society remained white determination to dominate—in all areas. While whites in power might not be able to control the internal workings of the Black family or church, they could intervene at will on issues of education and work.

Yet what remains most striking about this period, called the "nadir" of African American life by Rayford Logan, is the degree to which Black Americans would not give up, and the ingenuity with which they used their knowledge of white Southerners to open doors of opportunity, even if only slightly. It was never easy. There were far more defeats than victories. At every turn, the challenge to move forward required profound wisdom, as well as the patience of Job. But like agile acrobats, Blacks intent on widening the sphere of opportunities for their children walked the tightrope, seized every opportunity to inch forward, and with wily bravado helped to undermine their oppressor even as they pretended to walk the rope totally on his terms.

Pivotal to that process was engaging white power—those people who controlled the purse strings, either in their local communities or in Northern foundations. It was never easy to bring that negotiation to bear in rural areas. No matter how much Black parents wanted their children to learn to read and write, they needed to deal with the reality of putting food on the table. In agricultural areas especially, it was difficult for schools to remain open for more than a quarter of the year. Children were needed in the fields. The family depended on their labor. Poverty closed doors. Hunger took priority over learning the three Rs.

In cities, more options existed. Part-time work could go hand in hand with attending class. More jobs were available for people with literacy skills. But even then, opening new doors of opportunity required reaching out for white support.

Plessy v. Ferguson and the subsequent enactment of Jim Crow laws had created a prison cage that was virtually impossible to break out of, especially through any direct assault. Only by operating within the prison cage could one begin to accumulate the tools by which, someday, Blacks could challenge the legitimacy of the prison cage itself. That issue, of course, was what divided Du Bois from Washington. It would persist through all the struggles of Black Americans to achieve freedom in the twentieth century. But at the dawn of the century, it seemed to most Black community leaders that assaulting the foundation of Jim Crow would create nothing but greater repression. Measuring and balancing the risks in the world of education, they decided it made more sense to appeal for white aid to Black education on the grounds that such assistance would reinforce the status quo by training Blacks to more effectively enact the roles assigned to them under Jim Crow. The paradox, of course, was that the same skills acquired by new educational programs would provide the tools necessary to subvert the Jim Crow system at a later date. It was a tactic fraught with peril. No one could predict how many of the beneficiaries of an industrial education would become content with their lives, or with simply showing deference to whites. But most of those Blacks who negotiated the educational reforms remained confident that Blacks who benefited would continue the struggle forward, and when the time was ripe, assault the underlying premises of white supremacy.

In the world of work, as well, Jim Crow created categories that made open economic advancement impossible. Implicit in the entire structure of white power was the expectation that most Blacks would serve only as servants, sharecroppers, or marginal laborers. As with education, workers could not challenge directly that system of white supremacy. Deception might provide a means of securing a break, but confrontation would not. Black workers had to play at the edges, finding ways to move forward inch by inch in the knowledge that attempting more radical change would only call down decisive repression on them and their families. Only those few who were able to launch careers in the all-Black community could find a measure of autonomy.

All of this, in turn, highlighted the degree to which politics pervaded every aspect of Black community behavior. Ironically, in a world where the primary motive animating the creation of Jim Crow was to deprive Black people forever of the right to participate in the political arena, every activity of Black Southerners with regard to white Southerners would turn out to be political.

Chapter 5

Politics and Resistance

From 1900 to World War I

Not surprisingly, most observers have interpreted the 1896 *Plessy v. Ferguson* decision and the Wilmington race riot as the end of the Black struggle for freedom—at least until modern times. With enactment of poll tax legislation, literacy tests, and the grandfather clause, every state in the old Confederacy had eviscerated the political rights of Black Americans by 1902. Not until World War II would there be a significant effort to alter the law of the land on voting rights; and not until the heroic crusades of the civil rights movement in the 1950s and 1960s were the constitutional guarantees of the Fourteenth and Fifteenth Amendments restored in full. With the exception of the years during and immediately following World War I, Black Americans fought to defend their rights almost totally on their own. Yet fight they did. Denied citizenship rights, without recourse to the ballot box, and under constant threat, they persisted in defending their communities and working to advance their dignity and their rights.

For nearly half a century, no one dared assault the idea of segregation itself—the bastion of white supremacy. Arrayed against Black Americans was a solid wall of passive and active commitment to segregation. *Plessy* had left no room for maneuver. The most that Black Americans could do was to ask that the totally separate facilities legislated for them be made substantively equal to those set aside for whites. But segregation itself appeared impregnable, with little possibility of open resistance, or hope for change. The challenge of living within a world shaped by white supremacy boiled down to this: How would families, communities, and individuals promote their dignity, freedom, and economic security while residing in a society committed totally to denying all these things?

Meeting that challenge had not been and would not be easy. But in confronting that challenge, there was one constant throughout. Growing out of faith in a God of liberation and a community based on mutual support, Black Americans had always found the will—and the means—to defend their families and to push unremittingly for the full recognition of their humanity. To be sure, defeats exceeded victories by a substantial margin. The architecture of white supremacy prevailed more often than not, with mechanisms of social control sufficiently sophisticated, as well as brutally violent, to repel the plea for democracy that swelled from the ranks of Black people. But Black insistence never ebbed, and the willingness of African Americans to bear the risks of struggle never waned.

The lesson from that history—that the hope for equality within American democracy rested ultimately in their hands—would resonate again and again in the years after *Plessy*. However vicious and apparently total the triumph of white supremacy, Black Americans would not give up the fight. Even if some white allies joined them on occasion, this was preeminently an all-Black struggle. It might take new and different forms, depending on the context of national politics. Sometimes, Blacks were forced to use subterfuge as well as straightforward assault to challenge the status quo. But the fight persisted, African Americans waiting with both faith and hope for moments of possibility to carry forward their struggle for freedom.

Standing Up to White Power

Even in North Carolina—where white terrorism had crushed what seemed the last best hope for biracial democracy with the Wilmington race riot of 1898—resistance would not lay dormant. If white North Carolinians assumed that the events of 1898 would cow Black citizens into silence, they were soon proven wrong. Less than two years after the Wilmington coup d'état, African Americans gathered in Raleigh to commemorate Emancipation Day and, once again, reject the mantle of second-class citizenship. J. H. Shepard, the school president who had repeatedly affronted the General Education Board by trying to be "too free" in his proposals for Northern support for his college, derided North Carolina's attempt to disenfranchise his people: "We had not thought [it possible]," he declared, "that any considerable body of the people of this country would ever again seriously question the equal political and civil rights of any class of people." "[There] can be no middle ground between freedom and slavery," he went on. "[Hence, we] view with the greatest alarm the efforts now being made in this State . . . to deprive Negro citizens of the right of franchise which is guaranteed them by the Constitution."

At the same Emancipation Day celebrations, Bishop James W. Hood of the AME Zion church denounced his white contemporaries for seeking to undo the Thirteenth, Fourteenth, and Fifteenth Amendments. "Repeal them," Hood declared, "and slavery again becomes lawful." Blacks were not ready to accept such an outcome, and they showed their resistance across the state—from "paternalistic" Durham to belligerently racist eastern North Carolina. In 1907, Black women in Wilmington supported a boycott of city streetcars to protest segregated seating. Five years later, more than one thousand Black Wilmingtonians demonstrated their political determination by attending a rally demanding temperance and social reform. By calling out white duplicity, shaming white state leaders, then protesting through direct action the injustice of segregated streetcars, these Black Americans vividly demonstrated their commitment to stand tall and fight back against white racism—notwithstanding what had happened in their state in 1898.[1]

Continuity, rather than change, thus characterized Black response to white oppression—even after the dawning of the Jim Crow era. In 1896—the same year as *Plessy*—the National Association of Colored Men informed the US Congress that "while we are grateful for the millions which have been contributed North and South for the benefit of our race, we assert that it is not one-tenth of what [is] due us for the . . . value of soil tilled and watered with tears or our blood." When South Carolina senator Benjamin Tillman claimed in 1906 that Blacks were happy with segregation, the community had an instant response. "If the Senator don't know it," a local Black newspaper responded, "the Negroes of the South are as much dissatisfied with 'jim crow' humiliation as he is with [President] Roosevelt. Colored people in the south satisfied? Monstrous misrepresentation! Never was dissatisfaction more intense."

At no point were Blacks unaware of the consequences of fighting back. Birmingham's Black newspaper summed up succinctly how difficult it was under current circumstances to resist white racism. "Any show of resentment," the Birmingham *Wide Awake* wrote, "would cause [blacks] to be shot down like dogs." But there remained an insistence that Black aspirations—and outrage—be acknowledged.[2]

W. J. Campbell exemplified the continuity of Black determination to challenge the racial and class injustices of Jim Crow. Born a slave on an Alabama plantation in 1864, Campbell grew up as a farm laborer, went to school during Reconstruction, and soon became a teacher. Following a more general trend, he moved to the city of Birmingham in 1880, becoming a barber. But then he started to work in the coal mines of Pratt City, Alabama, and soon was appointed "organizer-at-large" by the Knights of Labor. Campbell then engaged in a region-wide campaign to organize workers on an industrial basis and ally with agrarian radicals. He was good at his job, founding Knights of

Labor lodges across Alabama, including one in Montgomery, and pioneering biracial alliances. After the Knights experienced a decline in membership, Campbell went to work for the United Mine Workers (UMW) to pursue his belief that interracial trade unionism offered the most effective way to end racial inequality. "You may speak of the school rooms," the former teacher argued. "They are the source of intellectual science, but the fact remains that the Negro must live . . . by the sweat of the brow. Hence his relationship to this avenue of life must be made [in coalition] with his co-workers. This [union] has done more to bring about that condition than any means known today."[3]

Throughout this period, Campbell remained a voice in traditional politics as well as union activism. A former secretary of the Alabama Republican Party in Jefferson County, Alabama, he became a delegate to the Republican national convention in 1892. Then, *after* the inauguration of Jim Crow and disenfranchisement, he helped secure enactment of a major reform bill in Kentucky in 1898 requiring that mine owners pay their workers every two weeks instead of monthly. By 1902, Campbell was secretary and treasurer of the UMW in Kentucky, administering a budget of more than $200,000 annually. The career of W. J. Campbell highlights the degree to which African Americans continued to battle for political power and economic justice well after the end of Reconstruction and the initiation of Jim Crow. Campbell's life also suggests the ways that unionism had the potential, at least on occasion, to serve as a cutting edge of interracial protest.[4]

Affirming their self-worth remained a vital precondition for African Americans to resist unjust laws and authority. Black Americans created a wide array of institutions that placed the dignity of individual and community above the crude racist calculus of Jim Crow. Blacks could sustain their faith in the future, Arkansas resident Money Allan Kirby explained, because "[white people] never did get down into the core of the black thinking to where they really brainwashed [us]. . . . We went to church conventions, lodges and so forth [and] we discussed that crap and it never did really soak in." Whatever white folks might have wanted to believe, Black Americans retained their own distinctive sense of self, and this infused their determination to fight for freedom. The solidarity experienced in unions, lodges, sharecroppers' quarters, churches, and women's clubs helped African Americans develop a way of life that allowed them to endure the spirit-crushing pressures of the society around them.[5]

During the Jim Crow era, as before, historical memory proved crucial to sustaining this communal vitality. Lodges, churches, and workers' associations ritually celebrated moments in time that kept alive a belief in the long arc of retributive justice. African Americans commemorated Emancipation Day, Decoration Day, and—in recognition of his iconic assault on Harper's Ferry in the prelude to the Civil War—John Brown's birthday. They used these occasions to pass on a sense of pride about their heritage—and mission. Such commemorations provided the perfect occasion for thinly veiled assaults on white rule, as well as the transmission, especially to the young, of the courage, moral imperatives, and ultimate vision of freedom that had come from their forebears. They also created new narratives that explained both Black defeats and the possibilities of resurgence—if only certain principles were adhered to. Instead of being cowardly in the face of white repression, Black newspapers editorialized, Blacks must look to the African American heroes of Reconstruction for inspiration.

Similarly, the passing of leaders like Frederick Douglass offered occasions for celebrating not just the political leadership of a fallen comrade, but hope for a future that would fully engage the next generation of leaders. As one news reporter described a church service in honor of Douglass, the minister called Douglass "the greatest man that ever lived or died in America, . . . a man who defended his race from . . . the time he broke the bar of slavery until his death." He was a "Prince among men," another person declared, with lessons for Blacks who followed him to learn. "Born under the yoke of an accursed slavery, he rose steadily above it, bursting its bolts and bars until he not only freed himself, but carried forward the conflict until the whole nation was emancipated." The lesson of Douglass's life was that his people could never give up the fight. In Douglass's own words, "Those who profess to favor freedom and yet deprecate agitation . . . want crops without plowing up the ground, . . . rain without lightning and thunder. . . . Power concedes nothing without a demand. It never has and it never will."[6]

With that kind of history, a new generation of Black leaders internalized—and perpetuated—a vision of a better America based on the democratic dreams that had been inscribed in the Declaration of Independence. As W. E. B. Du Bois said, the goal was *to reconstruct democracy in America*. People like Mary McLeod Bethune, a Black woman educator who would start her own college; James Weldon Johnson, a leader of the NAACP; Asa Philip Randolph, the founder and president of the Brotherhood of Sleeping Car Porters Union; Zora Neale Hurston, a Black woman activist; and Howard Thurman, a nationally known Black teacher, accepted that vision as adolescents and pledged to carry it forward, regardless of the brutality of white racists.

This was a generation of extraordinary courage. At no point since slavery were the powers arrayed against Black Americans so great. As a Black Arkansas newspaper had recognized in 1891, "Any Negro man who attempts to give expression to . . . the rights of his race becomes a victim, and is hunted until he is lodged in prison upon the most flimsy complaint." But notwithstanding that reality, another message was being transmitted in the churches, schools, and lodges of the Black community: it was the higher calling of Douglass, *never* to lose sight of the prize, and to make sure that whatever the temporary tactics used, the goal of ultimate freedom would never change.[7]

Different Expressions of Protest

Expression of that determination took many forms. One of these was through the Jeanes schools supported by the Rosenwald Fund, where teachers prided themselves on the quality of their instruction and the inclusion of Black history in their curriculum.

Throughout the South, more than two thousand of these Jeanes schools were built. They represented to tens of thousands of families a vehicle for young children to learn to read and write and to imagine a better life. The schools also suggested that at least *some* people—even if Northern philanthropists—shared their faith in equal opportunity, the idea that *all* citizens, regardless of their race or class, should have the opportunity to secure the educational foundation for advancement in the world.[8]

At other times, that determination to be free was reflected in the refusal of Blacks to accept customs that denigrated them. In Thomasville, Georgia, for example, the Black community organized a protest against the city's annual carnival because African Americas were ordered to stay away from the festivities. "The management tried to compromise," one reporter wrote. "It offered to admit both races on the holiday and to allow a special day for whites and another for colored. . . . The Negroes spurned the offer with contempt. . . . The Ethiopian half of Thomasville . . . stood firm on the rock of racial pride."[9]

A site of consistent protest—with significant political implications—involved African American streetcar boycotts in the early twentieth century. They represented one of the most extraordinary examples of Black protest, a wave of resistance to segregated transport in the early 1900s that anticipated the civil rights bus boycott movement in Montgomery and Tallahassee a half century later. Nearly every Southern city witnessed a streetcar boycott with entire communities mobilized for resistance, such as the women of Wilmington in 1907. Some of these efforts lasted a year or longer. Huge numbers of people were willing to engage in extraordinary sacrifice in the name of racial justice. Sometimes, they were even successful in forcing streetcar lines to back off on enforcing segregation ordinances.

Few Jim Crow laws were as explosive, denigrating, or dangerous as those of streetcar segregation. More likely to cross city zones than neighborhood buses, the streetcar was more often the site for visceral interracial conflict. The story of one Black rider in Jacksonville succinctly crystallized what would become a prototypical experience for Blacks in every state of the old Confederacy from 1900 to 1956. Albert Lewis, a chauffeur on his way home from work, handed a transfer ticket to the streetcar conductor. J. D. Cone, the conductor, refused to accept it on the grounds that the Negro had boarded the car at the wrong place. When Lewis argued with Cone, a physical struggle ensued. Cone pulled out his revolver and shot Lewis three times, killing him instantly. From years of experience, he understood that "the system" would protect him. Indeed, shortly thereafter, a grand jury exonerated the conductor.[10]

But in Jacksonville, as elsewhere, protests against Jim Crow streetcars were legion. In 1901, more than a decade before Lewis's killing, Blacks in Jacksonville had launched a boycott of the streetcar system. "We know from experience," Black citizens wrote, "that [the] authority given . . . conductors [to punish passengers] will be practiced almost exclusively on men and women of African descent to humiliate them." Although the boycott did not succeed, it set an example for others to follow. Two years later in Houston, Texas, the Black community met en masse to declare that they would not patronize a Jim Crow transportation network. Instead, like their descendants fifty years later in Montgomery, they organized an alternative transit system. As one Black news reporter wrote, "They called into service transfer wagons, fixed the price the same as streetcars, and make regular trips along certain [routes] where our people live." Wryly, the reporter noted that "prejudice is throwing into the hands of our people money that [otherwise] the white man would have had." Moreover, when some members of the Black community dissented from the boycott and attempted to ride on the white system, they were severely punished. "A black man is not allowed to ride on the cars," the reporter observed, "and if he should get on he is stoned, jerked off and thrashed or clubbed. Hence, he is not allowed to disgrace his race."[11]

In different places, the Black community played a variety of roles in the movement against Jim Crow rules. Even before a Jim Crow system was inaugurated, Blacks in Pensacola organized a preemptive boycott of local streetcars in 1905. "In Pensacola," the company manager reported, "90 percent of the negroes have stopped riding, even though the company has not [yet] issued an order . . . as to what they intend to do." Local committees of Blacks met other African Americans at the central station and presented each one with a button to be worn in the lapel of their coats. "WALK," the buttons proclaimed. In the meantime, organizations of African Americans hired a delegation of Black lawyers to travel to the state capital of Tallahassee to demand that the state reject the Florida Jim Crow law.[12]

Although whites in Pensacola insisted that the "better class" of Black African Americans supported the Jim Crow ordinance, the evidence did not support their claim. The local paper noted that Blacks in Pensacola who ignored the boycott paid a heavy price. "A number of negroes have been noticed on the cars," the *Pensacola Journal* noted, "but in each case, when they are seen by members of their own race, they are subjected to taunts of . . . 'Jim Crow.'" Even when a local segregation law was enacted, Blacks challenged its legality. "The colored people of the city immediately raised a fund to fight the law," a local Black paper wrote, "and one of their number, Rev. L. G. Croom, volunteered to violate the ordinance in order to make the test. He did so, was arrested, sentenced to thirty days at hard labor, and appealed the case, giving bond for his appearance." Exactly half a century beforehand, Rev. Croom had anticipated with precision the exact mode of protest taken by Rosa Parks in Montgomery, Alabama.[13]

There was no single method of protest that held sway. During the 1905 Jacksonville streetcar boycott, for example, Blacks employed numerous tactics, including legal challenges, oral persuasion, violent direct action, and sabotage. Initially, African American clergy and councilmen from the city's Black wards simply petitioned the mayor to veto the segregation ordinance. The following day the mayor announced he would sign the bill. That same evening, more than eight hundred African Americans met at the St. Paul AME church and resolved to initiate a boycott of Jacksonville's streetcars. While the clergy urged Black activists to remain nonviolent, other groups of African Americans initiated a hit-and-run campaign of firing into streetcars, harassing conductors, and tearing up rails. The second week of the boycott was marked by even more severe incidents of streetcar sabotage. Black middle-class leaders denounced these extra-legal tactics. Nevertheless, they reminded city authorities that the chaos had been ushered in by the segregation ordinances. Black professionals also informed the beleaguered city council that they were preparing a constitutional challenge to the ordinance. These seemingly contradictory tactics boosted the momentum of the boycott because they were launched from so many different social locations in the community and they kept white authorities off balance. Finally, the city relented on enforcing the measure. Temporarily, at least, African Americans had achieved a stunning victory against segregated transportation.[14]

Yet such victories were short-lived. The Supreme Court upheld Jacksonville's statute in 1905, paving the way for Jacksonville authorities to reinstate their segregation practices. Throughout the rest of the decade, state, municipal, and federal sanction of segregated transport made this a profoundly unequal battle. Individually and in small groups, Blacks continued to fight for decent seating and dignified treatment on streetcars and railroads. Black passengers often moved, or threw out, the hated Jim Crow signs, or refused to move to the rear of streetcars. They even fought physical battles with white passengers and drivers over seating arrangements. In such explosive settings, violence was always a danger. When a Black passenger on a New Orleans and Northeastern Road car in 1912 refused to pay his fare because a conductor forced him to stand while there were seats available in the white section of the car, a gunfight broke out. In 1917 the Atlanta *Constitution* reported that after Carrie Hill, a Black woman, refused to give up her seat to a white woman, a white man "jerked her from her seat and threw her to the floor, severely injuring her." Occasionally, Black anger at this kind of treatment turned into mob action. Thus in

Austin, Texas, after a white motorman ordered two African American women to move from the white section to the rear of the street car, Black passengers waited until he reached the end of the line in a predominantly Black section of town and then, after exiting, picked up rocks and hurled them at the driver.[15]

For African Americans, every moment in the Jim Crow South was rife with emotional pain. In the daily routines of going to work, walking on the street, entering through the back door at one's place of employment, or opening a tattered and torn school book, there were constant reminders of white privilege and white presumptions of Black inferiority. But few customs of the day so glaringly blasted the message of second-class citizenship as the Jim Crow railroad train or streetcar. Individually insulting and vividly symbolic, Jim Crow transportation rules slapped Black people in the face in a dramatic and deeply personal way; hence, the number of protests in response. And even though Black Americans were fully aware of the risks they were taking by protesting, they never stopped expressing their outrage at the treatment they received. By so doing, they gave the lie to those who professed that Black Americans were perfectly content with the way things were.

Rural Resistance

Although urban areas offered greater opportunities for Blacks to gather and share their collective anger at Jim Crow, African Americans who lived in rural areas developed their own ways of expressing resistance. They constituted the majority in most rural areas. The small towns where they gathered on holidays and weekends were places of intense religiosity, close-knit families, unchanging main streets with country markets where people gathered on Saturday to sell their crops. They were also sites for vicious racial animosities over who had the right to make a decent living, who could stand up for a family's ability to move to another county, and who could defend the idea of equal treatment both before the law and in the marketplace. In every rural county, an intense struggle transpired between whites and Blacks over the economic future of the region. It all boiled down to what W. E. B. Du Bois called the duel for labor control. African Americans wanted labor mobility—the ability to sell their skills at the highest price available; on the other hand, white employers—especially plantation owners, but also phosphate and turpentine owners—wished to chain their Black workers permanently to a given place.

During the first years of the twentieth century, Macon County, Alabama—located in the heart of the cotton Black belt—both embodied and distilled all of these struggles. Macon's white farmers were particularly upset by the propensity of Black farmers to sell their berries at the nearby Tuskegee Institute, thereby generating an independent source of income and reducing their dependence on large white landowners who sought to confine them to their own plantations. As the Montgomery *Advertiser* noted, "The negroes would go out and in a few hours pick enough berries [to get] more than the price paid for farm labor, . . . leaving the planters without labor." In response, Macon's plantation owners forced through a "trespass" law in 1912 that criminalized berry picking on land not on the owners' plantation. "Strict enforcement of the trespass laws caused [blacks] to return to the farm," the *Advertiser* wrote, thereby solving the owners' problem by denying Black workers the economic wherewithal to move to another location.[16]

As the Macon example suggests, African Americans defined freedom of movement as one of their most important rights. It was the precondition for economic independence. As one white plantation owner in Alabama said, "Mr. Negro wants to engage in raising cotton just the same as [me] and you cannot engage him to work for you on wages." Indeed, Black farm workers, seeking higher wages and better working conditions, fought white attempts to keep them tied to individual employers by moving as much as possible. In response, various Southern states enacted "vagrancy" statutes that empowered law enforcement officials to *force* Black farm workers to go back to their old plantation bosses. The intent was transparent to all. "Down South," the *Indianapolis Freeman* observed, "[they] are urging drastic town measures to force the 'negro loafers' back on plantations so that labor there will become more plentiful and cheap." Although the laws were theoretically "race neutral" in their language, white Southerners admitted that they specifically targeted African Americans. Across the rural South, whites were terrified that Blacks would flee their region for jobs in the coal mines of West Virginia or Pennsylvania. The myth of white supremacy confronted a simple, economic fact. "Should the exodus continue," one newspaper wrote, "farmers will not be able to employ enough labor to harvest their crops."[17]

Even in the face of vagrancy laws, rural Blacks sought valiantly to find ways to operate independently. While James Monroe Smith, a successful white planter described by his biographer as "a great medieval lord," insisted that "*his*" Blacks were content, he steadfastly refused to allow his Black tenant farmers to market their own crops. "Knowing when to sell cotton was not for everybody," Smith said, "and certainly not for Negro tenants." To his consternation, however, he soon discovered that his Black tenants had organized their own underground markets. Angrily, Smith noted that many of his workers "would, of nights in remote fields, gather corn . . . , pick cotton, [then] . . . take it off and sell it. Some of them would take my mules [and] . . . occasionally they would steal [my] plantation tools and sell them."[18]

What happened on James Monroe Smith's plantation was not an isolated event. A Black newspaper in 1905 reported that Black agricultural workers in one rural Kentucky county had formed a "Colored Labor Trust." Allegedly, the workers "entered into a combination and agreed not to work in harvest fields for $1.50 a day, the price offered by farmers." Moreover, reports of armed clashes between landlords and tenants hinted at Black efforts to sustain underground markets in cotton as a major cause. In response, ordinances in many rural Southern counties forbade African American tenants from selling cotton after dark. These so-called after-dark laws signaled that Black sharecroppers continued to find ways to wring a living wage out of a political and economic system intended to keep them working at near-starvation pay. Although legally disenfranchised and confronting a uniformly racist set of social and economic practices, rural African Americans aspired to control their own labor, to create safe social spaces in order to organize collectively, and to achieve a more just distribution of wages and land in the South. That they attained any measure of fairness was testament to their determination.[19]

Armed Self Help

Violence suffused a social structure defined by the racial ideology of Jim Crow. Whites took it as a given that they had the right to browbeat, maim, or kill *any* Black American, for whatever reason. Sometimes the reason was a failure of a Black person to move quickly enough to get off the sidewalk when a white person approached. Other times the rumor of a sexual assault on a white woman resulted in the torture and lynching of Blacks. And occasionally the threat was posed by Black people doing too well, daring to display their prosperity. In 1916, the *Southern Ploughman* reported that a white mob had whipped a Black minister in Edgefield County, South Carolina, because "the Rev. Mr. Blocker has a splendid home and two or three hundred acres of good land, good stock, horses, mules, hogs and cows." Not only was Blocker severely beaten, he was forced to sell his land and animals at a bargain price—all because he dared to succeed. "In the name of God," the *Ploughman* cried, "what is the Negro to do? They were advised to stay out of politics, and buy homes. This they are doing, and have been doing. . . . Are these people now to be driven from the homes that have cost them all their hard and self-denying toil for nothing, simply because THEY OWN TOO MUCH LAND AND ARE GETTING ALONG BETTER THAN WHITE PEOPLE? God forbid that such is the case." Over and over again, in every nook and cranny of the South, such violence occurred daily, arbitrarily, and with almost no possibility that white authorities would ever act to prevent it.[20]

Taking up arms became the ultimate expression of Black political activism in the face of Jim Crow. In an era defined by lynch law, some Black people used rifles to defend their farms, families, and communities against white violence, although this did not happen on a daily basis. Black Southerners needed to weigh carefully their ability to protect neighbors as well as strangers against white retribution. Still, Black communities periodically mobilized to act, particularly when it was clear that established police authorities refused to do their jobs. Thus in Guilford County, North Carolina, in 1895, armed African Americans surrounded the county courthouse to prevent Arthur Tuttle from being lynched. Tuttle had been accused of killing a police officer, and the county police force showed no interest in protecting the incarcerated man. "They hoped to lynch Tuttle," a participant wrote the Richmond *Planet*. "But . . . we had our Winchesters and revolvers in readiness and took our station near the jail. . . ." African americans in nearby High Point held a rally to support Tuttle's defenders, and Blacks across the region wrote the *Planet* to express their solidarity with those who acted to protect him.[21]

The *Planet*'s editor, John Mitchell Jr., was particularly committed to Black self-defense and became famous across the South for his advocacy. "Judge Lynch is relentless in his ravages," Mitchell editorialized, and if Blacks did not act in support of themselves, lynch law would spread everywhere. "The shot-gun, the repeating rifle is the first prerequisite to . . . checking [Judge Lynch's] progress [so that] a rigid enforcement of the laws will banish him from the land." If Blacks did not stand up and fight, he declared, they had only themselves to blame for the results. "The shooting of Mr. Edward Harris at Tuskegee, Alabama, by a mob of lawless white men was outrageous," Mitchell wrote, "[but] he should have been armed and have shot down his assailants." Significantly, some of Mitchell's chief supporters were also involved in leading streetcar boycotts, suggesting the degree to which protest against mistreatment of Blacks in one area naturally carried over into other areas as well.[22]

But it was not just Mitchell and his allies who believed in armed self-defense. After a Black man was burned alive for allegedly assaulting a white woman in Washington Parish, Louisiana, African Americans in the area armed themselves to prevent further violence. When a posse of white men tried to storm Duncan Chapel to disarm the Blacks, they met a volley of bullets in response. For several hours, the Rev. Alexander Connolly led a defense of the church. Ultimately, he and his neighbors were overwhelmed. The horrific armed clash led to seventeen deaths—two whites, and fifteen African Americans. Still, it testified to the determination of some Blacks never to acquiesce in silence to the brutality of white racism. In a world where weapons, power, and the force of the law stood overwhelmingly on the side of the white oppressor, there was little chance of ultimate triumph through forceful confrontation. Yet the fact that some were willing to try spoke worlds about the depth of anger and resistance that pervaded the Black South.[23]

Humor and Song

Given the risks and the near certainty of fatal consequences, very few Black Americans seized the opportunity to express their anger at Jim Crow with weapons. But there were thousands who used their voices, their songs, and their satire to mock their oppressors and signal their solidarity. These might not bring the same satisfaction as a blow to the jaw of Jim Crow. But they nevertheless provided an outlet for rage, a means by which Black Americans could say, to themselves, "There, you bastard, take that."

Throughout the Jim Crow era, dissent from Black workers rang loudly over the South's docks, forests, turpentine camps, and fields in the guise of work songs that questioned white authority and scored the harsh nature of wage labor. African American workers, the historian Raymond Gavins reminds us, developed a powerful "expressive culture" as a mechanism of psychic survival. By creating songs that both described the work culture they were immersed in and expressed in vivid terms their contempt for the system of Jim Crow, Black workers sustained their own morale, and put a spotlight on the material injustices at the heart of the Black work experience. As the singer and actor Paul Robeson later observed, work songs quickly transposed into tools of resistance, a mode of expression that eventually provided a foundation for the blues. "The work songs, as well as the songs of protest," Robeson wrote, "are the fruit of collective creation. Their rhythm is born out of the work process. . . . It may be the synchronized movement of dockworkers loading barges. It may be the hard, monotonous work of the cotton pickers." But wherever they appeared, such work songs amounted to a dramatic rite of community building, providing a badge of identity for the workers, an incisive depiction of economic reality, and a primal if sublimated scream of protest at the injustices they experienced.[24]

James Weldon Johnson brilliantly articulated how the work songs vibrated with a sense of communal purpose:

> All the men sing and move together as they swing their picks or rock-breaking hammers. They move like a ballet. . . . It is all in rhythm but a rhythm impossible to set down. There is always a leader and he sets the pace. A phrase is sung while the shining hammers are being lifted. It is cut off suddenly as the hammer begins to descend and gives place to a prolonged grunt which becomes explosive at the impact of the blow. . . . Just how long the hammers will be allowed to rest cannot be determined; nor, since the movements are not governed by strict time, can any exact explanation be given as to why they all begin to rise simultaneously.

Imbued with a powerful sense of participating in a larger whole, workers could then inject into their collective expression a new verse articulating their disrespect for the bosses who rode alongside as their overseers. By using music as their accompaniment, Black workers found their own way to control the pace of the job, and if a foreman fired the song leader for going too slow, workers would lay down their tools until the leader was rehired. Moreover, because these songs were rooted in the collective historical experience of slavery and oppression, they provide precious insights into how ordinary Black workers viewed the everyday realities of Jim Crow.[25]

Work songs blended themes of play, protest, and even thinly veiled threats of striking back. African American laborers in Alachua County, Florida, complained about long hours and no pay:

Cap'm, Cap'm, ya must be cross
Hit's done six a'clock and ya woan knock off.

Cap'm. Cap'm, ya must be cross,
Da money done come and ya woan pay us off.

But then came the threat:

One a dese mawnings, an twon't be long
Cap'm gonna call me, and I be gone.

Work songs similarly provided a means by which workers could communicate with each other about impending danger. Black celery harvesters and turpentine workers in Seminole County, Florida, were heard uttering the following "shout" to warn their fellow workers that the white "riding boss" was coming:

Boss man's a ridin' by;
Boss man's a ridin' by;
Look out, Boy, look out.

But more often than anything else, work songs offered a vehicle for describing with bitter satire how Blacks were being cheated by white bosses:

They worked this nigger all year long'
It's time for him to go home.
You hear the bossman say to the Book-keeper
"How do this nigger stand?"
The book-keeper go in the office,
He sit down and 'gin to figger;
Then he say to the bossman,
"That nigger's just even now."

Sometimes, songs conveyed a defiant wish to put an end to the white bosses' long-lasting abuse, as in this railroad verse:

Cap'n got a pistol and he try to play bad,
But I'm going to take it if he make me mad
Cap'n got a burner [gun] I'd like to have
A 32:20 with a shiny barrel.

Just as important, through their songs Black workers openly questioned the ability of whites to set the rules of their world:

De Cap'n can't read, de Cap'n can't write,
How do he know that the time is right.

Deceptively simple, such verses offered a searing indictment of white incompetence while highlighting the absurdity of white supremacist assumptions. Through such lyrics, Black work songs provided an important terrain for racial protest to find expression, as well as an enduring source of Black camaraderie. It might not be the same as going jaw to jaw with the white boss and calling him a fool; but it offered an outlet for expressing, in a voice heard by every coworker in the community, a collective affirmation that this was not the way life should be, and the belief that, sometime, justice would be won.[26]

Accommodation as a Road to Advancement

Nothing shaped the political options open to African Americans more than the daily occurrence of white racist oppression. Jim Crow was not just a set of customs and laws. It was a cruel and vicious system of denigration that infused each moment of every day where contact with white people occurred. Its essence was vividly encapsulated by a Black coal miner in Kentucky who was asked whether he and his fellow workers ever "made a little leeway against the company." "Well," he responded, "I tell you, if you're fighting a man and he got a double barrel shotgun and you ain't got nothing, you know who's going to come out ahead."[27]

That fundamental reality created ground rules for Black-white interaction that could be breached only at the risk of one's life. Jim Crow constituted a prison cage. It might be possible to improve one's position inside the cage, but before Blacks could break free of the cage itself, enough building blocks had to be put in place to make possible an open attack. That meant that in the overwhelming number of cases, Black advancement could occur only by giving the *appearance* of accepting the status quo, then using deception as a means of persuading whites to concede to a given program or opportunity, and then cloak the progress achieved by making it appear as simply an extension of the underlying status quo. Protest might occur, but never as a brazen assault on the structure of power itself.

Booker T. Washington personified that approach. Capable of playing a variety of roles, only he knew which ones ultimately defined his objective. On the surface, everything he did seemed intended to massage the egos of white supremacists. But behind the scenes, and even buried in his cultivation of white paternalists, he sought to lay the groundwork for challenging the very system he seemed to be endorsing.

Others learned the same lesson. A group of Methodist Black churchmen wished to hold a major conference in Kentucky. It was an insult to their intelligence and their standing in the community to accept the smoke-filled second-class accommodations of the Jim Crow railroad coaches. But the way out was not to challenge the existence of the Jim Crow cars and risk violent reprisals. Rather, the ministers made an arrangement with the Louisville and Nashville Railroad company to have a special train transport the conferees. It would be for Blacks only and would have first-class cars for everyone.[28]

Booker T. Washington himself pursued a similar course of action. On a train ride from Washington back to Alabama, Washington and a group of Blacks traveling with him stopped in Raleigh for rest and refreshment. Washington carried with him the kind of status reflected in the fact that Theodore Roosevelt, the president, had invited Washington to dine at the White House. So special arrangements were made. The proprietors of the Hamlet Hotel invited Washington and his associates to eat in the opulent splendor of their main dining room, while white customers were served in the hotel's front room where the furniture, by contrast, looked worn. Many white Carolinians were outraged, viewing the episode as proof that "negro socialism" was threatening the Tar Heel State with ruin.

In fact, there were two things going on. Washington was insisting that he receive the treatment his status earned him, all the while never questioning the idea of separate dining facilities. Meanwhile, whites were agreeing to provide a Black man first-class treatment precisely because he did not challenge their underlying ground rules. In the overall exchange, Blacks had more reason to be gleeful that Washington had demonstrated that he could secure first-class treatment than sorrowful because he had done so in a segregated dining room.[29]

Booker T. Washington, of course, excelled at playing duplicitous roles. At the same time he was persuading Southern white leaders that Blacks should pull themselves up by their bootstraps and accept the new system of Jim Crow, he secretly was bankrolling legal challenges to Black disenfranchisement. Thus, theoretically at least, the monies Washington was taking from whites to support Tuskegee's dedication to "industrial education" for Blacks were actually being reallocated to promote lawsuits challenging the very premises of Jim Crow. Washington was a perfect "spy in the service of God," to use the Danish theologian Soren Kierkagaard's phrase: while appearing to serve one master (an evil system of segregation), he was in fact serving a higher purpose (the universal dignity of man).

The 1906 commencement ceremonies at Tuskegee brilliantly demonstrated Washington's ability to play contradictory roles. He had invited two speakers to deliver the major addresses. The first was John W. Abercrombie, president of the University of Alabama. Consistent with the philosophy of those who had financially supported Tuskegee, Abercrombie told the large audience of African Americans that Black voting rights had been a huge error. "The sudden enfranchisement of a race comprising over three millions of people," Abercrombie declared, "was the colossal mistake of [our] times." The audience greeted President Abercrombie's address with uncomfortable silence.

Then came the second speaker. He was William Lloyd Garrison Jr., the son of the great abolitionist. "At once," the Birmingham Black newspaper reported, "the vast throng of Negroes in the chapel went wild," giving Garrison a five-minute standing ovation. Garrison did not disappoint. Refuting Abercrombie's presentation, he declared, "When I see this vast crowd of well-dressed, well-fed Negroes, I only wish my father were living to witness this scene. The best way to teach the Negro to vote is to put a ballot in his hand." The audience roared with approval.[30]

In this particular instance, Washington had perhaps risked going too far. He could not have failed to know that Garrison Jr. would say something critical about Jim Crow. Yet he had hedged his bets, choosing one speaker from the South whom he knew would endorse the existing social order and placate Tuskegee's supporters, and another from the North—a famous and well-respected white man—who had nothing to lose by making strong statements on race relations, and who, in the end, could say publicly what Washington believed privately.

What the Tuskegee commencement controversy did, in the end, was to underline the difficulty of arriving at any categorical labeling of African American behavior during the age of Jim Crow. Discussing the interior lives of enslaved African Americans, the historian Peter Wood writes, "To separate their reactions into docility on the one hand and rebellion on the other . . . is to underestimate the complex nature of the contradictions each Negro felt in the face of new provocations and new penalties. It is more realistic to think in terms of a spectrum of response, ranging from complete submission to total resistance, along which any given individual could be located at a given time."

In short, Black Americans played multiple roles during this Jim Crow period. Feigning obeisance to the rules of white supremacy, they simultaneously used every opportunity they could find to modify, weaken, and eventually undermine white control. If we freeze the frame on Booker T. Washington in 1895, he seems to be telling whites and Blacks at the International Exposition that African Americans should accept segregation. But move the frame forward to 1906 and the picture becomes fuzzier. Move it still further and we understand better the prescience of Peter Wood's description. Shortly before Washington died, he would join other Black Southerners in protesting D.W. Griffith's *Birth of a Nation* and urging African Americans to observe a national day of protest against segregation.[31]

Reflections

The variety of African American responses to Jim Crow captures the fact that there was no "correct" course of action. Every response needed to be calibrated by local circumstances, the exact nature of the situation, the dangers of physical harm, and the intensity of one's need to stand up for justice. Dissent did not and could not follow any preordained path. Regional differences mattered significantly. The Richmond *Planet* presented one frame of reference—relatively militant—for Blacks living in that border state. But Birmingham, Jacksonville, and New Orleans were very different, each place offering its own avenues for movement forward—factories in Birmingham, longshore unions in New Orleans, church assemblies in Jacksonville. The Delta counties of Mississippi and Arkansas, meanwhile, constituted a world of their own, with tighter social controls by whites and more reliance on separate institutions for Negroes. To complicate matters further, Blacks were divided by class distinctions, political disputes, and color conflict. Some communities had Black informants who shared information with white patrons. In others, the punishment for such betrayal was so severe that it would never even enter the realm of possibility.

What remained clear was that African American dissent in the Jim Crow South—in all its myriad forms—was as pervasive as the Jim Crow signs, laws, and separate facilities that covered the region. No one could deny the deeply personal pain that accompanied every racial insult, every act of denigration. Whether being pushed off a sidewalk, ordered to go in a back door, or bullied on a streetcar into giving up a seat to a white, not a single Black person could escape the slap in the face represented in every act of white supremacy.

But even in that context, resistance—whether overt or covert—was equally pervasive. It took many forms. The thunder of the mass streetcar boycotts was matched by quieter acts of resistance, large and small, that occurred wherever human dignity was upheld in the face of efforts to destroy it. Somehow, during the worst years of Jim Crow, Black Southerners found ways to sustain and nourish their democratic aspirations, as well as to organize the collective efforts needed to build the knowledge and create the community voluntary associations that could put into place the building blocks that eventually would culminate in an open demand to be free. Some insisted on moving each year, from total indebtedness to a white landlord to a new, potentially more promising farm. More and more Blacks started to contemplate an even larger possibility—leaving the South entirely for a Northern city where there might exist factory jobs, better schools, even the chance to vote.

Perhaps Henry Hooten, a Tuskegee, Alabama, resident, offered the best way of understanding and celebrating these multiple examples of endurance and protest. "Most times," he recalled, "we would use strategy rather than force [in dealing with whites]. Be very kind. Use psychology on them . . . the first thing the white man thought [was] that you knew less about . . . psychology [than he did]. . . . He knew it all. . . . He didn't think you had enough sense to [figure him out]. But you would listen to what he had to say . . . and at first you would tell him what he wanted to hear. . . ." And then, Hooten continued, you would pursue your own objectives in whatever way you could.[32]

Such a "strategy" made eminent sense. It helps to explain how and why African Americans kept alive their pride and activism in the years of the Jim Crow South. In truth, these multiple acts of resistance, subtle as well as overt, created the arsenal of tools that sustained the will to prevail, and that provided the instruments for taking advantage of the next stage of more radical, egalitarian possibilities in World War I and after.

Chapter 6

World War I

The eruption of World War I in 1914 created a huge dilemma for Black American activists. The president, Woodrow Wilson—a Southerner by birth and temperament—had already instituted a system of Jim Crow segregation in the government, creating separate eating facilities for Blacks and whites in the federal civil service. He had also praised the racist film *Birth of a Nation* (1915), calling it a brilliant historical depiction of the Civil War era. Indeed, the film drew on Wilson's own published scholarship. The president gave no indication of concern about the pervasive inequalities facing Black citizens.

On the other hand, he had also endorsed progressive legislation on wages, hours, and working conditions for American laborers. Furthermore, when Wilson—having declared American neutrality in the war between Germany, France, and the United Kingdom—was forced to change his stance after German submarines started to attack American ships, he did so with rhetoric that suggested a more idealistic and just world for all peoples. This was a "war to make the world safe for democracy," Wilson declared, a "war to end all wars," and to promote self-determination and equal rights around the world.

What to do in this situation? Was it possible that this might be the occasion for a breakthrough in American race relations, a road to true democracy and freedom? After years of federal indifference to the dilemma of racial inequality—when Blacks relied on their own families, churches, and community associations to carry on the fight for freedom—had the moment finally arrived when the US government would stand up for the ideals it was allegedly founded on?

W. E. B. Du Bois took a risk and encouraged African Americans to "close ranks" in support of the war effort. Writing in the NAACP journal *The Crisis*, Du Bois came down on the side of taking a chance that Wilson meant what he said about making the world "safe for democracy." If self-determination and an end to colonial rule were to be the result of the war, Blacks would gain immediately—indeed, they would be one of the prime beneficiaries of victory in the war. But Du Bois's support for the war was premised on the determination of Blacks to *insist* that victory would bring true democracy for Black people. "By the God of Heaven," he vowed, "we are cowards and Jackasses if [when] . . . the war is over, we do not marshal every ounce of our brain and brawn to fight a sterner, longer, more unbending battle against the forces of hell in our own land."[1]

As the war unfolded, it dramatized the volatile forces on each side of the struggle for racial justice. With energetic fervor, Blacks embraced the war effort. The changes that took place were dramatic—from increased membership and mobilization within the NAACP, to mass migration of Blacks toward the North and toward cities within the South, and greater employment opportunities for Blacks. On the other side, white Southerners—and Northerners—resisted Black demands for equity, violently repressed Black migrants, and defended the politics of white supremacy. Back and forth the battle went—a conflict as brutal as that which had occurred during Reconstruction and in the 1890s. Only with the dawning of a new decade would it be clear which side had come out on top.

The War

Most African Americans responded enthusiastically to Du Bois's call to "close ranks" and support the war. In many Southern counties, a higher percentage of African Americans registered for the Army draft than whites, while fewer claimed exemptions from the draft. In Jacksonville, the Associated Press reported that "the [army] registration booths were crowded throughout the day and at 9 o'clock tonight it was estimated that more negroes than whites had registered." Even in one Louisiana parish, where "a leading white man" was said to have declared that "this is a white man's country . . . [and] the Negro has no country and no rights," fewer Negroes claimed draft exemptions than whites.[2]

As it turned out, Black soldiers played a critical role in the US war effort at home and in Europe. The service of Blacks in the military went back to the American Revolution and continued forward to the highly decorated "Buffalo Soldier" regiments of the late nineteenth century. Indeed, General "Black Jack" Pershing, who commanded US forces in Europe during World War I, earned his nickname leading the Black troopers of the 10th US Cavalry regiment during the 1890s in the American West. The Black troops in the 10th later distinguished themselves in the Spanish American War as well as in border conflicts with Mexico during the early 1910s. One military officer found "the Negro soldier to be loyal to his flag, obedient to his officers and considerate to a captured foe."[3]

This despite the fact that African American enlistees entered a rigidly segregated military, and most were limited to service and supply companies. To be sure, this was essential work. In modern warfare, service and supply battalions are the lifelines of armies and naval fleets; without them, even the finest combat units are helpless. But Negro infantry units also built ammunition dumps, laid railroad track, and repaired roads—grueling work that mirrored their experiences in the South. "Worked often like slaves twelve and fourteen hours a day," according to W. E. B. Du Bois, "these men were ill-fed, poorly clad, indifferently housed, often beaten, always 'Jim-Crowed' and insulted." Nevertheless, they served proudly and well, anticipating that their service in helping America earn victory would translate into a new recognition back home of equal justice between the races.[4]

Nearly 400,000 African Americans enlisted in the US Army during the war. Roughly half saw duty in Europe. Not all of them did supply and support work. The 92nd Infantry Division repeatedly distinguished itself in battle. Hailing from West Palm Beach, Florida, L. A. Alexander served in the division's 167th Artillery Brigade, and by the end of the war, the young man had worked his way up to the rank of sergeant-major. During the Argonne-Meuse offensive, the 92nd's Black infantry and its machine gun and field artillery regiments pounded German defenses, endured gas attacks, and suffered more than 1,600 casualties. They knew what was at stake and explicitly discussed it. In October, L. A. Alexander reported that his artillery battery "took our position on the firing line, where we played our part in the great struggle for Democracy, and tried to measure up to the best that was in us, so that when we returned home it could not be said that we were shirkers and failed to do our duty."[5]

The Black soldiers clearly impressed their European counterparts. When they departed from one French town, the local mayor presented the unit with a letter that stated:

> From the very day of its arrival, your regiment, by its behavior and its military appearance, excited the admiration of us all. . . . From the beginning a real brotherhood was established between your soldiers and our people who are glad to welcome the gallant Allies of our France. . . . I hope that the white troops replacing your regiment will give us equal satisfaction, but whatever their attitude may be, they cannot surpass your 349th Field Artillery.[6]

Leo P. Dennis, a member of Bethel Baptist Institutional Church in Jacksonville, served with the 92nd's 350th Machine Gun Battalion. Dennis's battalion played a central role in the rescue mounted to save the 56th Infantry, entirely composed of white Americans, from annihilation at the base of the Metz fortresses on the Moselle River the day before the Armistice was signed. On that day, the 56th spearheaded an assault on the German stronghold of Pagny and got caught in a deadly crossfire, becoming hopelessly trapped. The Black soldiers of the 350th rushed into the face of murderous German fire, silenced the enemy guns, and rescued their white comrades from certain death. German leaders recognized the irony of Black soldiers sacrificing their lives for white soldiers. Hence, German airplanes dropped anti–Jim Crow leaflets on Black frontline regiments. "What is Democracy?," one leaflet read. "Personal Freedom, all citizens enjoying the same rights before the law. Do you enjoy the same rights as the white people do in America, the land of Freedom and Democracy, or are you rather not treated over there as second-class Citizens?" What the Germans did not understand was that the Black soldiers knew all this. That was precisely why they were fighting—to capture in their own lives at home the freedoms they were fighting for.[7]

The Black 371st Infantry Regiment from Pensacola served with the elite French 157th or "Red Hand" Division. Against terrific odds, the 371st breached the Hindenburg line at Monthois and fought heroically in the bloody Argonne Forest. French General Goybet was unreserved in his praise for the regiment: "Never will the 157th Division forget the indomitable dash, the heroic rush of the American (Negro) regiments up the observatory ridge and into the Plain of Meonthois. The most powerful defenses, the most strongly organized machine gun nests, the heaviest artillery barrages—nothing could stop them." In eight days of continuous battle beginning on September 28 in the Champagne, the regiment lost 1,065 out of 2,384 men.[8]

Jacksonville musician Eugene F. Mikell's regiment, the 369th Infantry, fought for 191 straight days in unbroken battle, the longest stretch of any US unit in World War I. Mikell's regiment earned the sobriquet "Harlem Hellfighters" for their bravery. They were the first Allied unit to reach the Rhine River. Their determination was unrivaled. The 369th's commander famously said, "My men never retire, they go forward or they die." The entire unit was awarded the *Croix de Guerre* by the French government for extraordinary courage in battle.

The idealism of these men, and their sense of accomplishment, was palpable. To believe that they would return to America and accept second-class citizenship was incomprehensible. "I saw the towns of desolated France," wrote Private Henry Rivers to his mother, "the fruiting trees destroyed in senseless hate." Lest his mother believe his service had been in vain, the poetic Rivers declared:

> My Mother, cheer your heart and dry your tears, for after awhile, God willing I will return. We sacrifice today that through the years we may enjoy the peace for which we yearn, We fight for every mother as she sings her baby to sleep upon her throbbing breast. Battle for womanhood of the earth, for liberty, for honor and for right. Be proud, oh Mother, dear, that you gave birth to one son who answered such a fight.[9]

Still, Jim Crow followed African American soldiers to Europe. Despite a record of exemplary service for their country, they were often vilified by their white officers, most of whom hailed from the Jim Crow South. White commanders told French citizens that Black troops were "inferior" and warned the French to avoid them. "American white officers fought more valiantly against Negroes," W. E. B. Du Bois later remarked, "than they did against the Germans." And back home, the majority of white Americans were determined to uphold the racial status quo regardless of Black sacrifices. As one newspaper in Tampa, Florida, warned:

> The Negro returned soldier who is full of the "equal rights" treatment he got in Europe during the past months will do exceedingly well to remember that for every one of him there are about a thousand white returned soldiers who were completely fed up on the same equal rights stuff over there, and they are not going to stand for one moment any internal rot started by any yellow-faced coon who has the hellish idea that he is as good as a white man or a white woman.

Yet Sergeant Major L. A. Alexander, the Black artillery soldier from West Palm Beach, had a different viewpoint of the war's outcome. Proudly noting that "we played our part in the great struggle for Democracy," the veteran declared, "I voice the sentiment of every colored soldier in the United States when I say that we are hoping and expecting to reap the benefits of our toilsome struggles and that Democracy in its fullest meaning will be for the betterment of the negro race as it will be for all other races."[10]

Back Home

What would happen back home depended on how the citizens and politicians of the country responded to the role of Blacks in the war, both at home and abroad. That became the cutting edge. The pace of domestic change accelerated dramatically. What was later called the "Great Migration" helped transform the demographics of the country. In 1910, 90 percent of all African Americans lived in the South, mostly in rural areas. Over the next twenty years, prompted mostly by World War I and a changing economy, 1.3 million Blacks moved from rural areas in the South to urban areas in the North. Detroit alone saw its Black population soar from 6,000 to 120,000. Blacks moved to cities in the South as well. Most the migrants took jobs in the steel, automobile, shipbuilding, and meatpacking industries. Overall Black industrial employment skyrocketed from 500,000 in 1910 to 901,000 in 1920. Migration, unionization, the growth of the urban Black population, and the increase in membership of the NAACP all contributed to a faith among many Blacks that this could be a turning point, a start to the end of Jim Crow. As 147 African Americans from Hattiesburg, Mississippi, crossed the Ohio River on their way north, they stopped to pray, then sang, "I done come out of the land of Egypt, ain't that good news?"

Most of the migrants were open about their reason for leaving. "In colored localities, we have very bad streets, no light, no sewage system," one migrant wrote. Another said, "all [we]ask is fair treatment . . . living wages . . . the right to make an honest living. . . ." Sometimes whole communities went north. One minister in Ocala, Florida, discovered that his entire parish was moving to New York. And once they got to their new homes, they created community centers and churches that were a mirror image of where they had come from.[11]

On occasion, the migration north helped create better conditions in southern African American urban centers such as Birmingham, Norfolk, and Richmond. Black factory workers were sometimes able to join and organize trade unions, on occasion in tandem with white workers. Sharecroppers and tenants in Arkansas, Florida, and east Texas who "stayed behind" began to form cooperative organizations and plan for strikes. The NAACP also increased its ranks dramatically, building on its 1915 victory in the Supreme Court in *Guinn v. United States* which invalidated the "grandfather clause" that denied Black men the right to vote if their grandfathers could not vote. In three years, the NAACP went from having 8,642 members in 68 branches in the South to having nearly 100,000 members in 342 branches.[12]

By 1919, even "moderate" Black leaders were sounding more militant. Urban League spokesman Eugene Jones, for example, warned African Americans to beware of the white capitalist. In the past, Jones noted, "it used to be said that the rich white man was the Negro's best friend" and poor white man his enemy. "But I want to tell you that the rich white man is no friend of the Negro. The only way for the colored man to get a foot hold in industry is to organize."[13]

So change was in the air. But Black activists would soon learn what North Carolina Blacks had discovered in 1898 at the time of the Wilmington race riot. The "best white men" were not to be trusted.

After the War

But what would happen if white supremacists prevailed, if whites in the North as well as the South resisted Black demands for changes in housing restrictions, racially segregated schools, access to the ballot box and to political office-holding? Racial distinctions, after all, defined American society—who could do what, associate with whom, hold office, have freedom of choice. These questions would define whether or not World War I, and Du Bois's call to "close ranks," might lead to a new era of racial quality.

It was clear that many Black Americans were intent on pressing forward with their demand for independence. In April 1918, the women teachers of Wilson, North Carolina, revolted openly against the dictates of the white school board. One of them, Mary Euell, had been called to task by the Black principal of her school for leaving school an hour early. No, Euell said, she had left on time. Daylight Savings Time had started and she had come in an hour early, and then left an hour early. The principal took her to the white superintendent—a friend of Booker T. Washington. He ordered her to shut up when she started to make her case, then slapped her in the face when she continued. After Euell told her colleagues what had happened, eight resigned on the spot and three more quit soon after. The entire Black community united in protest and treated the teachers as heroines, hosting a banquet in their honor. Black leaders called the superintendent and principal "brutes, worse than the Kaiser." Black churches and lodges supported the teachers as they went on strike. Soon, African American parents and the Colored Business League started to raise funds to support their own school, and just weeks later eight Black teachers welcomed three hundred pupils to the new Independent School they had created.[14]

Indeed, Black women throughout the South were active participants in social movements. In Florida, women launched a statewide voter registration campaign as part of the battle for women's suffrage. In Jacksonville, one reporter wrote, "they began to arrive at 8 o'clock [in the morning], and many of them sat down on the curbing to rest, so many hours were they in line." Another eyewitness declared: "Some went with babies in their arms, and took their lunches so that they would not have to fast while waiting." The local newspaper noted that more than seven thousand women had registered—over half the female Black population in the city.[15]

Elsewhere, similar Black protests occurred. James Bray was a well-respected Black minister in Birmingham, Alabama. A former college president who held a doctorate, he was known for his decorum and dignity. But one day on a Birmingham streetcar crowded with Black passengers coming home from a hard day working at a local steel factory, he protested when the driver ordered Blacks to move to the "colored" section of the packed car. When Bray said no, the conductor attacked him. Bray then responded with an uppercut to the jaw of his attacker. The passengers openly rejoiced at his bravery, and the local Black newspaper declared "these [Jim Crow] signs should be pitched out of the window and burned."[16]

Similar episodes of protest against Jim Crow occurred throughout the country, each one highlighting the contrast between Black insistence on honoring the democracy they were fighting for in the war against Germany and the insistence of whites in the United States on suppressing Black freedom. A number of industrial labor unions undertook interracial organizing campaigns in Chicago, Birmingham, and other urban areas. The NAACP's James Weldon Johnson, for one, sensed a revival of hope among African Americans as he traveled across the country. "Everywhere," he said, "there was a rise in level of the Negro's morale. The exodus of Negroes to the North . . . was in full motion; the tremors of the war in Europe were shaking America with increasing intensity; circumstances were combining to put a higher premium on Negro muscle, Negro hands, and Negro brains than ever before; all these forces had a quickening effect that was running through the entire mass of the race."[17]

But alas, such optimism turned out to be short-lived. In the end, white racism prevailed, easily and quickly. Throughout American history, rising Black aspirations had been met with white violence. Now, that pattern resumed. Between 1917 and 1923, African Americans experienced a new wave of riots, massacres, and acts of racial terrorism. The peak of recorded violence occurred during the tumultuous months between April and October 1919, a season that Black leaders soon dubbed the Red Summer. During these months, race riots broke out in Washington, DC; Charleston, South Carolina; and Longview, Texas, among other places; casualties were in the thousands. Lynching became especially prevalent in 1919. Eleven African Americans were burned alive at the stake. In the same months, lynch mobs murdered sixty-nine Black people, including ten World War I veterans whose military service was viewed by whites as a threat to the racial status quo. During Red Summer, anti-Black race riots raged across several cities and garnered national attention. Along with physical injuries to hundreds of Blacks, the riots inflicted incalculable property damage, mostly borne by Black Americans. The riots also undermined the political and economic status of African Americans in communities across the nation.[18]

The whites who brutalized Black citizens enjoyed almost universal immunity from prosecution. Their Black counterparts, on the other hand, were often hauled off to jail cells just for defending their homes and neighborhoods. White citizens who shot or beat a Black person to death in broad daylight had little to fear from law enforcement authorities who often participated in vigilante activities themselves. The rule of law in the United States—from the courts to the local police to the attitude and actions of federal institutions—was used as an instrument for maintaining Black subordination and to prop up white supremacy, not let it be weakened.

The race riots of 1919–1923 were not inspired solely by racist hatred. Rather, they highlighted the ongoing connection between white resistance to Blacks seeking economic advancement as well as political rights. The East St. Louis riot, for example, was aimed at keeping African Americans from moving up the occupational ladder, as well as preventing them from going to the polling place. To achieve the same result, the Tulsa, Oklahoma, riot of 1921 concentrated on destroying a thriving Black business district, a bastion of Black capitalism and one of the most prosperous Black neighborhoods in America. The Tulsa riots highlighted the link between issues of class and race. Properties and businesses owned by African Americans were explicitly targeted by white rioters. Remembering the years she spent building up a successful hairdressing practice in Tulsa and then seeing it destroyed, Mabel Little recalled: "At the time of the riot we owned ten different business places for rent. Today, I *pay* rent." Riots in small towns and rural areas drove African Americans off the land and often allowed white residents to take control of Black property for drastically reduced rates or for nothing at all. The massacre and forced removal of the African American community during the Rosewood, Florida, riot of 1923 wiped out generations of Black landownership.[19]

Soon, "Red Summer" was reinforced in national politics by the "Red Scare." Even as President Wilson traversed the country urging support for the Treaty of Versailles, conservatives were zeroing in on political progressives, using the rise of communism abroad to attack working-class and Black militancy at home. J. Edgar Hoover, soon to be head of the Federal Bureau of Investigation (FBI), spread the word that radicals were trying to destroy America. Hoover and his allies arrested, detained, and ultimately expelled thousands of "alien" (i.e., immigrant) political activists. As appeals to "law and order" ensured the ascendancy of Hoover and similar reactionaries, the possibility for social and economic reform disappeared. Eventually, the Red Scare resulted in the deportation of more than three thousand supporters of communism from the country. Progressives who advocated social and economic change, including a greater commitment to racial justice, were condemned and persecuted.[20]

As state and federal authorities used powers gained through the Espionage and Sedition Acts of 1917–1918 to undermine legitimate protest groups, they ignored the harrowing crimes committed by whites seeking to reinforce Jim Crow. In the two years leading up to the Chicago Race Riot of 1919, scores of African American homes were bombed. Yet state authorities conducted no meaningful investigations, nor did they ever identify any of the perpetrators. The same scenario played out in Miami. When similar bombings occurred there, undercover federal agents seemed more interested in spying on African Americans than in catching those responsible. In contrast, Blacks who participated in the 1917 Houston race riot were vigorously prosecuted. Some were even executed.[21]

A race riot in Ocoee, Florida, on election day in 1918 perhaps best highlighted the linkage of political rights with economic opportunity. After being denied the right to vote, Mose Norman, a Black activist, was chased away from a polling place, and fled to the home of July Perry, a well-off Black who owned a substantial house on a small lake across from the Ocoee courthouse. A mob of more than a hundred whites chased him, and when they tried to break down the front door, Perry fired his gun at the intruders. In response, fifty carloads of whites laid siege to the well-off Black neighborhood. They destroyed the local fraternal lodge building, set fire to local Black churches, and killed fifty-six Black citizens. July Perry was captured and lynched. Mose Norman was never found. For days afterward, hundreds of African Americans fled the city, never to return. When the light-skinned Walter White of the NAACP—posing as a white person looking for property—came to Ocoee a week later, his white driver told him the massacre had occurred because of white jealousy of Black landowners like Norman and Perry who were judged to be "too prosperous" by their white peers.[22]

Federal indifference—and complicity—reinforced this upsurge of racism. The federal government turned a blind eye to the growth of the Ku Klux Klan. By contrast, federal authorities harassed the Industrial Workers of the World, a union of immigrants, migrants, and Mexican and African American workers that was seeking to transform labor-management relations. Wilson's attorney general, Thomas W. Gregory, did not investigate the disenfranchisement of African Americans in the South or anti-black violence in the North. Instead he launched an investigation into alleged illegal Black voting in the Midwest. Prominent members of the Wilson administration even claimed that Black migration to the North had been motivated by "sinister forces" bent on undermining the nation's political system. Meanwhile the larger public was encouraged by the mass media to see Black people coming North as subversive interlopers out to destroy white communities. Hence, sensational headlines such as: "Negroes Flock in from South to Evade Draft" (*St. Louis Times*); "North Does Not Welcome Influx of South's Negroes" (*Chicago Herald*); "Negro Migration: Is It a Menace?" (*Philadelphia Record*); and "Negro Influx On, Plan to Dam It" (*Newark News*).[23]

Factory owners recruited Blacks to come North to take jobs they desperately needed to fill, then used racial tensions between white and

Black workers to fight against unionization of their factories. "Large numbers of Negroes were brought from the South by the [meat] packers," the NAACP's Walter White noted, "and there is little doubt that this was done in part so that the Negro might be used as a club over the heads of the unions." In East St. Louis, site of one of the largest race riots in the World War I era, these tensions were rife, particularly at the Aluminum Ore factory, one of the largest employers in the city. When the workers at Aluminum Ore went on strike, historian Elliot Rudwick writes, "the union members remembered only that Negroes had taken their jobs. In their frustration they seized upon this single point: if Negroes had not come to East St. Louis the union could not have been crushed."[24]

In the end, the very hint that a change in America's race relations might be in the offing seemed sufficient to trigger anxiety, apprehension, and anger among large numbers of white Americans. Blacks continued to protest, to rally their communities and institutions in support of breaking down the rules and regulations of white racism. World War I had brought some progress. But in the absence of intervention and support from the government and local authorities, breakthroughs were few and far between.

The 1918 Philadelphia race riot spoke as powerfully as any event to the underlying dynamics that shaped the possibility that World War I might bring significant change. The riot started after African Americans began buying homes in the city's predominantly white residential neighborhoods. It was the newly purchased home of Adelia Bonds, a Black probation officer, that would become the flashpoint for the Philadelphia race riot. Bonds had violated an unwritten rule by purchasing a house in a predominantly white area. Mrs. Bond's neighbors began harassing her immediately, continuing on a daily basis. On July 16, a group of white citizens gathered in front of her residence at 2936 Ellsworth and began throwing large stones at her house. Mrs. Bonds fled to the top story of her house, and then, armed with a rifle, fired warning shots at the crowd. One of these rounds hit Joseph Kelly, a white man, and the riot began. The Philadelphia police were unable to quell the violence, in part because they sided openly with the white rioters. The Philadelphia race riot resulted in multiple casualties. Four people were killed, and approximately sixty were wounded.[25]

Leaders of Philadelphia's Black Methodist Ministers Meeting lodged a formal protest with the mayor's office, stating:

> We desire you to understand that we put the whole blame upon your incompetent police force. But for the sympathy of the police, their hobnobbing with the mob, what has now become the disgrace of Philadelphia would have been nothing more than a petty row. Your police have for a long time winked at . . . the beating up of Negroes, the stoning of their homes and the attacking of their churches. . . . In nearly every part of the city, decent law-abiding Negroes have been set upon by . . . irresponsible white hoodlums, their property damaged and destroyed, while your police seemed powerless to protect them.[26]

Many of the racial dynamics featured in the Philadelphia race riot would be repeated in the much larger Chicago race riot the following year, as well as in others during Red Summer. In the Tulsa race riot, for example, state guardsmen contributed to an already disastrous situation by failing to disarm white citizens as they looted Black property. Some white troops openly referred to Blacks as "the enemy." In East St. Louis, state troopers openly fraternized with rioting whites, even on occasion joining them in attacking the Black enemy.[27]

African Americans attempted to defend their neighborhoods—sometimes using arms—but that could often precipitate even more violence against them. The Tulsa race riot, for example, began after a group of armed African Americans gathered to help law enforcement officials prevent the lynching of a young man accused of bumping into a white woman in an elevator. But when whites in Tulsa realized that the Black community was organizing to stop the lynching, they attempted to disarm a group of Black veterans. Soon, gunshots broke out, and one of the worst race riots of the decade erupted.

Reflections

In all of this, Black America's hope that "closing ranks" and fighting a war to "make the world safe for democracy" might bring a breakthrough in race relations quickly evaporated. Black protests continued. African Americans had done their part—indeed, much more than their part. But in the larger scheme of things, white Americans proved unwilling to sacrifice their privileges based on race. The apparent turnabout in vision that accompanied Woodrow Wilson's decision to go to war turned out to be an illusion. The president who praised *Birth of a Nation* remained a white supremacist, notwithstanding a rhetorical vision that seemed to prophesy a different world, dedicated to human rights.

One more time, Black Americans would have to deal with a government and social structure dedicated to defending white supremacy—not equal rights for all human beings.

Chapter 7

The 1920s and 1930s

By the early 1920s, it was clear that World War I had done little to change the lives of African Americans. It had raised hopes, only to have them dashed almost immediately after the armistice. W. E. B. Du Bois's call to enter the war full-gear had produced nothing but disillusionment. Whether one cited the vicious race riots, intensified Jim Crow laws, or the federal government's indifference, the plight of Black people in the South deteriorated once the soldiers came home. The political message that nothing would ever change in American race relations slapped Du Bois in the face, sending him in a new direction. He now came to believe that Black separatism was the only answer to the "Negro problem." The Great Migration northward offered a respite for some, or at least the opportunity to fight an old war on a new battlefield. But for most Blacks in the South, the only solace to be found was in mutual self-help and community institution-building.

When the Depression swept the land in 1929, it created an even greater level of despair. For the most part, Franklin Roosevelt and New Deal Democrats—especially in the early New Deal—refused to alter the Jim Crow system of segregation. Most felt dependent on Southern Democratic votes to secure any kind of congressional action. Only when it became clear that Black suffering was the most prominent example of the South's being the nation's number one economic problem did they recognize that federal *intervention on behalf* of Black Americans would be essential to produce a brighter future for the region, and the race. In the meantime, the struggle continued, fueled by the adamant refusal of Blacks to give up, no matter what the odds in favor of white racism.

Two realities shaped the ongoing plight of Black people in the South: the first was the persistence of racist violence, the second the overpowering influence of the South's sharecropping and tenant farmer system. While physical brutality constituted one white response to Blacks at the end of the war, persistent economic oppression represented the other. Ever since the dream of "forty acres and a mule" had evaporated in 1867 in the face of powerful white opposition, subsistence farming had become the norm for almost all Black people living in the South, condemning virtually the entire Black population to a life of poverty and despair. Indeed, only 1 in 100 Blacks in the South owned their own land.

To be sure, there were occasional stories of success. James Hall, who started off as a tenant farmer, eventually bought two mules and a two-horse wagon. With the support of his wife and family, he eventually saved enough to buy his own sixty acres, then two hundred more. Ned Cobb, the hero of Theodore Rosengarten's *All God's Dangers*, also struggled successfully to purchase land, grow decent crops, and eventually, buy a Model T Ford.[1]

But Hall and Cobb were the exceptions. In most instances, Black sharecroppers and tenant farmers were mistreated by their white landlords. When it came time to tally up how much the tenant farmer owed the planter for supplies he had purchased, the verdict in almost every instance was that the Black tenant farmer owed the planter money, and thus ended up deeper in debt. Even if his own figures were different from those of the boss, he had no basis on which to challenge the person who controlled the lives of his wife and children. The pervasive power of the white landowning class, often the same people who served as furnishing merchants for the supplies purchased by the tenant farmer, offered no opportunity for rebellion.

To make matters worse, the health of Blacks in the South continued to deteriorate. Venereal disease was pervasive, reducing life expectancy among African Americans in the South by 17 percent. Blacks tested positive for syphilis at a rate of 27 percent, six times the rate for whites. Less than 15 percent of Black births took place in hospitals. Not surprisingly, Black women were twice as likely to die from complications of childbirth than whites. In 1920, one hospital bed existed for every 1,941 Black people, versus 1 for every 139 whites. Even in a relatively well-off state like North Carolina, 34 of 100 counties had no hospitals at all.[2]

A dearth of educational facilities made it impossible for most Blacks to lift themselves up by school achievement and advance to high school and college. The duration of the school year for most Black children was under four months. In most cases, per-capita expenditure on a Black child's education was a tenth of that for a white child. Schoolbooks, when available, were hand-me-downs from white schools, often full of racist taunts, since white children knew whose hands their books would end up in. Few high schools were available to Blacks; and even where they existed—most often in cities—the facilities were atrocious. Often, students had to buy their own books. Overall, only half the children under eighteen in the South were enrolled in school by 1930, with the Black percentage far less than that for whites.

With outside support from Northern philanthropies, some gains in education were made in the 1920s. The Rockefeller General Education Board tried to help, as did the Jeanes Fund, a philanthropy started by Julius Rosenwald, the Sears Roebuck entrepreneur. Through their efforts, more than two thousand new schools were created in Southern states by the mid-1920s. New sanitary programs were started as well, seeking to cut back on Black vulnerability to hookworm and venereal diseases. At least some of this charitable work reflected the efforts of Jewish activists. Julius Rosenwald was denounced by his enemies as a "semitic Santa Claus." Yet such intervention did, occasionally, make a difference. In places like Durham, North Carolina, Jeanes Fund schools helped create the foundation for a significant leap forward in the Black education system. Still, given the dimension of the problem that Black families faced, the Jeanes funds barely made a dent overall in the education system.[3]

Thus by the early 1920s, Black activists had started to give up on the dream of integration. The ardor of Du Bois's enthusiasm for Black participation in World War I quickly faded into bitter anger. More and more during the 1920s, DuBois focused on the idea of "pan-Africanism." He urged American Blacks to make common cause with their brothers and sisters four thousand miles away. Reality had hit home. "[We] must start on the earth where we sit," he declared, "and not in the skies whither we aspire. . . . We are segregated. We are a caste. This is our given and at present unalterable fact. Our problem [now] is how far and in what way can we consciously and scientifically guide our future, so as to ensure our physical survival, our spiritual freedom, and our social growth." Integration, he now observed, would require "long centuries and not years. [Yet] we live in years, swift-flying, transient years." What had once been a fervent hope for rapid change now appeared a distant dream. If a war to "make the world safe for democracy" produced no progress toward racial justice, it was time to turn to other strategies for moving forward.[4]

Close Up

Those who occupied the highest status in the Black community built their prosperity and power through control of institutions that were primarily Black—hence in some ways "separatist." These included churches, hospitals, medical practices, and Black colleges. They catered to an all-Black constituency, in some case mandated by law, as in institutions of higher education or hospitals; and they flourished because whites could not control their clientele or take it away from them. Nowhere was this more evident than in the case of the Black church. But an even more outstanding example was the Black funeral home. Death was a community experience focused in the family, the church, and the neighborhood. The Black funeral was intimate, painful, and profound in its emotional impact. Losing a loved one could never be shared, let alone supervised and controlled, by an alien population of whites. Hence it was not surprising that Black funeral homes occupied a venerated place within the community, or that the directors of those funeral homes stood at or near the top of a business elite. That was one reason that for generations, single Black families managed funeral homes and no one dared touch those establishments. They were sacred. They were inviolable.

For the same reason, funeral homes helped provide a birthplace for other Black institutions that needed a safe haven. The place that helped bury family members could also serve as the home for Black institutions that needed safety and protection. It was not surprising, therefore, that when a new NAACP chapter was started in a city, its home base was either a church or a funeral company. The NAACP "was born in our funeral home," Zechariah Alexander from North Carolina told an interviewer. Local chapters of the YMCA also had their origins in groups that met in churches and at funeral homes. Both institutions were autonomous. Whites could not control them, except by burning them to the ground. Even the most vicious white racist might hesitate before torching the place that prepared Black bodies for burial.

But most Black elites developed through interlocking family directorates in which relatives looked after each other, paved the way for the success of their kin, and created a world unto themselves, largely protected and closed off from racist interlopers. In some of the most notable instances, white power brokers played an important role in creating the circumstances in which Black elites developed, facilitating businesses, providing initial funding, building a closed circle that protected the members of the Black elite from being assaulted or undermined by whites who were not part of the upper class.

Nowhere was this more evident than in Durham, North Carolina. There, in the early twentieth century, the Washington Duke family, the white creators of the American Tobacco Company and eventually the founders of Duke University, helped sponsor a cadre of Black business and professional people who dominated the Black community for decades. The Duke family helped to create the North Carolina Mutual Insurance Company, the largest Black insurance company in the world; then the Mechanics and Farmers Bank, one of the largest Black financial institutions in the country; and a whole series of subsidiary institutions for middle-class Black Durham residents, which, by virtue of their ties to prominent whites, were virtually off limits to white attacks. As one leader of North Carolina Mutual recalled, "It's all tied together. . . . They know each other . . . they stick together. . . . It's as easy as that." It was a revolving, self-perpetuating circle. Still, once you joined the family, you were protected as long as you did not attack the white elite.

It all started with the Duke family. Washington Duke had a barber named John Merrick. He was talented, bright, and creative; soon, Washington Duke saw his potential for becoming much more than a person who cut hair. Eventually, Duke suggested that he help Merrick start an insurance company to cater to the needs of Southern Blacks who needed protection. One thing led to another. Financial managers were hired, accountants, doctors, and pharmacists—as well as salespeople who traveled across the region. Soon the families started to intermarry. The business grew, and by the mid-1920s the North Carolina Mutual Insurance Company had become the leading Black business in the United States.[5]

In some respects, the Durham story was both bizarre and unique. That kind of relationship between the white elite and their Black colleagues did not exist in many places. But in Norfolk, Virginia, and in Winston-Salem, Greensboro, and Durham, North Carolina, the presence of a Black business class made a difference. Black businesses flourished in the Durham Black neighborhood called "Hayti"; soon, nightclubs and bars proliferated. The community had a distinctive vitality. In Durham one group started the Biltmore drug store. It had a back room, with comfortable chairs and couches—in effect, a lounge—where the Black elite, "mostly professionals and business people, who were officers with big jobs at the Mutual or the Bank," gathered each evening to talk about issues facing the community. They would then arrive at a consensus on how *they* wished to proceed. Their decisions were binding, and quickly were communicated to the community at large. It was one part of the story of the 1920s and 1930s—a far better story than was true for virtually all the rest of the Black population. Indeed, ultimately, it was the exception that proved the rule, since so few other communities could boast parallel stories of success.[6]

In the meantime, unmitigated poverty was the experience of almost all other Southern Blacks. Whether it was as sharecroppers, servants, tenant farmers, or service workers in lumberyards or tobacco factories, Blacks struggled just to survive on annual incomes that averaged under two hundred dollars. Almost no one enjoyed electricity, indoor plumbing, the opportunity to go to high school, or the possibility of imagining an independent life. The entire South, historian John Egerton wrote, was "a feudal land. . . . It was rural, agricultural, isolated. It had its ruling nobles, its lords of the plantation manor—and its peasants, its vassals." And despite the efforts of some, white supremacy and racism reigned supreme.[7]

Still—and notwithstanding the renewed rule of white supremacy after World War I—Blacks would not cease protesting. On January 1, 1922, more than one thousand African Americans came together in Raleigh, North Carolina, to celebrate Emancipation Day. Focusing on a demand for a federal anti-lynching bill and equal educational appropriations for Blacks, the group denounced Jim Crow, resolved to continue supporting the NAACP, and insisted on their right to "vote our honest convictions on every issue." The number of NAACP chapters in the South grew from three in 1910 to fifty in 1919. Continuing a tradition of political activism that had started in Reconstruction—and persisted through the Readjuster and Populist movements—Blacks in North Carolina created their own Twentieth Century Voters Club. By doing so, they joined fellow activists in East Texas; the Virginia tidewater (especially Norfolk); Birmingham, Alabama; and even parts of Mississippi, in challenging Jim Crow laws and seeking to reassert their voting rights. The 1922 Emancipation Day resolutions, the Twentieth Century Voters Club, and the upsurge in African American political organizations all challenged traditional assumptions about the quiescence of Black political life during the Jim Crow period. While federal, state, and local governments might exclude African Americans from electoral politics, they could not silence Black Southerners. In Magnolia County, Arkansas, Money Alan Kirby, a community leader, explained that Blacks persisted in their demand for freedom because whites "never did get down into the core of . . . Black thinking [while] trying to brainwash us."[8]

The story of one Black family in North Carolina illustrates how family commitment to a better life for the next generation helped animate protest in the larger community. Howard Monroe Fitts Jr. grew up in the town of Wilson. Both his parents were teachers, and his father regularly worked with Black associates to provide relief packages of food to the poorest residents. Blacks lived on one side of the railroad tracks, with dirt roads; whites on the other side, with paved roads. Wilson spent $8.59 per year on each Black child in its schools, $33.91 on whites. The average value of white schools in the district was twenty times that of Black schools. Fitts's parents provided their son with a strong religious and educational background. Each summer, they supplemented their income from teaching. Although paid far less than their white counterparts, they worked in the tobacco fields and factories during the summer to increase their son's chances to advance. Active members of the local NAACP, they provided a model for their son of standing up for racial justice. Through their dedication, they enabled him to go to the North Carolina College for Negroes and earn a teacher's certificate. Eventually, he pursued a doctorate, carrying forward to the next generation the commitment to racial progress that his parents had instilled in him. "My father was never . . . very vocal," Howard Jr. recalled. "My mother showed more anger . . . at the racial situation than he did." But both parents promoted the NAACP and made sure that their son witnessed firsthand the model he should follow.

Fitts went on to become a leader in the Black protest movement of the 1940s in North Carolina.[9]

During the 1920s, another mass-based expression of Black protest occurred with the United Negro Improvement Association (UNIA) headed by Marcus Garvey. Born in the Caribbean, Garvey quickly became a cause célèbre when he came to the United States and attracted thousands of Black supporters with his vision of African Americans moving back to Africa. With a strong base in New York and powerful chapters of the UNIA throughout the South, Garvey stirred strong passions—especially among Blacks who had migrated to the United States from the Caribbean—with his vision of a new Black republic in Africa. Especially in the early 1920s, Garvey became a sensation in cities like New Orleans and Miami and a variety of communities in Virginia. Thousands of Blacks bought shares in his Black Star Line shipping company, envisioning a mass migration of Blacks from America to Africa. For a significant period of time, the UNIA became an umbrella activist group that offered a utopian goal for those who saw little hope in fighting for freedom within the United States.

But in the end, Garvey and his followers were more dreamers than people engaged in social change. Membership numbers fluctuated wildly, depending on the news coming out of the UNIA. Within a few years, Garvey's shipping company—and then its successor, the Black Cross Navigation and Trading Company—collapsed in bankruptcy, their ships making only one or two journeys. Some of the UNIA chapters, especially in the South, developed partnerships with right-wing white supremacists, whom they cultivated for their support of a back-to-Africa movement. There was little if any cooperation between the UNIA and the NAACP, with Du Bois and Garvey more often cast as foes. By the 1930s, the up-and-down volatility of the UNIA had ended up very much on the down side, with little evidence that the UNIA was engaged in social activism for racial justice *within* the United States.[10]

Throughout the 1920s and 1930s, well over 70 percent of Black Southerners continued to live in rural areas. Despite exceptions such as James Hall and Ned Cobb and the emergence of a Black bourgeoisie in places like Durham, the vast majority worked as tenant farmers or sharecroppers in situations that offered little hope for advancement. While the Great Migration shuttled tens of thousands of Blacks to cities, South as well as North, trying to survive on the farm remained the life challenge confronting most African American families. Poor health and malnutrition afflicted hundreds of thousands, particularly in cotton-growing regions. Malaria was a constant affliction, with ten times as many Blacks dying from the disease as whites.[11]

If everyday life during the 1920s was a struggle for survival, the onset of the Great Depression created a downward spiral that proved even more devastating. One simple statistic said it all. At the end of World War I, cotton sold for forty cents a pound. By 1927 that price had fallen to twenty cents a pound. And with the onset of the Depression, it plummeted to six cents a pound. How could Black families survive, let alone prosper, in such conditions?[12]

The answer was very simple: mutual self-help—sharing and caring for each other. It was a long tradition. Throughout the late nineteenth and early twentieth centuries, Black farmers had moved from their own work to help their brothers and sisters if they finished planting or harvesting a crop and their neighbor needed assistance. Now, that tradition became an exercise in sharing. "If we ran out of something," one sharecropper told an interviewer, "we could borrow. Yup, that's what we did. We borrowed from each other all through them days." Another woman noted that "everybody was going through the same thing [so] if we had a piece of bread here [and] next door didn't have any, we'd give him a piece of our bread. . . . That's the way that things worked. . . . I can remember children coming to play with us, being in the backyard playing, and when my mother cooked, she'd feed all those children." Local Black storeowners allowed neighborhood residents to take home supplies if they had no money, trusting that they would be repaid in time. "Yes, they did help one another a lot," one woman told an interviewer. "They had their troubles, your trouble was their trouble."[13]

One other response made equal sense: buy as little as possible, grow enough food to feed your own family (and share with others), and rely on creative handiwork and initiative to keep the family clothed and sheltered. "We grew all our [own] food," sharecropper Arnette Davis said. "Grew everything. . . . Nothing to buy except clothing." Another tenant farmer told an interviewer: "We could almost live off the earth instead of going to the store. . . . You shuck the corn and then get the kernel off the cob, carry it to the grits mill and make corn meal. You could just about get everything you need except sugar and flour and black coffee."[14]

Inventiveness also helped meet needs that otherwise would go unfulfilled. One sharecropper's son told how his father dealt with a clothing crisis. "My daddy . . . had a lot of get-up about him," the son said, "and he knew how to do a lot of things. For instance, he'd buy us shoes . . . and when we'd wear them out, he would go up in some of those alleys and find some automobile tires that the white people had thrown away. And he'd . . . cut out soles for our shoes. He had a little old gadget he called a shoe lass, and he would cut that sole out and nail it to these shoes, and they would last for a lifetime."[15]

Still another option was to parse resources carefully to make them fit your needs. Blanche Davis recalled that a white woman paid her a dollar a week to do all her washing. Davis would then take the money and buy three yards of cloth at twenty-five cents a yard. After that, she would go home and sew clothes for her two little daughters. Others simply combined their resources. In one family, all the kids worked from sun-up to sun-down. "You had to be sitting in the field when the sun comes up," one young man said, "and you stay there until the sun goes down." For all that work, each of the children received twenty-five cents a day. But then, the young man said, "We'd pool that money . . . and my daddy, they would go into town and buy enough [supplies] to last you all week, and then some, with that money." Staying alive—keeping the family clothed, sheltered, and fed—was never an easy task. With the Depression it got worse and worse. But persistence, caring, and fortitude came together to create a path whereby people could help each other to survive for another day.[16]

The New Deal

By most accounts, the election of Franklin D. Roosevelt to the presidency in 1932—and the liberal policies of his New Deal—started the process by which the federal government became an instrument for change in race relations in America. But in the beginning, Roosevelt faced a political conundrum. A Northerner with a bachelor's degree from Harvard and a law degree from Columbia, he had risen to political prominence in New York understanding the need to listen to his urban constituencies, including the powerful Black community in Harlem. On the other hand, FDR was dependent throughout his presidency on support from Southern Democrats who constituted a majority of his Democratic support and were committed to racism and segregation. Democrats from the South also controlled most of the key committees of Congress.

FDR determined that the only way he could promote his legislative agenda was through trying to appease those Southern Democrats. When it came to most issues related to race, FDR chose to chart a course that would not personally alienate those committee chairs. Even on a subject as morally indefensible as hanging Black men and women from trees, FDR refused to support a federal anti-lynching law. He might denounce lynching as a "vile form of collective murder," as he did in 1933, but he never endorsed national legislation outlawing the practice. "If I come out for the anti-lynching bill," he observed, "[Southern legislators] will block every bill I ask Congress to pass to keep America from collapsing. I just can't take that risk." Especially in Roosevelt's first term, most New Deal legislation on minimum wages, agriculture, and industrial recovery contained measures that minimized benefits for Black Southerners, often excluding them from becoming beneficiaries of programs designed to help people in agriculture and industry.[17]

Nevertheless, Franklin Roosevelt's new administration brought more positive news on federal government policies toward Blacks than had been seen since 1867. To be sure, the New Deal put into place a series of government regulations that spelled disaster for hundreds of thousands of Black sharecroppers. But in the end, the good outweighed the bad, especially for the long-range future of federal intervention in support of Black citizenship rights.

The bad news came early. The 1933 Agricultural Adjustment Act (AAA) was one of the biggest initiatives undertaken by the New Deal. Farmers throughout the South were plunging into bankruptcy. The price of cotton per pound had fallen to one-eighth of what it had been just a dozen years earlier. Struggling to come up with an answer, the Roosevelt administration, as was its wont, pieced together proposals from various groups lobbying for specific solutions. But its central point was clear: the New Deal would save farmers in the nation, especially in the South, by reimbursing them for taking land out of production. Indeed, under the AAA, the acreage devoted to cotton production plummeted by 40 percent.

The legislation accomplished two things. First, it put money directly into farmers' pockets through paying them to stop working the land. Second, and equally important, by reducing the production of farm goods, it lowered the supply of food and produce, hence raising the prices of those goods being marketed. In the supply-demand equation, lower supplies inevitably generated higher prices. The AAA thus had an immediate impact, reducing the bankruptcy rates of established planters. Even after the law was ruled unconstitutional by the Supreme Court in 1936, the laws that were passed to replace it created a federal floor under farm prices that made subsidized agriculture a permanent feature of the American political landscape.

Yet an act that immediately benefited white American farmers did irreparable harm to Blacks. Taking land out of production, and paying the owner of that land to do so, did nothing for the overwhelming numbers of Black sharecroppers and tenant farmers, who by virtue of the legislation lost their only source of income. *Their* land was taken out of production. Nor did the Roosevelt administration propose additional legislation that addressed the rampant poverty that existed—and that now grew dramatically—among Black American tenant farmers. In the end, the federal government paid relatively well-off families a small fortune to eliminate one million acres of agricultural land from cotton production. But it did nothing for the Black (and some white) poor people who had labored under the old tenant system. Relatively well-off white planters had been saved from ruin. Those who rented or sharecropped their land, by contrast, were left with nothing. As a result, the number of sharecroppers in the South fell from 400,000 in 1930 to 300,000 in 1940, and fewer than 200,000 in 1950. What was to happen to them? Who would provide the help they needed?[18]

Similar disappointments beset African American factory workers who initially believed that the National Recovery Administration (NRA) would improve their wages and hours by setting national standards for compensation. Throughout the country, the NRA set codes for industries, designed to increase pay rates and regularize workers' rights to an eight-hour day, thereby increasing the purchasing power of laborers while creating healthier conditions in the nation's factories. The NRA set thirty cents an hour as a minimum wage in most industries, a significant increase, especially in the South.

Initially, Blacks were encouraged by news reports of the NRA's policies, seizing on them to initiate their own collective protests against existing working conditions. On Saturday morning, August 26, 1933, for example, more than 200 Black women workers at the Charleston, South Carolina, Bagging and Manufacturing Company shut down their factory. The strike began in the weaving room where more than 130 women worked. Quickly, it spread. "After the work had ceased [in the weaving room]," the local newspaper reported, "the agitators went into the spinning room, where a like number of workers" walked off the job. Eventually, 800 women workers abandoned their posts, completely shutting down the plant. For years, the women had labored for over sixty hours a week, their pay averaging less than six dollars, or tencents per hour. According to the *Charleston News and Courier*, the "workers threatened violence to those who would not cease work." Soon, the manager ordered the power turned off and called the police. But the women defended their action, facing the police with bobbins and knives. Temporarily at least, they forestalled police brutality. As they sang spirituals, the women workers seemed infused with a passion and determination that shocked the white press. Newspapers responded editorially with racist headlines like: "Spirit of Jungle Animates Negroes in Strange Strike," claiming that the walkout "resembled a jungle scene."[19]

In fact, the Black women at the bagging plant were acting out of the belief that the NRA was about to pass a code for the textile industry that would guarantee a minimum wage of twelve dollars a week for all employees on the factory floor. Like countless others in the country, these women saw the federal government's intervention as a pivotal step toward greater dignity and justice in the workplace. Even local politicians had argued for the need to give workers more money so that they could rejuvenate the economy through consumer spending. On the day of the strike, the local newspaper ran an ad featuring a white stenographer complaining about being paid only ten dollars a week, with the message—endorsed by twenty-one Charleston businesses—that low wages were a scourge on society.[20]

But the reality was that under the early New Deal, Black workers were *intentionally not covered* by these NRA guidelines. Blacks *throughout* the South—and North—might presume that federal regulations were intended to apply to all citizens. But in the industries where most Blacks worked, that was not the case. In nearby Edisto Island, Black domestic workers also went on strike, believing that they would receive the NRA's minimum wage of thirty cents an hour. But domestic workers too were excluded from the NRA codes. The same reality faced female laundry and cafeteria workers in Birmingham, who launched wildcat strikes for better wages and working conditions, citing NRA codes. Instead of helping Black factory workers, overall the NRA simply heightened Black workers' awareness of how little the government was doing to bring improvements to their work in industry. Tragically, that help was not forthcoming to most Black workers. White stenographers, yes. Blacks in the bagging industry, no, Before too long, Black workers simply referred to the NRA as the "Negro Run Around."[21]

The Better Side

On the other hand, New Deal welfare policies did help Black citizens sometimes, and on occasion, significantly. Many poor Blacks, often for the first time, became beneficiaries of federal aid. Blacks made up a significant proportion of those receiving welfare checks from the Federal Emergency Relief Administration (FERA)—including 55.6 percent of Black families living in the mid-Atlantic states. To be sure, they often received less than whites—in Atlanta, for example, the average monthly relief checks were $32.66 for whites and $19.29 for Blacks. But at least there were federal relief checks.[22]

When the Works Progress Administration (WPA) was established, Blacks were hired to do public works chores alongside whites. The WPA's successor, the Public Works Administration (PWA), did the same. Both organizations made a huge difference in the South. Its workers created twenty thousand miles of new or reconditioned sewer lines. More than two million new "privies"—outdoor toilets—were built in the South. Black healthcare benefited substantially through malaria control programs and new sanitation services. Even if segregation remained, Blacks received recognition in both hiring and in managerial posts. The Federal Employment Relief Administration (FERA) had established all-Negro units—still segregated—in every Southern state by the end of 1934. The Public Health Service (PHS) focused its energies on diseases that disproportionately affected Black citizens—diseases such as hookworm, syphilis, and tuberculosis.[23]

When the Social Security Act was passed in 1935, it also helped, though once again, unequally. For example, Social Security payments did not go to farmers or domestics, a group that constituted 65 percent of all African American workers. Still, federal funds from Social Security accounted for more than one-third of all public health spending in seven Southeastern states by the end of the decade, and one study of 96 Southern counties found that by 1939 one-third of all the counties employed Black public health nurses.[24]

Perhaps most important, many of Roosevelt's appointees were committed liberals on issues of race. Harold Ickes, secretary of the interior, had earlier been president of the NAACP chapter in Chicago. Ickes ended segregation in the Interior Department's cafeterias and restrooms, reversing Wilson's Jim Crow segregation in those facilities. He also insisted that the PWA hire Blacks who were skilled as well as those who were unskilled. Under Ickes, Blacks occupied one-third of the housing units built by the PWA in the mid-1930s; and he ordered that jobs created under the PWA be allocated, county by county, according to the percentage of Blacks and whites in the local population.

Rexford G. Tugwell was another liberal Democrat on issues of race. When the Farm Security Administration (FSA) was created in 1937, Tugwell made sure that it focused most of its energies on the problems of sharecroppers and tenant farmers, a predominantly Black group. Heading up the FSA was Will Alexander. A former trustee of the Rosenwald Fund, which had done so much to enhance Black education and healthcare in the 1920s, Alexander sought to ease credit for beleaguered Black tenant farmers and sharecroppers. Across many sectors of the economy, Black workers and their families were given explicit aid. "We have tried to give Negro nurses every consideration in new positions being created out of Social Security and other funds," one Public Health Service worker reported to his boss in the late 1930s. In North Carolina, nearly fifteen thousand expectant mothers and twenty-two thousand young children, most of them Black, attended health clinics funded by Social Security between 1936 and

1938, while overall, Southern state funding on maternal and infant health quadrupled from 1930 to 1940.[25]

The Federal Writers Project became a particularly powerful magnet for Blacks. People who soon became internationally known authors—individuals like Zora Neale Hurston, Richard Wright, Ralph Ellison, and Arna Bontemps—joined the project. By the end of the 1930s, a critical mass of Black leaders had also been appointed to key positions within the New Deal. People like Mary McLeod Bethune and William Hastie served in prominent positions in the Roosevelt administration and worked closely with white allies like Virginia and Clifford Durr, Aubrey Williams, and Will Alexander. The National Youth Administration, under Williams, ensured that Blacks made up 10 percent of those enlisted, while under Will Alexander, head of the Farm Security Administration, Blacks comprised a higher percentage of supervisors in the agency than any other New Deal department. Indeed, by the end of the 1930s, most federal agencies whose activities were most relevant to Black Americans were headed by people for whom racial justice was a priority.[26]

Cities with liberal local governments also provided room for innovations promoted by federal bureaucrats. The Public Housing Authority, for example, built a huge housing project in Memphis where Blacks could live. Not only did "Dixie Homes" provide a place for local Negroes to reside; it also provided Blacks with jobs as part of the construction crew. Local unions tried to keep them out, but the federal government insisted that builders had to employ a certain number of Blacks to construct the new housing.[27]

Indeed, powerful policy positions in New Deal administrative offices were headed by a new breed of socially liberal activists. Robert Parran, the US Surgeon General in 1937 and an ardent proponent of economic and social justice, declared that "we must accept as a major premise that citizens should have an equal opportunity for health as an inherent right [along] with the right of liberty and the pursuit of happiness." Special funds were set aside for an adviser who advocated on behalf of Black interests. Secretary of the Interior Ickes appointed a liberal white Southerner, Clark Foreman, in 1934 to work specifically on civil rights issues. A former leader of the Commission for Inter-racial Cooperation, Foreman focused on the economic conditions of the South, especially those facing Blacks. He worked closely with Robert Weaver, a Black Harvard economics graduate, who led the fight against discrimination in housing and employment.[28]

All of this reflected, more than anything else, the liberal leadership of First Lady Eleanor Roosevelt. As a daughter of one of New York's oldest and richest aristocratic clans, Roosevelt had grown up with traditional upper-class attitudes toward the poor and toward minorities. But both her parents had died by the time she was ten, and when she was sent off to an English boarding school, she encountered a totally different world. Allenswood, her school, was led by a liberated woman—Marie Souvestre—who emphasized the importance of social justice, commitment to social change, and independence for women. After three years of tutelage from Mme. Souvestre, when Eleanor returned to New York for her debutante party, she quickly demonstrated that her interests had turned from those of a spoiled aristocratic daughter to those of an engaged woman reformer. Soon she was working in Lower East Side settlement houses, dedicating her life to the well-being of the urban poor. Although she married her distant cousin Franklin and spent most of the next two decades raising five children and being a "political wife," she returned to the activism of her earlier life during World War I and after. She participated in coalitions with the Women's Trade Union League, the Consumers Union, and a variety of women's reform groups to work on issues of social justice. When her husband was struck down by polio, she became his surrogate in countless political activities. But she also continued her activities with women reformers. She actually extended those activities, helping to forge her husband's reputation as a liberal. Once ensconced in the White House, she recruited countless activists to Washington to help manage such agencies as the WPA, the Social Security Administration, and the Labor Department.

More than anyone else, Eleanor Roosevelt proved critical in developing what became known as Roosevelt's Black Cabinet, an array of Negro officials who helped run New Deal agencies and raise repeatedly the issue of advancing Black rights. The Black Cabinet spent hours each Saturday morning formulating plans for how to influence other New Dealers to pay more attention to issues of racial justice. Robert Weaver was one member, Mary McLeod Bethune of the National Youth Administration another. Persistently, effectively, and with shrewd political insight, Roosevelt's Black Cabinet became a hitherto unknown presence in Washington circles, the "go-to" group whenever any issue of substance related to race appeared on the national agenda.

The Black Cabinet came to maturity at the same time that the Southern Conference on Human Welfare (SCHW) rose to the fore. Started by liberal Southern whites, the SCHW became, for the first time, a dramatic alternative to the Jim Crow conservatism of the Southern white ruling class. Although the SCHW did not explicitly advocate an end to segregation, it came close, urging abolition of the poll tax, a substantial increase in the living standards of both Black and white Southerners, enactment of a national healthcare system, and improvement of living conditions throughout the region. The rise of the SCHW coincided with the election of two outspoken Southern white liberals to the US Senate, Claude Pepper of Florida and Lister Hill of Alabama. Although neither embraced desegregation openly, or directly advocated for Black civil rights, both insisted on improving the social and economic conditions of the entire South, Black as well as white. Such was the only path, they argued, if the South were to become a healthy, contributing member of the larger society.[29]

The new liberalism of the Roosevelt administration became most evident in the work of the Resettlement Administration (RA). Working closely with the Farm Security Administration, the RA made a concerted—albeit belated—attempt to correct the racial insensitivity of the first Agricultural Adjustment Act which had led to the expulsion of so many Black sharecroppers and tenant farmers from large white-owned farms. Now, instead of watching out only for the interests of the white elite, the RA set out to make it possible for Blacks to become independent farmers—providing them loans and grants—tilling land that they now could own themselves through federal loans and grants.

The Farm Security Administration was also willing to make loans to Black families so that they could purchase farms. Often, a Black person was on the staff at the RA and FSA offices. Indeed, in Athens, Georgia, a Black administrator was in charge of the office. As one person securing a loan noted, this would never have happened had it not been for the New Deal. "Black man running it. It was four of them, three whites, one colored. I got there and told my story. Man, that Negro went to raising sand," providing the money almost immediately.[30]

In the meantime, Eleanor Roosevelt continued to sanction—and accentuate—the Black protest movement. In 1936, the National Negro Congress (NNC) was formed in Chicago. It brought together over eight hundred delegates primarily from Northern cities, many of them products of the Great Migration. Pullman porters, Black clubwomen, meatpackers, and steelworkers aligned with the union movement; these delegates represented a commitment to greater militancy in the struggle for equal rights. In a demonstration of her independence, and of her commitment to racial equality, the First Lady was a keynote speaker at the 1938 convention of the NNC. Roosevelt demonstrated the same nationally visible leadership on behalf of equal rights when she resigned from the Daughters of the American Revolution (DAR) after the DAR refused to allow Black contralto Marian Anderson to sing at Constitution Hall in its national headquarters; instead, she arranged for Anderson to perform at the Lincoln Memorial, where she drew a crowd of seventy-five thousand.[31]

All of this reflected the opening that the Roosevelt administration—with Eleanor Roosevelt in the forefront—gave to white liberals and to Black activists. To be sure, FDR continued to refuse to take positions that would alienate Southern whites, such as endorsing federal anti-lynching legislation. On the other hand, when the president described the South as the "nation's number one economic problem," and urged Congress and the American people to commit themselves to addressing its plight, he unleashed a barrage of liberal programs, headed by reformers now acting with a mandate from the most powerful person in America. Their work inevitably affected Black Southerners in a positive fashion. It was not a solution to the race problem—not even an explicit recognition that race remained the foundation of the South's economic plight. But it was a start—an effort to "humanize, to moderate" a problem that for the entire twentieth century had assaulted the rights and opportunities of Black Americans. If no one was yet willing to state explicitly that the central issue was race, at least now there were efforts to work on the issue, in the process offering a modicum of hope that a new age might be coming. After 1936, Blacks comprised nearly 20 percent of WPA workers. The federal civil service had 150,000 Black employees, three times the number under President Hoover. And at the 1936 Democratic convention, Franklin Roosevelt chose a Black minister to offer the invocation.

Not surprisingly, the Black population responded at election time. In 1928, the Democratic nominee, Al Smith, had received only 28 percent of the Black vote. Now, in 1936, 75 percent of Black Americans voted for Franklin Roosevelt. Perhaps—just perhaps—there was some reason for hope.

Reflections

Still, no matter how encouraging it might be that a "Black bourgeoisie" existed in Durham, or a "Black Cabinet" operated in the New Deal, the overwhelming majority of Black Americans continued to live in a world hostile to their own pride and self-advancement.

The stories of white racist exploitation of Southern Blacks were endless, and powerful. Cleaster Mitchell grew up in Arkansas during the 1930s. Her mother cooked for a rich white family. On Christmas

Day 1936, Mitchell recalled, her mother was cooking dinner for her sisters and father when suddenly, her white boss came into her kitchen and ordered her to come to his house and prepare *their* holiday feast. "Well, I can't [do that]," her mother responded, "[because] I always fix my children's Christmas dinner." The man left, furious. An hour later he returned. "I want you to get out of my house," he declared, "I want you out of here tomorrow." "Yes, sir," her mother responded, and the next day they moved, "all because . . . she was cooking *our* Christmas dinner."[32]

Even in relatively more liberal places like Memphis, Blacks continued to suffer. Black students were given no books to use in school until they went to high school, and even then, the books they received were sent from white schools, and were full of degrading racist remarks written by students who knew their hand-me-down books would eventually go to Black students. While Blacks comprised a substantial part of the population, there were only two high schools for Blacks in Memphis, while there were nine for whites. Black schools had no ball fields, no playgrounds—and all this, in a relatively progressive place.

On balance, then, while the Depression years offered Black Americans some encouragement for the future, patterns of racial oppression remained in place. Blacks who hoped for a new era of cooperation with whites could take pride in the election of US senators like Claude Pepper of Florida and Lister Hill from Alabama who aimed to improve the position of Black people. During the New Deal, new, bolder interracial groups took root, seeking to promote racial equality. Frank Porter Graham, an outspoken progressive, became president of the University of North Carolina and invited the distinguished Black poet Langston Hughes and other liberals to speak about racial issues on campus. Addressing the Southern Conference on Human Welfare, Graham declared: "The black man is the primary test of American Democracy and Christianity. . . . Let us raise the flag of freedom and democracy where it counts most." Eleanor Roosevelt attended the meeting, refusing to abide by local segregation ordinances, and placing her seat with one side on the "white" side of the aisle, the other on the "Black" side. "It was a love feast," white liberal Virginia Durr observed. "We had a feeling of exhilaration, like we had crossed the river together and entered the Promised Land." The truth, however, was that America was still very distant from any such promised land, with even the SCHW proving reluctant to condemn segregation outright.[33]

For the most part, even those whites who prided themselves on being "moderates" on the race issue failed to intervene in any significant way to improve the situation of Blacks. Jonathan Daniels, editor of the *Raleigh News and Observer*, and subsequently a White House aide to FDR during World War II, typified the limitations of being a "moderate." Daniels had no problem with segregation per se—only with the fact that separate Black facilities were so unequal they could never pass the "separate but equal" test of *Plessy.* Daniels opposed federal anti-lynching legislation, did not believe that Blacks should serve on juries, and expressed serious doubts about poor and ill-educated Negroes being able to vote. Overall, his goal was to defuse racial tensions, not to promote racial equality. While he might on occasion work with Black reformers, his biographer writes, he sought only gradual change through compromise, and consistently refused to denounce white racists. Even if white moderates like Daniels proved more genteel in their politics than Ku Klux Klan members, they could not be called supporters of racial justice.

Overall, then, despite some progress, racist politics continued to be a powerful presence in government. Some Southern newspapers particularly singled out the First Lady for their attacks, featuring Mrs. Roosevelt "going to nigger meetings, with two escorts, niggers, on each arm," and Black people being invited to dine at the White House as honored guests. Senator Herman Talmadge of Georgia blasted gatherings where "our college girls sat elbow to elbow with Negro men," and a local WPA insisted that officials address Blacks as "Miss" or "Mrs."[34]

Thus, despite some significant steps forward—a degree of greater support from the federal government with the WPA, Social Security, and the RA, and the existence for the first time of a "Black Cabinet"—the future remained uncertain. When FDR attempted to unseat racist white Democratic senators from the South in 1938, he failed miserably. Meanwhile, white politicians like Theodore Bilbo from Mississippi continued to compare the New Deal to Reconstruction, and to mobilize their comrades to resist "lefty liberals."

If nothing else, the experience of the 1930s demonstrated the importance of three critical forces in Black lives: the overall state of the economy, the persistence of Black protest and community-building, and the willingness of the federal government to support those who demanded racial justice. The 1930s proved that forward progress could occur when Black demands remained high, and there existed a willingness on the part of those in power to offer reinforcement to those demands. But it would take much more before real change could occur.

Chapter 8

The Persistence of Struggle, the Beginning of Hope

African Americans and World War II

As the first decade of the Great Depression came to a close, African Americans confronted a divided political world. For the first time in generations, the administration in Washington was more friendly than unfriendly. Blacks were recruited, along with whites, to build roads, save forests, and serve the public welfare. Even though Franklin Roosevelt had repeatedly declined to openly embrace Black initiatives, his wife, Eleanor Roosevelt, worked effectively and openly to bring civil rights violations to the attention of federal officials. Then there was the Black Cabinet, a group of African Americans largely recruited to the administration by the First Lady, to systematically advance, and defend, the cause of African Americans.

Now, a new crisis loomed on the horizon. From the time Adolf Hitler took office in Germany, Franklin Roosevelt had understood that Nazi ideology would have to be confronted someday. Japanese imperialism in Asia made the global situation even worse. Americans were tired of war, reluctant to get involved. But in 1939 Germany had invaded Poland, and Japan was moving aggressively into Southeast Asia. Once again, the questions arose: How would African Americans respond? What should you do when your country goes to war? It had never been an easy choice. Why fight on the side of a government that had always oppressed you? Yet war, by definition, set in motion changes in the economy, in where people lived, in who performed which tasks, and in who paid the price of battle and earned the fruits of victory.

The Civil War had brought freedom. Blacks from the North and former slaves from the South comprised 10 percent of the Union army. They also suffered 10 percent of Union casualties. In the beginning, at least, the Civil War had generated a new set of possibilities—the right to vote, biracial governments during Reconstruction, progress in education, social welfare, even the possibility of land reform. Yet soon Blacks were betrayed—by the party that, theoretically, had "saved" them. Still, they had made a start.

World War I carried with it the same kinds of tension. But the war had not lasted long enough for systemic change to occur. Anger and resentment greeted returning Black troops. Race riots broke out across the land, repressing those Black citizens who dared raise their voice in a plea for democratic rights. After a promising beginning came a disastrous end, renewed repression, political disillusionment, and a turn, by at least some, to the ideas of Marcus Garvey, who argued that it was long past time for American Blacks to go "back to Africa."

Now, a new war was on the horizon. This time, once again, the war appeared to be about noble ideals: to fight Japanese imperialism, Nazi dictatorship, and Hitler's drive to exterminate the Jews. The allies were battling to defend the "four freedoms" that Franklin D. Roosevelt and Winston Churchill declared to be the purpose of fighting—freedom of speech, freedom from want, freedom to determine one's own destiny, freedom of worship. Could this be different, a moment of real possibility?

The War Begins

From the beginning, many Black activists were intent on using the impending crisis to drive home their demands for change. Throughout the 1930s, one of the most encouraging developments had been the growing strength of industrial unionism. A new labor organization, the Congress of Industrial Organizations (CIO), spearheaded bold attacks on corporate power. Starting with a sit-down strike at the General Motors plant in Flint, Michigan, in December 1936, the newly formed United Automobile Workers (UAW) demanded recognition as an industry-wide union. It embodied a brand-new approach to labor management relations, one that featured ground-up activism from all industrial workers, not top-down skilled craftworkers' control. Significantly, the government refused to intervene on behalf of management as it had in the past, and the strike was successful. Soon the UAW was joined by electrical workers and steelworkers. Union membership skyrocketed from two million in 1932 to eight million by 1940. The CIO, with at least tacit support from the federal government, was challenging corporate power and securing greater rights and freedoms. Moreover, the new unions were more open to Black Americans. Their leaders had been active supporters of Black civil rights, and they adopted a more aggressive stance on political as well as economic issues, fighting for healthcare, higher minimum wages, and safer factory conditions.[1]

Although not a part of the CIO, the Brotherhood of Sleeping Car Porters Union, an all-Black labor organization, exemplified the new energy surging through the labor movement. A. Philip Randolph, the president of the union, was a brilliant tactician as well as radical activist. He made sure that his union became instrumental in vastly expanding the national reach of the Black press. Papers like the *Chicago Defender*, the *Amsterdam News*, and the *Pittsburgh Courier* had become a rallying force for Black protest, highlighting the courage of those who stood up against racism, and inspiring others to do the same. By the early 1940s, Black newspapers had four million readers, nearly a third of the nation's Black population. Randolph and the Brotherhood of Sleeping Car Porters were largely responsible for delivering the papers to Black communities across the nation where they traveled by train. Because these Pullman porters distributed the papers, more and more Black workers—cooks, elevator operators, truck drivers, maids, and housekeepers—now could share the latest news of Black insurrection.[2]

With the shrewd insight of an activist political leader, Randolph immediately seized the opportunity provided by the likelihood of wartime mobilization. If Blacks were to support the war, he insisted, the federal government must act to address employment discrimination against Negroes. And he backed up his demands with an astute political threat. "I suggest that ten thousand Negroes march on Washington," he declared. "We *loyal* Negro Americans demand the right to work and fight for our country." As in all skillful activism, Randolph's timing was perfect. Threatening to bring his marchers to the nation's capital in the midst of a congressional debate on military preparedness, he brilliantly used the lever of the war crisis to drive home his demands. Eleanor Roosevelt soon joined the cause, as did Roosevelt's Black Cabinet. The First Lady insisted that her husband meet with Randolph and other Black leaders. Randolph continued to increase the pressure; by now the size of the proposed march had risen to fifty thousand. Intentionally, Randolph and his colleagues insisted that this would be a march of Black people only, highlighting the degree to which *race* discrimination was the key and Blacks were determined to lead the crusade for equal justice.

Roosevelt finally gave in and invited Randolph for tea. At their meeting, Randolph made a simple demand. "We ask no special privileges," he said. "All we ask is that we be given equal opportunity with all other Americans for employment . . . and that you make it a requirement that [employers] hire [their] workers without regard to race, creed, or color." Shortly thereafter, in June 1941, the White House issued Executive Order 8802 establishing the President's Fair Employment Practices Commission (the FEPC) "to receive and investigate complaints of discrimination" against Black workers. The intent of the executive order was explicit. "There shall be no discrimination in the employment of workers in defense industries or government because of race, creed, color or national origin."[3]

Whatever the eventual deficiencies that emerged in the way the FEPC enforced its mandate—it had only six full-time staff, and an annual budget of just $80,000—never before had there been such decisive federal intervention on the issue of economic equality. Using the positive changes that had occurred in the New Deal in the late 1930s as a foundation, Black leaders now pushed the ball forward, focusing on increasing Black employment in war industries, securing union endorsement for civil rights regulations by the government, and supporting candidates who embraced government regulations designed to guarantee racial equality. If in the past race relations had taken two steps backward for every step forward, Randolph—and virtually all his colleagues in the CIO—were determined to use the crisis of a second world war to make the leap toward a dramatically different future for Black citizens.

Consistent with that hope and the new FEPC ban on discrimination, the onset of war caused Black employment to increase dramatically. Between December 1941 and August 1942 the number of Black men employed in manufacturing went from 500,000 to 1.2 million. The change occurred most visibly in defense industries. The number of Blacks working in shipyards climbed from 6,000 to 14,000. The change was even more dramatic in aircraft factories. There, Black employment went from zero to 5,000. Overall, the Black share of defense jobs increased during the war from 3 percent to 8 percent of the total—Blacks coming much closer in their munitions employment to their proportion of the larger population.

The war also kick-started a second Great Migration. Between 1917 and the stock market crash in 1929, 15,000 Blacks per month had left the South. Now, that figure almost doubled. In Detroit, 60,000 Blacks came to town, and the percentage of Blacks in the auto industry rose from 3 percent to 15 percent in just five years. In Pennsylvania, New Jersey, and Delaware, the proportion of defense workers who were Black doubled. Georgia and Alabama lost nearly one-third of their Black population between the ages of fourteen and thirty-four to the North, while in Mississippi the proportion lost was one half.[4]

Government employment figures also skyrocketed. The number of Black civil service workers leapt from 60,000 to 200,000. Indeed, overall the number of Blacks employed in manufacturing grew from 500,000 to 1.2 million, with the proportion of African Americans in the iron and steel industries growing to more than 25 percent.[5]

Black women in particular experienced dramatic change. During the Great Depression, over 70 percent of employed Black women had worked as domestic servants in private homes. With the sudden emergence of the war crisis, those figures shifted radically. In response to the call for new workers, over 400,000 domestics left their former jobs, and the number of Black women who held positions as housemaids and cooks fell from 72 percent to 48 percent. By contrast, the proportion of Black women working in factories went from 7.3 percent to 18.6 percent. Overall, the number of Blacks employed as skilled crafts workers and supervisors doubled from 1940 to 1944. Many of these new jobs were in industries dominated by the new CIO unions, and as a result, Black membership in labor unions more than doubled.[6]

Helping to create an atmosphere conducive to racial progress, the entire government propaganda machine was mobilized to preach a doctrine of unity and brotherhood in the aftermath of the Japanese attack on Pearl Harbor and the German declaration of war against the United States. All Americans, the Office of War Information insisted, should come to the aid of the war effort. The identity of the nation was at stake. Democracy, and all it stood for, risked being overrun by totalitarianism.

Once again, Black Americans responded enthusiastically. As one Black woman in New Iberia, Louisiana, told an interviewer, the local men at her college left the classroom "wholesale" to join the army. "Just every day we would see the young men dragging their trunks across campus" on their way to enlist. While one group of white and Black soldiers were getting ready to board a ship for Europe, the crowd on the dock started singing the World War I ballad, "Over there, over there, and you won't come back until it's over over there." A Black soldier on the ship could not believe his eyes. Everyone was crying, whites and Blacks alike. Perhaps, African Americans allowed themselves to imagine, this could be a new day after all.[7]

But then reality hit home. Although Blacks enlisted at a rate far higher than their proportion of the population, they met segregation and prejudice immediately at training camps. All military bases were segregated. When Black soldiers tried to go to town for recreation, they were heckled, forced to sit at the back of the bus, and denied service at local eating establishments. The prevalence of bases in the South made this army-wide discrimination acute. Training camps were infamous for their discrimination against Blacks. When one off-duty Negro MP was shot by a white law-enforcement officer, a local jury quickly acquitted the sheriff of any wrongdoing. In Fort Benning, Georgia, a Black private was lynched; and when a Black army nurse was brutally beaten for defying Jim Crow seating rules on a Montgomery, Alabama, bus, military officials did nothing. Soon enough, some Black soldiers started carrying baseball bats to ward off attacks by white soldiers. Church services on bases were segregated, with signs directing people to separate worship places for Catholics, Jews, Protestants, and Negroes. Southern white political leaders, like former Louisiana Governor Sam Jones, accused Roosevelt of trying to "force social equality" of the Negro upon the South, making the perpetuation of white supremacy "the true patriotic crusade."[8]

One base in Wilmington, North Carolina, exemplified the insidious consequences of persistent Jim Crowism. Soldiers might have a night of leave, but Black soldiers had to wait until all the whites had taken buses to town before they could depart; on the other end, they were not allowed to make the return trip until every white had been accommodated. Even in non-Southern camps, Blacks were given strict instructions. A white officer in California told Black troops that they should "know their place," and never "get out of line." On the battlefield itself, Jim Crow often remained intact. As one Black soldier was walking over dead bodies during the invasion of Normandy, he jumped into a foxhole to seek cover, only to be told by two white soldiers, "This is [our] hole." The draft could even be used to punish those who openly resisted white control. At one point, Blacks in Tennessee demanded that the governor appoint Negroes to the State draft board, since they made up such a significant portion of those drafted. The governor retorted, "This is a white man's country. . . . The Negro had nothing to do with the settling of America." In New Iberia, Louisiana, one Black person was known for packing a gun and standing up to white authority. "If you keep messing with me, I'm going to use [my gun] on you," he told the white sheriff. Shortly thereafter, the Black rebel was drafted and sent off to camp. He was forty-seven years old, more than double the age of the average draftee.[9]

In some ways, it seemed that nothing had changed. The Red Cross, for example, segregated "white" and "colored" bottles of blood plasma, ignoring the fact that a Black scientist, Dr. Charles Drew, while perfecting methods for preserving blood plasma, had determined that there was no difference in the plasma of whites and Blacks. This advance of science confronted—but could not overcome—centuries of belief in the myth of white supremacy. Leading the opposition to change was Congressman John Rankin of Mississippi, who denounced "the crackpots, the communists, and the parlor pinks" of America for attempting to alter the labeling system on blood supplies so that "it will not show whether it is Negro blood or white blood. That seems to be one of the schemes of those fellow travelers [who are trying] to mongrelize this nation." Indeed, a growing number of white conservatives in the South insisted that Blacks who protested were Communist agitators.

There were even worse examples of persistent belief in white supremacy. When Black soldiers entered a lunchroom in Salinas, Kansas, the manager said, "You boys know we don't serve colored folks here." Indeed, they did know, so the Black soldiers just stood there, "inside the door, staring at what we had come to see—German prisoners of war who were having lunch at the counter. . . . It was no jive talk. The people of Salinas served these enemy soldiers and turned away Black American GIs."[10]

The heightened racial tensions caused by wartime changes inevitably affected civilians as well. When one woman from the NAACP wrote a letter to the superintendent of schools, she failed to address it to the "Honorable Lawrence C. Porter." So infuriated was the superintendent that he ordered the letter writer to leave town by sunset. In Memphis, Tennessee, a young Black woman came to town to sell quilts and food that she and her parents had made on their farm in the country. "Just picture [this]," she told an interviewer, "[three of us black girls] walking down the street . . . and here comes three white persons." The whites locked arms to form a chain and filled the sidewalk from edge to edge. "That means either you walk up [on someone's] yard, or you walk out on the street. But you will not pass me on the sidewalk. You don't belong there." She went on: "Sweetheart, I promise you [Memphis] was not always sweet. . . . They believed in kicking people, . . . [and we] were tired [of it]." It appeared that the more things seemed likely to change, the greater the resistance to change became.[11]

But change there was. After basic training in Southern army camps, when Blacks had free time to go into town, they encountered rampant hostility, including, in one veteran's words, "a rash of bitter beatings" by both local police and MPs. But eventually, most soldiers were transported elsewhere, and although they were still in segregated units, for the first time many Black soldiers experienced a very different world from that which surrounded them in the Jim Crow South. Howard Fitts was a twenty-year-old who grew up in Wilson, North Carolina. "All my years here," he told an interviewer, "I knew where I could not go, I knew what I could not do." Then, after basic training, he was shipped to San Bernardino, California. Suddenly, he recalled, "[I was] able to sit where I wanted to on a bus, and not . . . have anybody look at me strangely. I could move with a kind of freedom I didn't have [in the South]." One time, Fitts remembered, "I was in my uniform [at a lunch counter] eating whatever I had . . . and the waiter told me that the gentleman [at the other end of the counter] had paid for it. I didn't see the gentleman. . . . He just saw me as a soldier. And I don't know whether he saw me as a *black* soldier or not, [but] that kind of thing, it gave you some satisfaction . . . and a good feeling about [California]."[12]

The kind of "new world" that Fitts and others experienced in Western cities in the United States only intensified when they went abroad. In England, France, and Africa, Black soldiers were greeted as liberators; treated with dignity; and welcomed to social hours, pubs, and interracial gatherings. In Algeria, Fitts noted, "as black troops we were accepted anywhere we wanted to go. . . . We could go to any restaurant . . . or nightclub [we wanted to]." Charles Lewis, another Black soldier, recalled the upward mobility he experienced because of the war. He had lost all his savings during the Depression, then became a mess hall cook in the army until he was promoted to stevedore, unloading ships, and eventually became part of a combat unit in Europe. He recalled vividly the pleasures of attending integrated nightclubs in London, Paris, and then Germany. His experience in Europe was so different from his experience in the South that Lewis re-enlisted in the army and went to Japan for two years, where once again he was well treated.[13]

Some Black soldiers also saw changes in their white counterparts during the war, especially in Europe. "I think that whites and Blacks sort of felt that we were fellow Americans in a foreign setting," Howard Fitts recalled. "[We felt] an identification with each other." Tensions remained, and there were brawls between whites and Blacks, especially when Black soldiers took out white women—a not uncommon occurrence in Europe. But the shared experience in Europe, and the growing frequency with which whites and Blacks fought together in combat, or at least in complementary roles, helped create a more positive tone for interaction between the races. "Opportunities . . . began to open up . . . to join outfits that were fighting," Fitts noted, "with the infantry, the cavalry . . . and some fellows from our outfit who were impatient with the kinds of roles we [had] played [in the past, now] did join fighting units." Nor was the perception of new attitudes limited to Black troops.

"White boys who have seen Negroes die to save their 'buddies' and to help keep America free," one white observed, "are [no longer] in favor of . . . Jim Crow." Another white soldier noted that "forcing [blacks] to ride in the rear of buses and stand for whites to sit down, I realize now is narrow-minded childishness." The change was not from night to day; and for every step forward, there was always the possibility of a step back, a reminder of how deeply entrenched systemic racism was. But something was happening.[14]

In fact, the key to all that occurred during the war was the combination of some progress taking place even as pervasive racism remained. It all amounted to a peculiar chemistry—the glimpse of a new day, juxtaposed almost immediately with understanding how much still needed to be changed. Yet the combination possessed its own animating dynamic, heightening the commitment to persist with protest and to demand change immediately, all the while confronting, on a daily, minute-by-minute basis, the power of structural racism. A shift in momentum had occurred. Enough positive change was happening—with more seeming possible—for Blacks to remain fervently committed to pushing forward, even in the face of ongoing racism.

Nevertheless, the negatives were powerful, even given the tantalizing promise of equal opportunity. Thirteen national AF of L trade unions, including some of the strongest, continued to exclude Blacks from membership. For every integrated UAW or United Steelworkers Union, there were craft unions carrying an all-white sign. Moreover, despite some new job possibilities, most openings were at low levels, with Blacks primarily hired as janitors or scrubwomen rather than as technicians or skilled craftsmen. In addition, when efforts were made to promote Black employees, whites often rebelled. In Mobile, more than twenty thousand white workers rioted and walked off their jobs when efforts were made to hire twelve Blacks as welders in a local shipyard. Nor was this kind of response limited to the South. A similar reaction occurred when the city of Philadelphia attempted to promote eight Blacks from working as porters to being bus drivers on the public transport system.[15]

Even the FEPC often failed to live up to expectations. Notwithstanding the importance of a presidentially signed executive order mandating an end to discrimination in hiring practices based on race, the agency remained anemically staffed, underfunded, and without real enforcement power. The FEPC's leadership waffled more often than it acted decisively, and the White House provided little reinforcement or encouragement. On at least one occasion, administration officials advised the FEPC not to publish a summary of hearings on discrimination, instead urging that the agency use "private persuasion" to make its case. In the end, the administration cared more about filling jobs quickly, even if that meant sanctioning racial prejudice. The FEPC failed to persuade Southern railroads to hire Blacks as engineers or conductors, and even proved ineffective when it came to integrating Blacks into the transit system of the nation's capital. Overall, the agency successfully resolved only 20 percent of the complaints brought to it from the South.[16]

All of this exemplified the fundamental dynamic at work: significant steps forward took place in the midst of ongoing racism.

Yet on balance, progress was occurring. There were opportunities to be seized, gains to be solidified, and protests to be mobilized. The shifting demographics of the nation highlighted the possibilities. More than two million Blacks migrated from the South to the North and West, while thousands more moved from the countryside into Southern cities. Sometimes the motivation was an order from the Selective Service, other times the chance to take a job in a munitions factory in the North. Whatever the case, hundreds of thousands of Black Americans boarded trains and buses to move to a new home. More often than not, they found the living situation at their new destination less attractive than they had hoped. Urban ghettoes, with their overcrowded housing, hard-pressed social facilities, and persistent discrimination, proved to be not much better than what they had left behind.

Still, just being in a new place created a difference. There was more psychological space, more opportunity to talk freely. Northern urban political bosses reached out to court the Black vote. The community was new, perhaps not as warm or supportive as where you came from, but with more and better opportunities to explore new options, less of the imminent tyranny of small-town authority. There were now new ground rules, plus an independence from the overwhelming social constraints that had been enforced in rural Southern communities. Racist control might still exist, but in new forms, with the possibility of mounting different responses, and more opportunities to try to carve out a better life.

The combination of change, some improvement, and daily reminders of ongoing oppression created a perfect incubator for renewed protest. Simultaneously, hundreds of thousands of Black Americans were experiencing a new world; the possibility of a better job; and exposure to new customs, people, and institutions. Yet they also encountered the persistence of Jim Crow discrimination in the Armed Forces, housing, and on the job. That juxtaposition spawned anger, frustration—and hope. If some improvement occurred, that generated an expectation that still more might come, and if those expectations were then dashed, a rising tide of protest was inevitable.

The March on Washington movement led by A. Philip Randolph was simply the beginning. The National Negro Congress came out of the 1930s with a radical set of demands for change in both the economy and government. At the beginning of the 1940s, Ella Baker had taken on the task of organizing NAACP chapters throughout the South. Now her efforts redoubled, producing stunning results. Local NAACP chapters multiplied by more than 300 percent during the war years. Meanwhile, national membership in the NAACP increased by 1,000 percent, skyrocketing from 50,000 in 1940 to 500,000 in 1945. The war itself provided the key slogan for mass protest. If the United States was fighting to save democracy abroad, why should it not devote as much energy to achieving democracy at home. "Double V"—"victory at home as well as victory abroad"—became the slogan for Black citizens across the country. "If racial discrimination under Hitler is wrong," one NAACP pamphlet declared, "racial discrimination in America is wrong." Picturing Black men in uniform, the pamphlet went on to directly link the issues. "Policies of racial discrimination divide us and aid the enemy. . . . The man who discriminates against Negroes is a Fifth Columnist."[17]

Black newspapers blazoned the demand for victory at home as well as victory abroad on a weekly basis, in the process increasing their circulation by more than 40 percent. Roy Wilkins of the NAACP returned from a visit to North Carolina proclaiming that "Negroes are organizing all over the state to secure their rights. They are not frightened." In Winston-Salem, North Carolina, a dedicated group of Black tobacco workers, led by African American women, launched a huge strike against the American Tobacco Company after a co-worker collapsed and died of a heart attack because he had been hounded by his foreman and not allowed to go home sick. The strike shut down the company and led to a National Labor Relations Board (NLRB) election. Mostly Black workers systematically lobbied their neighborhoods to secure Black votes. The result was an unprecedented turnout of Black employees and a victory for a powerful new progressive union—a biracial union—that now was certified.

The Black women who had been on the cutting edge of the labor protest then turned to political organization, registering voters and mobilizing enough political energy to elect a Black alderman in Winston-Salem right after the war—a first in North Carolina history, and the first elected Black official in the South since the disenfranchisement of the early 1900s.[18]

In Washington, DC, an interracial group of students—anticipating a form of protest that would galvanize the nation a decade and a half later—staged a sit-in at a segregated downtown restaurant. "We die together," the picketing students' signs said. "Let's eat together." Southern Black leaders met in Durham, North Carolina, in October 1942 to demand complete equality for the Negro in American life. "We are fundamentally opposed to the principle and practice of compulsory segregation in our American society," the Durham meeting declared. Mainstream Black leaders were now issuing clarion calls for change that five years earlier only the radical National Negro Congress would have demanded. It seemed to many that every day brought new, more militant statements, each proclaiming that the time had passed for token gestures. Substantive reform must happen, and happen soon. Typifying the new mood, Pauli Murray, a bold North Carolina radical who tried to integrate the University of North Carolina Law School, marched with a group of other young radical women across 125th Street in New York City's Harlem, shouting, in jitterbug rhythm, "Hey Joe—Whaddyeknow—old Jim Crow—has got to go."[19]

In 1943 whites and Blacks convened in Richmond, Virginia, to plan for the future. "The South must save the Negro or itself be lost," NAACP leader Gordon Hancock declared. "Men must be brotherized or they will be brutalized. . . . The time is at hand when we of the South must decide what we are going to do, . . . [and] if we have the moral courage to follow through." The next year, this series of meetings came to fruition when Blacks and whites came together to form a brand-new organization, the Southern Regional Council (SRC), which would now seek to speak on behalf of creating a new, multiracial society. Largely a group made up of white Establishment leaders, this one also fell short of what most Black activists wished for. The SRC chose not to assault the idea of segregation directly. It continued to be beholden to "moderate" whites who cared more about consensus than moving boldly to attack racism. Nevertheless, it represented a step forward, protesting overt discrimination, police brutality, and second-class schools and facilities for Blacks.[20]

Culturally, while most American films in the 1920s and 1930s continued to presume a system of white supremacy, movies produced during World War II embodied an entirely different message. *The Emperor Jones*, starring Paul Robeson, a Black celebrity, celebrated the talents of an independent Black man. The anti–Ku Klux Klan film *The Black Legion*, starring Humphrey Bogart, represented a denunciation of white racism. Lillian Smith wrote a best-selling novel called *Strange*

Fruit, which portrayed a secret love affair between a white man and a Black woman. Billie Holiday then recorded a song with the same title that swept the country with its story of a lynch victim hanging from a tree. W. J. Cash's now-classic *Mind of the South* appeared in 1941, highlighting the fact that even though lynch mobs often consisted of working-class whites, it was in fact upper-class whites who inspired and controlled white racism. Just three years later, Gunnar Myrdal, a Swedish sociologist, published his magisterial *An American Dilemma*, which surveyed with brutal candor the history of white supremacy and the degree to which racism remained the "original sin" of America's history.[21]

The most notable feature of the new era of protest was the persistence of demands for change. This generation of activists would neither back down nor be satisfied with mealy-mouthed excuses. The experience of one group of Black soldiers in Macon, Georgia, typified the new strength that spread throughout the Black community as the war unfolded. Black soldiers at a segregated training camp went on leave to the town of Macon. They encountered a rash of assaults, not just from white citizens, but from police and white MPs as well. When they returned to camp, the soldiers protested the treatment they had received to their commanding officer. They also demanded a meeting to confront the issue. Finally, the officer in charge approved a meeting. But he insisted that the soldiers must make a choice—either go to the meeting or gather at the lunchroom for their noontime meal. To lodge their complaint, they would have to forgo their chance to eat. To the amazement of everyone, no one chose to eat that day. "Not a soul was standing at the mess hall," one Black soldier recalled. "That was the highest point of my life . . . because it was something that the men decided for themselves." The sense of racial self-empowerment was growing.

Then, it turned out that the meeting was surrounded by MPs with their guns drawn. It was clear that their intention was to intimidate the Black soldiers. But the soldiers would not back down. "I made a speech," Harvey Johnson, one of the leaders of the Black soldiers recalled, "that I don't think I'll ever be able to make again. . . . I spoke of the horrible war and the mistreatment of American people, American soldiers . . . not knowing if they are going to survive, [surrounded] by MPs pointing their guns at us." Even as Johnson spoke, and the Black troops were surrounded by MPs, a truckload of German prisoners passed by with *only one* MP guarding them. So the Black soldiers demanded that the MPs at their rally be withdrawn. And in response to their persistent demands, the MPs *were* removed. "The result," Johnson said, "was that things changed at that base . . . they cleaned the base out because of [our] activity. It [all] ended positively."[22]

That kind of response became as much the norm as the exception among Black soldiers. They took inspiration from each other as word spread of Black soldiers standing up to white racism. Yes, it was still there. Yes, it remained pervasive. But this time, it did not go unchallenged. And all it took was one story of Black troops succeeding when they stood up for their rights to reinforce the determination of countless others to make sure that this time, a war for democracy abroad must also bring progress toward achieving democracy at home.

Nevertheless, the tension between some progress, on the one hand, and renewed expressions of racist hatred, on the other, remained an ongoing dilemma. Nothing better exemplified the problem than the racial conflicts in Detroit. Tens of thousands of Blacks moved north to this, the nation's third-largest industrial city. Yet when they arrived, they were more likely to encounter frustration than progress. Advances, when they came, took place incrementally, and often over massive resistance. When three Black workers were promoted at one factory, three thousand whites walked out in protest. It was also almost impossible to find housing, and most Blacks huddled together in "Paradise Valley," a Black slum, where rents were high, housing substandard, and recreation difficult to find. (According to a 1941 study, 50 percent of all Black dwellings were substandard in contrast to only 14 percent of white dwellings.) When Blacks finally secured apartments at the Sojourner Truth Homes—a new, federally financed housing project—they had to be protected by federal troops.[23]

It was no surprise, then, when on one hot summer day in 1943, the racial situation exploded. At Belle Isle Park, a nearly thousand-acre water refuge much used by city residents, whites and Blacks ordinarily swam in different areas, each race supposedly familiar with the boundaries of their area. But then one day, whites started to stone a Black swimmer who had wandered into a predominantly white area. Quickly, rumors spread, telling of murderous attacks by each race on the other. Violence escalated, sweeping the city, until hundreds were injured—both Black and white—and more than seventy killed. Soon federal troops were mobilized to suppress the killing and looting. But the Detroit race riot—like those in New York and elsewhere that soon followed—highlighted just how raw race relations still were in America. Like a mirror, Detroit reflected both a new spirit of militancy and assertiveness among Black Americans, and the degree to which whites everywhere resisted the change they were witnessing.[24]

The contradiction between the national rhetoric of fighting a war to preserve democracy abroad and the reality of pervasive antidemocratic racism at home galvanized Black anger. "Our war is not against Hitler and Europe," one Black columnist proclaimed, "but against the Hitlers in America." A Black citizen pinpointed the same issue in a letter to President Roosevelt. "Hitler has not done anything to the colored people—it's the people right here in the United States who are keeping us out of work and keeping us down." Epitomizing the ideological irony at the heart of America's war was a slogan that circulated among Black draftees being sent to fight in the Pacific: "Here lies a Black man killed fighting a yellow man for the glory of a white man."[25]

Yet that very irony fueled African American determination not to give up, but instead to redouble their generations-long protest against racism. As one returning soldier said, "I'm over there putting my life on the line . . . to help save a country that's going to segregate me back home. . . . I didn't want my sons and daughters to grow up and see those kinds of conditions." So he dedicated his life to creating change. The war experience had given him no other choice. "Something was wrong with our society," he declared. He had experienced life in England and France where, like many Black soldiers during World War I, he had been treated as a liberator. "You were somebody there," he recalled. Now, he would devote his life to making sure his children could be "somebody" in America as well.

Another soldier reflected the same determination to act. In England, he recalled, "Blacks could go in any place . . . they seemed to accept Blacks with pride." So when he returned to Clarendon, South Carolina, he joined the NAACP and determined to make a difference, even if that involved getting into a war with the local white establishment. Clarence Marable came back to Birmingham from the war with the same commitment. Although his grandfather had been unable to read, he had become a landowner. Now, the grandson joined the NAACP, determined to prove that he and countless others had "won the right to vote" by their service. He enrolled at Morehouse College in Atlanta, where he heard Black speakers like Roland Hayes, Ralph Bunche, and Howard Thurman inspire the war generation with their challenge to the young to go out and make a difference. Large numbers of Black veterans, like Marable, used the GI Bill to go to college, where they joined the NAACP and, with their classmates, continued the protests they had begun during the war. In countless communities, from Clarendon County, South Carolina, to Patoutville, Louisiana, Black veterans were often the leaders willing to challenge school boards on improving Black schools, and to buy the school buses that made it possible for the young to get to high school.[26]

In at least some cases, they received encouragement from whites. Before he left Europe to return home, Emmett Cheri, an African American soldier from New Orleans, recalled the words of a white officer. "The war is over," the officer had said. "You've put your lives on the line for this country. So you have the same rights as anyone in this country. . . . Don't take a step back." The same veteran recalled going into a drugstore after returning to New Orleans and being ignored by the white clerk, until a white soldier told the clerk she was disrespecting him. "He said, look at yourself, if it wouldn't have been for him, you probably wouldn't be here." In some places, like Memphis, progressive unions such as the United Auto Workers campaigned to change the customs of downtown department stores and treat Blacks the same as whites in all areas of the store, including where customers tried on clothes. In response, the department stores opened all their dressing rooms to Blacks as well as whites.[27]

But Blacks themselves bore the brunt of challenging long-standing racial customs. In the process, they displayed a courage and determination that dismayed white people previously accustomed to whites being totally in charge. Again, veterans led the way. Before he even took off his uniform, future civil rights leader Medgar Evers went to register to vote at the county courthouse in Jackson, Mississippi, notwithstanding the fact that whites had warned that they would shoot him if he tried to cast a ballot. (They did not shoot him, but refused to register him to vote.) In Terrell County, Georgia (long known as "terrible Terrell"), Black soldiers came back intent on challenging the oppressive structure of power in the country. In Columbia, Tennessee, violence erupted as whites attacked Black veterans for rejecting "business as usual" and insisting that there would have to be a "new deal" in the jobs they held.

Blacks zeroed in on voting as the key to progress. After all, it represented the most visible symbol of equal citizenship—something Black soldiers had risked their lives to defend through their service in the Armed Forces. More than eighteen thousand Blacks registered to vote in Atlanta in the year after the war. In Winston-Salem, three thousand registered, and they then elected a Black alderman. A few miles away, in Greensboro, a voter registration drive doubled the number of Blacks on the voting rolls, and a Black citizens group mounted a war against the system whereby "establishment" whites in the city sought to buy Black votes, and then proceed to ignore Black interests. As a result of these efforts, the overall number of Blacks registered to vote in the South increased from 2 percent of the population in 1940 to 12 percent in 1947. The 12 percent remained a shockingly low figure, and a testimonial to the degree to which whites were still committed to denying Blacks their civil rights. But a sixfold increase in seven years also testified to the determination of Black Americans to challenge pervasive racism and demand compliance with democratic values.[28]

In truth, the success that Blacks achieved paled beside the overwhelming intransigence of whites. In Georgia, Eugene Talmadge won his race for governor in 1941 by proclaiming that "no Negro will vote in Georgia for the next four years." He was true to his word. Afterward, the only Black to vote in one district was murdered in his front yard by four white men. In Walton County, not far away, whites shot and killed two other Blacks. In a horrific aftermath, when the wife of one of the victims recognized a member of the shooting gang, two wives were also murdered. In Mississippi, when Medgar Evers and five other veterans went to the courthouse to vote, white men with pistols drove them away. And in Columbia, Tennessee, whites rioted in protest against "uppity" Blacks who were insisting on their rights. Seventy of the Black protestors were arrested, and a mob broke into the jail to murder two of the prisoners. As if that were not enough, Isaac Woodward, still dressed in his army uniform, stepped off a bus in South Carolina after a dispute with the driver, only to be confronted by police with billy clubs who poked out his eyes and blinded him. All this in the first eight months of 1946.[29]

As if vicious beatings and murders were not enough, whites employed scores of subtler means to quell Black dissent. The head of the White Citizens Council in Mississippi pointed out that 95 percent of Blacks were employed by whites. Hence, if any Blacks dared to try to register to vote, they could simply be told to "take a vacation." When Blacks insisted on pursuing their rights nevertheless, their insurance was canceled, their credit cut off, and sharecroppers were evicted from their land. Moreover, the procedures for voter registration were loaded with obstacles. Blacks understood that if a registrar asked a Black applicant to define the meaning of "habeas corpus" as part of a citizenship test, the real message was: "Habeas corpus—that means that this black man ain't going to register to vote today." Even supposedly procedural laws were infused with racist bias. In Alabama, a Black voter was required to get two whites to vouch for his citizenship in order to be enrolled as a voter. The head of the Alabama Bar Association summed up the chances of that ever happening: "No Negro is good enough and no Negro will *ever* be good enough to participate in making the laws under which the white people of Alabama have to live." For those who did not understand the message, Mississippi senator Theodore Bilbo made it crystal clear. "If there is a single man or woman serving [as a registrar]," Bilbo said in his 1946 re-election campaign, "who cannot think up questions to disqualify undesirables, then write Bilbo or any good lawyer and there are a hundred good questions which can be furnished. . . . But you know and I know what is the best way to keep the nigger from voting. You do it the night before the election. I don't have to tell you any more than that. Red-blooded men know what I mean." Bilbo then winked at his audience and left the stage.[30]

Reflections

Three things were abundantly clear by 1946, a year after the war had ended. America's involvement in World War II had triggered a huge convulsion in American race relations. It was simply not possible to fight a war for the "four freedoms" and against Nazi fascism, with its planned genocide of European Jews, without confronting the reality of racism in America—a racism that directly contradicted everything America was telling the world that it stood for. The war also created an avalanche of opportunities on the home front that brought change to every family, homestead, and city in America. Hundreds of thousands of new jobs were created. There was mass migration to the cities to fill those jobs. New possibilities opened up. Most importantly, Black Americans were ready to seize those changes, to assert themselves in brand new ways, to demand rights that had been denied them for decades, but that now became attainable because of the crisis at hand. They grasped the crisis of another world war, wielded it as a weapon, and insisted that they be heard. A. Philip Randolph's March on Washington movement was only the beginning, for beneath that very public confrontation demanding an end to economic discrimination against Blacks in war industry jobs lay a thousand communities of citizens ready to embrace the war effort as a means to finally advance their rights. The whole Black community was involved—churches, unions, self-help associations, lodges, and women's groups. A rising tide of protest gained momentum, and nothing was going to stop it.

On the other side, most whites, especially in the South, were committed to resisting change. Whether through murders, beatings, court-martials, or economic intimidation, they would not give an inch. To be sure, there were some who recognized that the time had come for change. But in the white South, they were vanishingly few, and when it came to issues like voting rights, the likelihood of concessions was almost nonexistent. The drumbeat for change among Blacks unleashed by the war would not go away. But neither would the determination by Southern whites to keep intact the racist regime of Jim Crow, a system of white superiority and control.

In the end, the federal government continued to hold the wild card. That had been the case during and after Reconstruction, in the era of spreading segregation at the dawn of the twentieth century, during World War I, and afterward. Now once again, the federal government had to answer the question: Did it believe in equal rights for all citizens?

No longer did anyone doubt that Blacks were going to fight to the death for their equality. The combination of some change, and continued resistance, guaranteed that this time, there would be no retreat from the battle. Just as clearly, it was obvious that whites who held power in the South would fight with all their might to resist these demands for a new world of equal rights. They would use whatever means they had to battle back, including murder, intimidation, and brutal repression.

Now the question was what Washington would choose to do in the face of a new determination by millions of Black Americans to finally claim their share of the American Dream.

Chapter 9

Postwar Protest

The immediate message from Black Americans following World War II could not have been clearer: "We want our freedom, and we want it now." From Terrell County, Georgia (long known in Black circles as "terrible Terrell"), to Pensacola, Florida, to Winston-Salem, North Carolina, and to Chicago, Illinois, Blacks took on the most oppressive structures of white power. Rejecting "business as usual," Black veterans in Columbia, Tennessee, demanded that there be a "new deal" in the jobs they held and the way they were treated. Cities like Greensboro, Detroit, and Atlanta started to build Black political machines that would choose candidates to run for public office.

But if Black determination demonstrated one side of the story, repeated instances of white resistance documented the other side. Racist violence occurred almost everywhere in Jackson, Mississippi, when Medgar Evers and five other Black veterans went to vote; in Georgia, where the only Black to go to the polls in one district was brutally killed in his front yard by four white men; in Columbia, Tennessee, where whites rioted against "uppity" Blacks who insisted on their rights, breaking into jail to murder two Blacks who had been arrested while fighting against a white mob; and fifty miles outside of Atlanta, where two dozen white men ambushed and executed two Black army veterans and their wives in broad daylight.[1]

But this time, Blacks refused to back down. The "double V" campaign—"victory at home as well as victory abroad"—had animated protests across the nation; now, the protests grew and grew and grew.

With the extraordinary experience of World War II as a backdrop, the modern civil rights movement now began. The fundamental question was how white America—and above all the federal government—would respond.

The Early Postwar Years

The theme that dominated race relations in America during the years after World War II was both simple and profound: Blacks demanded immediate action to create a more equal society in politics, the economy, the courts, and education. Whites who held power resisted consistently. If they conceded on some issues, they did so only after being pressed, and never to the extent that meaningful change occurred. The tension created by this dynamic generated ever more determination—and increasingly innovative tactics—by civil rights activists. Finally, in the mid-1960s, twenty years after the end of World War II and confronted by nationwide activism, the government was compelled to act. It had no choice but to embrace laws that advanced the cause of racial justice. It was a long struggle, featuring massive suffering among Black protestors, as well as constant innovation in tactics and strategy. And although the activism of Black protestors eventually paid off, the ongoing reluctance of powerful whites to take meaningful action spoke powerfully to how central racism was to American society.

No single white individual better illustrated the complexity of the struggle Black activists faced than President Harry Truman. For his entire political life before becoming vice president, Truman had done the minimum necessary to appease his Black constituents in Missouri. In the Senate he had voted to end the poll tax, to enact anti-lynching legislation, and to appropriate funds for the Fair Employment Practices Commission. But he also reportedly told a Southern Senate colleague: "You know I'm against this [anti-lynching bill], but if it comes to a vote, I have to vote for it. My sympathies are with you, but the Negro vote in Kansas City and St. Louis is too important." Skeptics viewed Truman as "a borderline Southerner with a slaveholding heritage . . . ; the word 'nigger' rolled off his lips as easily as it did those of his Southern poker playing cronies on Capitol Hill." One indicator of his ambivalence was his characterization of Eleanor Roosevelt in a letter to his sister before he was to appear with the former first lady at an NAACP event. "Mrs. Roosevelt has spent her public life stirring up trouble between whites and blacks—and I'm in the middle." The *Pittsburgh Courier*, one of the leading Black newspapers in the country, described Truman's selection as vice president to replace the liberal incumbent, Henry Wallace, as an "appeasement of the South." Indeed, when Truman ascended to the presidency after FDR's death, one Southern senator said: "Everything is going to be alright now—the new president knows how to handle the niggers."[2]

Truman's response to liberal efforts to create a permanent Fair Employment Practices Commission illustrates his penchant for *seeming* to be liberal, rhetorically, while doing little of substance to back up his words. Thus, he impressed supporters of civil rights with his endorsement of FEPC legislation, but he did nothing to persuade recalcitrant Southern senators to vote for the bill. This echoed Truman's wartime behavior, when he had also refused to allow the FEPC to order the Washington, DC, transit system to hire Black bus and trolley operators. In response, Charles Houston, a prominent NAACP lawyer, had resigned from the FEPC.

Black activists were quick to recognize the president's waffling. Truman seemed to respond only to ever-increasing protest. As pickets mobilized outside the White House carrying signs saying "SPEAK, SPEAK MR. PRESIDENT," and fifteen thousand people marched to the Lincoln Memorial to protest racial violence in Georgia, Tennessee, and South Carolina, Truman felt compelled to listen. After meeting with one NAACP delegation protesting the racist violence in Columbia, Tennessee, in 1946, the president declared, "My God, I had no idea it was as terrible as that. We have to do something."[3]

And this time he did. In December 1946, Truman created a national Committee on Civil Rights. Its distinguished members included Charles Wilson of General Electric, Frank Porter Graham, president of the University of North Carolina, and Franklin Roosevelt Jr. After thoroughly surveying the entire spectrum of evidence on race relations, the committee declared that race relations in America were deeply troubled. The committee made a series of strong recommendations, including creating a permanent civil rights division in the Justice Department, enacting anti-lynching legislation, supporting legal action against segregated housing, and abolishing the poll tax. Truman endorsed all the commission's recommendations, and then became the first president ever to address an NAACP convention, where he echoed points that had been made by generations of African Americans. "There is a serious gap between our ideals and some of our practices," Truman declared, "and this gap must be closed. Every man should have the right to a decent home, . . . the right to a worthwhile job, the right to an equal share in making public decisions through the ballot. . . . We must assure that these rights—on equal terms—are enjoyed by every citizen." Blacks were pleased, even more so when, the day after the commission's recommendations were released, Truman ordered the Justice Department to file a brief with the Supreme Court supporting the NAACP in a case seeking to invalidate any restrictive racial covenant clauses in housing contracts.[4]

Yet Truman soon retreated to his more traditional and ambivalent stance of combining rhetorical support for racial justice with almost no substantive follow-through. Politics again won out over principle. In the spring of 1948, white Southern politicians were threatening to bolt from the Democratic Party, while white newspapers accused Truman of "stabbing the South in the back." Displaying his moderation, Truman introduced no new civil rights legislation, and failed to issue the executive orders the Civil Rights Commission had recommended for ending segregation in federal employment. As one Truman aide later explained, "The strategy [was] to start with a bold measure and then temporize to pick up the right-wing forces. Simply stated, backtrack after the bang." The NAACP's Walter White quickly learned the lesson, declaring that asking for a meeting with Truman would simply give the president another occasion "to tell us that I am still for civil rights." Instead, White said, "the time has come for him to *do* something . . . instead of telling us how he feels personally." The burden of forcing the president and the federal government to act would once more fall to African Americans and the civil rights movement.[5]

From Truman's perspective, the politics of gesture ended up working to his advantage. Over the eight years preceding the election of 1948, the Black population in the North had increased by two million. Black voters held the potential balance of power in states like Ohio, New York, New Jersey, Pennsylvania, Michigan, and Illinois. Although Truman opposed a strong civil rights plank in the Democratic platform in 1948, in the end he was forced to accept the ringing commitment to civil rights that Minneapolis mayor Hubert Humphrey and others insisted on writing into the party's platform. Moreover, he became the first president to campaign vigorously in Black communities like Harlem. In effect, Truman was threading a needle, trying to sustain support from all sides: while avoiding a substantive battle, he could make ritualistic gestures in a speech here and there that would appeal to liberals, all the while continuing to appease conservatives by not following through on his rhetorical commitments with substantive action.[6]

The strategy worked. Although most Black newspapers endorsed Republican candidate Thomas Dewey, Truman narrowly won the 1948 presidential election. Indeed, the key winning votes were cast by new Black voters, especially in Western states such as California. But while African Americans were pivotal in handing the presidency to Truman, their daily lives had not changed very much. Two months before the election, Isaac Nixon, an army veteran, was warned by whites in Wrightsville, Georgia, not to go to the polls. When he ignored their warning and went to vote, he was murdered before sunset. The next week the president of the local NAACP chapter was driven from his home into exile in Atlanta. Shortly thereafter, the men accused of murdering Nixon were acquitted by an all-white jury. For these Black victims of white supremacist violence, the politics of gesture was not enough.[7]

The issue of how to proceed was soon complicated even further by the rise of anti-communist hysteria. The objectives—and tactics—of civil rights activists were denounced as leftist and pro-Soviet by conservative whites who appeared before groups like the House Un-American Activities Committee (HUAC). Racial equality ranked high as an objective among many CIO unions that had flourished during World War II. But now, many of those unions came under attack because communists had gained entry into their leadership ranks. Under the 1947 Taft-Hartley Act, all union leaders were required to sign a loyalty oath and forswear any relationship with communism. If they refused to do so, their unions would lose their legal status and crumble. In those unions where this happened, their ranks were decimated. Thus, some left-leaning unions that had joined the movement toward racial justice—and had recruited the most Black members—suddenly were seriously weakened because of their "communist" sympathies.

In 1947, Truman himself declared a Cold War against the Soviet Union and created a Federal Employee Loyalty Program that sought out civil servants who might have expressed interest in left-of-center political values. By his actions, Truman helped to legitimize a new kind of inquisition—all in service to a political orthodoxy where any questioning of America's society and declared values was defined as treasonous.[8]

In the South, Blacks were the primary victims of this new wave of anti-communism. This tactic was explicitly used to dismiss demands for increased rights—even to push back against the modest gains that had been achieved in prior years. In 1943 Black workers in Winston-Salem's tobacco factories had stunned the owners by organizing a CIO union. They then used that union to mobilize Black voters and elect the first Negro alderman in the history of twentieth-century North

Carolina. Now, that union was pilloried for being pro-communist and in 1948 lost its ability to represent the workers at Reynolds Industry. Georgia's governor, Eugene Talmadge, blamed "Communist doctrine from outside the state" for civil rights protests inside the state. Indeed, Talmadge sought to restore the all-white primary as a way of combating "foreign influences." Merely to associate with a person of a different color was deemed suspect—and potentially a sign of Communist Party sympathies.

In a letter to Truman, the NAACP's executive secretary, Walter White, noted that government agents "have been asking white persons whether they associate with colored people," and Blacks "whether they have entertained white people in their homes." Indeed, the association of civil rights activism with communism became so extreme that people were asked whether they ever owned a Paul Robeson record album. Robeson, the Black singer, had exhibited sympathy for the Soviet Union during World War II. Machismo, patriotism, opposition to social protest—these were the values that defined "true" Americanism, according to white Southern conservatives. It might still be possible to seek racial reform, but only on terms that could never be interpreted as questioning the fundamental soundness of American democracy.[9]

This anti-communist hysteria posed a strategic dilemma for civil rights activists. For years, progressives in labor and politics had been among Black America's few partners in the pursuit of freedom and justice. Was it now necessary for them to forswear any coalition with progressives and operate solely within the politics of the "establishment?" More broadly, during a moment when any questioning of American policies was being portrayed as "un-American," could they persist in raising issues about the problem of inequality within the larger distribution of social and economic power in America?

The answer was soon in coming, especially among the more prominent civil rights groups. The NAACP made the decision to expel all communists from its membership. Other civil rights organizations narrowed their focus to one that advocated only those reforms that could take place within the existing structure of laws, not on larger issues of race and class. The Cold War thus limited both the tactics and the objectives of Black protestors. It was no longer feasible, politically, to talk about transforming the political and economic structure of American society. Left-leaning groups, such as the National Negro Congress, found it increasingly difficult to retain credibility—with the press, with churches in the Black community, and with whites who were moderate to mildly liberal. In this context, more "establishment" groups like the NAACP and the Urban League held sway, working within existing legal and economic structures to seek reform *within* the system, rather than taking on the system itself. Just as Booker T. Washington had avoided direct confrontation with those in power in the nineteenth century, another generation of Black activists now felt compelled to tailor their confrontation with white racism inside boundaries deemed safe by white America.[10]

But even as the power of anti-communism undermined more radical Black protestors, what remained astounding was the ongoing strength of postwar Black activists in the South as well as the North. With unmitigated determination, they fought harder and harder. If public officials seemed more committed to the politics of gesture than to substantive change, Black activists refused to settle for symbolic victories. They would push and push and push until ultimately, the political establishment was compelled to change. As Bertha Gober, a Black woman activist, wrote in 1961, "We've been 'buked and we've been scorned, We've been talked about, sure's you're born, But we'll never turn back, no We'll never turn back. . . . Until we've all been freed, and We have equality."[11]

The Movement Begins

Ella Baker was there from the beginning. Reared at the turn of the century in the Black belt of North Carolina, she learned from her mother the importance of standing up for herself and fighting for her rights. A proud and independent woman, Baker's mother instilled a sense of pride and determination in her daughter. After graduating from Shaw University in Raleigh, Ella Baker went to work in New York City, and among other things took a job for the Works Progress Administration during the New Deal. Then, in 1940, she became a field secretary for the NAACP. Traversing the South, she organized countless local branches of the NAACP, including a youth chapter in Greensboro, North Carolina. Through her recruitment campaigns, she helped boost NAACP membership from forty thousand in 1940 to five hundred thousand in 1945. Although she was quiet in demeanor, her strength and persistence inspired everyone she met. Ella Baker was there for it all. She, and the people she touched, would shape the history of the 1950s and 1960s.[12]

J. A. DeLaine, pastor of an African Methodist Episcopal (AME) church in Clarendon County, South Carolina, typified the kind of local people whom Ella Baker galvanized. He was a successful pastor and teacher, one who could not be blamed were he to just sit back and enjoy his success. But that was not J. A. DeLaine. He had a fire burning within him. On Sunday mornings, he drew constant parallels in his sermons between the liberation promised in Scripture and the need to change the reality of everyday life in the South. In fact, Clarendon County was one of the most racist and conservative places in America—where life among Blacks had changed least since Reconstruction. In 1949, the county spent $179 per white child in the public schools, $43 per Black child.

J. A. DeLaine and the NAACP set out to change that. A schoolteacher as well as a pastor, DeLaine and his allies sought to buy a school bus to transport Black children so that they would not have to walk miles on dusty roads to reach their classrooms. When the school board refused, they then sued the county for its failure to provide anything near equal education for Black children.

The white response was simple. DeLaine was fired from his job teaching at the school. His house was burned down. Everywhere he turned, segregationists were determined to shut him up and put an end to his challenge of their authority and prerogatives. But DeLaine would not quit; and because of his persistence, the NAACP was able to bring the Clarendon County school suit to the Supreme Court as one of the five cases that were ultimately combined into *Brown v. Board of Education.*[13]

Amzie Moore grew up a thousand miles away from Clarendon County in rural Mississippi. After returning from the war, he, like Medgar Evers in Jackson, was determined to finally make things right in his home town of Cleveland, Mississippi. As he wrote before he joined the fight, "Here I'm being shipped overseas, and I've been segregated from this man whom I might have to save, or he save my life." It was a point he did not fail to make repeatedly. Now, with his own gas station and store, Moore became president of the local NAACP, in a state where murdering Black people was commonplace.

Despite the routine use of lethal violence against them, Mississippi Blacks refused to be intimidated. Amzie Moore became the backbone and bedrock for protesting white racism in the state. Outside activists interested in fighting for racial justice in Mississippi always came to Amzie Moore's house as their first stop in town. Moore would put them up in his home, then introduce them to members of the community. Soon, they would hold group meetings together, discuss the latest examples of white racist cruelty, then decide on the most effective way to protest, going to the registrar to demand the right to vote, or petitioning the school board for more equal rights for Black students. The partnerships that Moore generated would ultimately transform the nation. From Moore, the activists learned to go to the homes of grassroots activists, organize the community, and generate a new sense of collective commitment to the cause of racial justice.[14]

Amzie Moore, Ella Baker, J. A. DeLaine—three names, three people—but three representatives of a legion of local activists who helped build the civil rights movement of the 1940s and 1950s and 1960s from the ground up. They tried voter registration, were beaten back, and tried again. When the federal government practiced the politics of gesture, they fought for direct legislation. When politicians offered no help, they went to the courts. When the courts failed them, they went back to their communities and started all over again, this time taking their fate into their own hands, registering to vote, and directly challenging the reign of establishment white conservatives. They created a movement that would transform a nation and inspire the world.

The Movement Takes Off

To an increasing extent, civil rights activists focused on two issues: the right to vote, and challenging the constitutionality of segregation in schools, buses, and public accommodations like hotels and restaurants. They did this in the courts, and through direct action demonstrations. Significantly, campaigns on these issues operated within the existing structure of laws and values, rather than seeking to transform or overthrow that structure. This strategy made it much more difficult for white conservatives to smear civil rights protestors as subversive leftists. Equally important, it allowed civil rights advocates to argue that their basic objective was to make America live up to its claim to be the most enlightened democracy in the world.

The cause of voting rights had appeared to make some progress during World War II. In *Smith v. Allwright* (1944), the Supreme Court ruled that the "white primary," a device Southern states had used to exclude Black voters from the only election that really mattered in the one-party South—the Democratic Party's primary—was unconstitutional, and a direct violation of "one person, one vote." If the only real election was the Democratic primary, from which Blacks were excluded, and if Blacks could not participate in choosing the only candidates who would appear on the ballot in the general election, they were, in effect, disenfranchised.

Soon, however, it became clear that the Court's decision would mean nothing without follow-up action by state governments and federal officials. Southern white politicians who were smart simply created new obstacles to Black voting, convinced that Washington would never do anything to alter the situation. The federal government did not disappoint them, and it would take a massive campaign by the civil rights movement in the 1960s before voting rights could be sustained through federal legislation.[15]

Opposition to government-mandated segregation offered a more promising road. In its 1896 *Plessy v. Ferguson* decision, the Supreme Court had ruled that there was nothing illegal about requiring segregation between the races, but the Court premised its decision on the notion that while Black institutions could be separate from white institutions, they also had to be equal. The "separate but equal" ruling bequeathed two legacies to civil rights activists: first, it invited lawsuits that could prove, decisively, that segregated schools were never equal; and second, it took off the table, at least in theory, the argument that segregation by definition created inequality, and therefore was unconstitutional. How then, given *Plessy*'s affirmation that segregation was constitutional, could the NAACP and others get to the point of challenging segregation directly, overturning *Plessy*, and establishing that segregation per se was unconstitutional?

The struggle was never easy and took decades to complete. It began with NAACP attorneys taking on the first, and easiest, task—demonstrating repeatedly, in specific instances, that separate was not equal. Thus, in 1939, in *Missouri ex. Rel Gaines*, NAACP lawyers argued that Missouri could not claim that it provided equal opportunities for a law school education to its Negro citizens if it segregated them in a one-room "law school," without adequate library or faculty resources; or if it sent them out of state to another institution. The court agreed, ordering that Missouri create a fully equal law school, in state, for Blacks. The pivotal point was the principle involved. If the *Gaines* decision were to hold, should not the same doctrine of full equality apply to high school facilities as well? And if the doctrine of full equality were to apply to other segregated institutions, might this not destroy so many Jim Crow laws that segregation itself would be threatened?[16]

Still, the NAACP had to proceed cautiously. At the end of the 1940s, it pushed the Court further than it had ever gone before on how to define "separate but equal." In *Sweatt v. Painter* and in *McLaurin v. Board of Regents*, it contended that equality could not be measured by dollars or physical plant alone. Just as important was the reputation of the faculty, the stimulation of intellectual exchange with fellow students, and the quality of the academic experience. Here, the key issue was how a Black student was treated in an otherwise white-dominated institution.

Based on the *Gaines* decision, the University of Oklahoma had accepted a Black applicant, George McLaurin, to its law school, but on a segregated basis. McLaurin could take classes with whites but was forced to sit in a separate, roped-off area of the classroom. He might eat in the school cafeteria, but in a separate alcove. Yes, he could use the university library, but he had to sit at a dingy, segregated desk. All of this, NAACP attorney Thurgood Marshall argued, created a "badge of inferiority which affected [McLaurin's] relationship, both to his fellow students and to his professors." Here, the NAACP was asking the Court to confront the *psychological* as well as the physical consequences of being treated as a different kind of human being. Marshall made a compelling case, and for the first time the Court was forced to grapple with the personal—the existential—consequences of segregation. The Court agreed with Marshall's arguments, acknowledging that the definition of equality had to include psychological, social, and spiritual considerations.[17]

But now, the NAACP confronted a dilemma. Should it continue to win cases based on proving that "separate" was not "equal?" Or should it challenge—directly—the now half-century-old doctrine of *Plessy* and contend that segregation *itself* was the problem? Stated in another way, would the NAACP continue to operate on the enemy's turf, or should it take a chance on calling into question the turf itself, attacking the *very doctrine* of segregation? If the NAACP won, it could destroy a keystone of white supremacy. If it lost, on the other hand, the legal underpinnings of racism might well last another fifty years. After all, the judicial system was conservative, and bent toward upholding the precedents of previous decisions. But in the end, the NAACP concluded that it had no choice but to throw down the gauntlet.

The history of *Brown v. Board of Education* demonstrated the risk that the NAACP was taking. Many judges were wary of reversing half a century of law. As Justice Robert Jackson asked at the time, was the Court really the venue for eliminating the "fears, prides and prejudices on which segregation rests"? Indeed, based on the kinds of concerns Jackson had raised, the NAACP repeatedly had backed away from seeking any decision that would call into question the Court's finding in *Plessy*.

By most estimates at the time, the justices were divided 6–3, with the majority favoring the NAACP. But in a case so pivotal to American history—and American politics—change really required a unanimous, or at least near unanimous, decision. So the Court asked attorneys to address the question of whether deliberations over the Fourteenth Amendment, guaranteeing "equal protection" to all citizens under the law, ever contemplated the issue of school segregation itself. Marshall and the NAACP engaged historians John Hope Franklin and C. Vann Woodward to research the question. But they could find no definitive answer as to whether Congress had ever in the 1860s considered segregation as an issue when the Fourteenth Amendment was passed.[18]

But then, by a stroke of luck—at least from the point of view of the NAACP—Chief Justice Fred Vinson, one of those opposed to overturning *Plessy*, died from a sudden heart attack. Faced with this sudden vacancy, President Dwight D. Eisenhower appointed Earl Warren, the former governor of California, to take Vinson's place. Warren had always been a "progressive" Republican. But he had one keenly felt regret about his political past. After Pearl Harbor, Warren had led the movement to deprive Japanese American citizens from the West Coast of all their civil and political rights. Instead, they would be incarcerated in massive internment camps. They lost their property, their wealth, their independence—even though no one ever produced any evidence that they were a threat to the country. Warren profoundly regretted his decision—one that was based solely on the race and ethnicity of those who were interned, not on their actual behavior or political viewpoints.

Now, he had the chance to redeem himself. Carefully, the newly appointed Chief Justice led the court through the process of re-arguing *Brown*. He talked daily with his fellow justices. Politically shrewd and psychologically brilliant, he carefully cultivated their allegiance. When the Court gathered to consider the new arguments each side had made, Warren went out of his way to listen thoughtfully, and through his questions to pose the issues in the simplest, most fundamental terms. During oral arguments, it looked like Justice Robert Jackson and Justice Stanley Reed were still on the fence. But clearly, a majority favored overruling *Plessy* and making segregation by race unconstitutional. Warren assigned himself the task of writing the decision.

Carefully, he took the cultural high ground. He avoided tendentious nitpicking over legalistic issues. Instead, he asked his colleagues to accept a simple affirmation of basic principles—that equal protection under the law meant equal facilities. Within this framework, separate facilities were, by definition, unequal. Warren personally brought a draft of his decision to Robert Jackson, hospitalized after a heart attack. He engaged in long conversations with Stanley Reed, a Southerner, about the importance of having a unanimous court behind its decision.

On May 17, 1954, Warren read the Court's decision to reporters and lawyers. Education, he began, represented a central experience of life. The fundamental question before the judges, he went on, was whether "segregation . . . on the basis of race" deprived minority group children "of equal education opportunities." "We believe that it does," he declared. "To separate [those children] from others of similar age and qualifications solely because of their race generates a feeling of inferiority as to their place in the community that may affect their hearts and minds in a way unlikely to be ever undone." Consequently, Warren concluded, "in the field of public education the doctrine of 'separate but equal' has no place. Separate educational facilities are inherently unequal. . . . Any language in *Plessy v. Ferguson* contrary to these findings is rejected." The decision was unanimous.[19]

Seven years after J. A. DeLaine had agreed to challenge the Clarendon County School board, fifteen years after *Gaines*, and almost sixty years after Jim Crow was established as the law of the land, the Court had declared segregated schools to be a violation of the right of African Americans to have equal rights under the law. It was a "second Emancipation Proclamation," the *Chicago Defender* proclaimed. Thurgood Marshall, the NAACP's lead attorney, predicted that all segregated schools would be abolished within five years. The Supreme Court, it appeared, had done what politicians had adamantly refused to do.

The Aftermath of *Brown*

The problem, of course, was that political leaders were the ones who had to implement the decision. They bore the responsibility of acting to desegregate public schools. Now, *they* had to respond, and respond decisively.

Initially, at least, there seemed some basis for optimism. Although some Southern governors, among them James Byrnes of South Carolina, Herman Talmadge of Georgia, and Hugh White of Mississippi, rallied white segregationists by denouncing the decision, others called calmly for acceptance of its consequences. "Big" Jim Folsom of Alabama declared, "When the Supreme Court speaks, that's the law." Arkansas governor Frances Cherry echoed Folsom. "Arkansas will obey the law," he declared. "It always has." One of the South's leading newspapers, the *Louisville Courier Journal*, called the *Brown* decision simply "an acceptance of a process that has been going on for a long time." In Greensboro, North Carolina, the school board voted almost unanimously to accept the decision and initiate the process of compliance. So too did school committees in Louisville, Kentucky, and Little Rock, Arkansas. The Southern Baptist Convention, the largest religious body in the South and home to a theologically conservative constituency, declared at its June 1954 meeting that the *Brown* decision "is in harmony . . . with the Christian principles of equal justice and love for all men." One white Southern expert on race relations estimated that 75–80 percent of white Southerners fell into the "silent majority" category—people who would go where they were led, but who were willing to be led.[20]

Yet without leadership from the top, the decision existed in a vacuum. As one legal scholar wrote, "The law is a landing force [of change]. It makes the beachhead." Yet unless it was "broadened by forces from behind," nothing would happen. Where these forces did not exist, the scholar concluded, "the law has been unable to hold its beachhead and the legal action becomes a kind of military monument on which is only recorded 'we were here.'" Tragically, it soon became clear that "the forces from behind" were not willing to act; and so in cities throughout the South, school boards that had been willing to comply with *Brown* when it was announced—and there seemed no other choice—suddenly discovered that there was no outside pressure to desegregate. Indeed, if they had proceeded, conservative white supporters who embraced segregation were likely to unseat them and destroy their political careers.[21]

The one person who had the moral authority to move the country decisively forward on desegregation was Dwight David Eisenhower. "Ike" was a revered figure. The hero of D-Day and America's victory over Nazi Germany in World War II, he was venerated by his fellow citizens. If he had acted immediately and declared, "The Supreme Court has spoken, integration is now the law of the land, and I will enforce the decision with all the energy at my command," Southern governors would have had little choice but to comply; the commander-in-chief had issued an order, and even if they disagreed, they could have said that they had no choice but to obey the highest authority in the land. The situation resembled that which existed right after the South's surrender in the Civil War. At that moment, President Andrew Johnson could have imposed any civil rights reforms he chose, and those reforms would have been accepted. He had total control. So too did Eisenhower in the aftermath of the Supreme Court's decision.

But instead of acting decisively in support of *Brown*, Eisenhower did nothing. Instead, he waffled. Over and over again, he said that he would express neither approval nor disapproval of the Court's action. Except that he did observe: "I don't believe you can change the hearts of men with laws or decisions." In truth, Eisenhower deeply regretted the Court's action. Whatever enlightenment he brought to decisions on foreign affairs or the economy, Eisenhower was an uninformed opponent of the struggle for racial equality. "All [that whites] are concerned about," he once said, "is to see that their sweet little girls are not required to sit in schools alongside some big overgrown Negroes." It would be difficult to imagine a statement less informed by rational judgment, or more shaped by racial bigotry. Indeed, he later claimed that appointing Earl Warren as Chief Justice was the "biggest damn mistake" he had ever made. Far from advancing race relations, he later told an aide, "the Supreme Court decision set back progress in the south at least fifteen years. . . . The fellow who tries to tell me that you can do these things by force is just plain nuts!" One observer overheard Ike telling Warren at a White House reception to show some sympathy for segregationist whites. To which Warren reportedly responded, "You mind your business, and I'll mind mine."[22]

Repeatedly, Eisenhower refused to take action in Southern states, even to enforce recent federal court decisions ordering desegregation in specific communities such as Mansfield, Texas. And although he finally did order federal troops into Little Rock, Arkansas, after Governor Orval Faubus barred seven Black students from entering Central High School in 1957, it was primarily because he was outraged that Faubus, a political subordinate, had broken his promise to the president to ensure peaceful compliance at the school. It was less the principle of equality that spurred him to act than the fact that Faubus had committed an act of military insubordination and needed to be punished by his commander-in-chief.

Rather than stifling white resistance to *Brown*, then, Eisenhower encouraged it by his refusal to take a stand on the issue. In doing so, he deprived moderate state officials of the principal excuse they could have used to defend compliance with the Supreme Court's decision. This was the law of the land, they could have said. But through his inaction, Eisenhower had created a vacuum in which massive resistance could quickly flourish, because there was no one standing in the way.[23]

Soon, legislatures throughout the South enacted resolutions calling for total resistance. States such as Virginia, Alabama, and Mississippi claimed the right to "interpose" themselves between the people and the federal government, and declare *Brown* "null, void, and of no effect." Even "moderate" states like North Carolina—called by Harvard political scientist V. O. Key "an inspiring exception to Southern racism"—moved to deny the possibility of desegregation. Governor Luther C. Hodges promised to provide state money to any white student who was threatened by integration and wished to go to a private white school. Even though Hodges's own staff reported that white North Carolinians were indifferent on the issue of desegregation, the governor chose to inflame racial hostility by suggesting that Blacks wished to intermarry with whites. There were two extremist groups in the state, Hodges declared: the KKK and the NAACP. Only those who followed his plan could achieve "the middle way." As Hodges described the dilemma, Black citizens were the cause of the crisis, white citizens its victims. Hodges's ingenious efforts resulted in North Carolina having a lower desegregation rate—0.026 percent in 1961—than Virginia, Texas, Tennessee, or Texas. As one Little Rock school official observed, "You North Carolinians have devised one of the cleverest techniques for perpetuating segregation that we have seen."[24]

"Nothing could be worse," Supreme Court Justice Felix Frankfurter observed, "than for this court to make an abstract declaration that segregation is bad and then have it evaded by tricks." Yet this is exactly what had happened. If Black Americans had been betrayed by the very processes they had been told to believe in, then they would be forced to take action on their own terms, and to express their anger in a way that could no longer be ignored or misunderstood.[25]

The Movement Responds

Starting soon after white resistance to *Brown* became clear, Black Americans reverted to the grassroots activism that had always sustained—and animated—their drive for freedom. The determination to fight back took inspiration from the horror of a lynching in Mississippi in 1955. Racial murders were commonplace in the South, and especially in Mississippi. But this time, the courage of the victim's mother—and the horror of the murder now blazoned across the national news media—made this lynching somehow different.

In the summer of 1955, Emmett Till, a fourteen-year-old who now lived in Chicago, came South to visit his mother's family. One day, he went into a white-owned store in the local neighborhood for a snack. He had been told by his relatives how to behave around white people, but according to local gossips, Till made loose remarks about sex to the woman running the store. (According to a subsequent oral history interview, the woman denied that this had ever happened.) That night, a white gang seized Till at his relatives' house. They drove him to a local watering hole, tore out his eyes, ravaged his body, and sent him hurling to his death in the Tallahatchie River.

Under ordinary circumstances, Till's murder would have been ignored by local officials and the media. But this time, the teenager's brutal death became a national scandal. Till's mother took his body back to Chicago. But in the process, she insisted on dramatizing the racist brutality that led to the death of her son. She insisted on having an open casket, with the horrific dismembering of his body on display for all to see. Overnight, pictures of Till's ravaged body appeared on the front pages of Black newspapers throughout the country. Soon, *Jet* magazine—a national color-photo magazine—published the same photos. Those pictures of Emmett Till helped galvanize the nation.

Everywhere, average citizens—some white as well as Black—were brought face to face with the horrific truth that lay at the heart of race relations in America. Black lives did not matter.

Soon, the story of Till's death and the visceral reality of racist intimidation spread across the land, helping to set the stage for what, by the end of 1955, led to the first stage of what became a nationwide movement to strike back at patterns of racism that already existed everywhere. They now had been driven home with brutal gravity in pictures of Emmett Till's ravaged body.[26]

One of the first manifestations of the new protest movement occurred in Montgomery, Alabama.

It was only natural that Black protestors should mobilize around issues that highlighted the absurdity of the Jim Crow system, a system epitomized by the Jim Crow bus system. Blacks were supposed to pay the driver at the front of the bus, then get off the bus and re-enter through the rear door, occupying those seats at the back of the bus that were allocated to Black passengers. Sometimes the line between Black and white seats was flexible, but whenever white customers remained standing, Blacks were expected to give up their seats to accommodate them.

For decades, Blacks had protested the cruelty of the Jim Crow bus system. Sometimes, they would pay their fare up front, only to have the driver pull away before they could re-board the bus at the rear door. When Blacks protested, drivers would call the police. On occasion, they would pull out a gun and shoot the protestor. During World War II, protests multiplied so rapidly that the governor of North Carolina admitted that it was just as likely that the Jim Crow bus system would not function as that it would. Blacks were simply refusing to comply with segregation on the buses.[27]

Not surprisingly, then, the Jim Crow bus system was the first object of direct protest after it became clear that little positive would be done on the issue of school desegregation.

It is at this point that mainstream American history books have often distorted what really happened. The typical grade school version of the ten years between 1955 and 1965 goes like this: Rosa Parks was too tired to give up her seat on the bus. Martin Luther King Jr. came in and started the civil rights movement. President Lyndon Johnson eventually responded, and Congress passed the Civil Rights Act of 1964 and the Voting Rights Act of 1965. Racial equality had been achieved and the civil rights movement came to an end.[28]

Not true. Rosa Parks was indeed a well-respected, genteel member of the Black community in Montgomery. But she was also an exemplar, in her generation, of the leadership within the Black community that from Reconstruction through World War II had never given up the fight for freedom. Based on institutions within the community—churches, women's clubs, neighborhood associations—these individuals insisted on their rights, refused to be silenced, organized community self-help organizations, and did anything and everything they could to advance the cause of Black freedom. It was never easy, but for generations, people like Rosa Parks had carried the struggle forward, never admitting defeat or succumbing to the horror of white supremacy.

Black people rallied to the cause of Rosa Parks when she was arrested for refusing to give up her seat precisely because she was so well-known to her peers for her record of leadership in the freedom struggle. For fifteen years, Parks had been a dynamic activist in the civil rights movement in Alabama. She served for more than a decade as secretary of the NAACP in Montgomery. In 1944, Parks courageously galvanized Blacks in a city three hours distant from Montgomery after a Black woman was raped by six white policemen. Through her persistence and strength, Black activists forced the local government to indict the officers and put them on trial. (Not surprisingly, they were acquitted by an all-white jury.)

After returning to Montgomery, Parks continued her efforts to invigorate the local civil rights movement.

Instead of being an accident of history, a woman who just happened to be too tired to give up her seat on the Montgomery bus that day, Rosa Parks very consciously became the catalyst that sparked the direct-action revolution. Parks had carefully calculated and planned what became a sustained strategy of targeted protest. She had recently returned from a meeting of Black activists at Hillandale, a Tennessee retreat center where, for a week, civil rights leaders gathered to plot how to organize this kind of venture. On two occasions in the weeks before Parks's arrest, the community of civil rights activists in Montgomery had contemplated a bus boycott. But on both occasions, the civil rights leaders of Montgomery felt that the risks were too high. In one case, the person taken into custody was an unwed pregnant teenager who refused to move to the back of the bus to provide a white person a seat. In a second instance, the person arrested came from a family with a criminal record. What was missing both times was a person with impeccable credentials who could be a focal point for protest—someone who was universally respected—someone whom everyone would rally around, immediately and with enthusiasm.

If Parks's history of activism and her recent participation at the Tennessee meeting of Black protestors were not enough proof that her action was carefully calculated, her immediate response upon being arrested for refusing to give up her seat sealed the issue. What did she do that afternoon? First, after being arrested for refusing to give up her seat to a white passenger, she went to the home of Virginia and Clifford Durr, long-standing white activists in the community who had served in the New Deal and were known for their strong defense of Black activists. Then she contacted E. D. Nixon, the head of the local NAACP, who was already prepared to mobilize the union members of the Brotherhood of Sleeping Car Porters Union—an all-Black union—on her behalf. Finally, she contacted Jo Ann Robinson of the Women's Political Council, the Black equivalent of the League of Women Voters.

That weekend night, Robinson gathered her colleagues from the Council at a local Black women's college. Together they worked through the evening to print forty thousand leaflets calling for Montgomery's Black citizens to boycott the city's Jim Crow bus system. By the next day, those leaflets ended up in the hands of virtually every Black family in Montgomery. That Monday, not a single Black individual rode the public buses in Montgomery.

It was only *after* the boycott had been successful on its first day that thousands of Blacks in Montgomery gathered at an evening meeting in the Holt Street Baptist Church. There, they were greeted by a brand-new minister in town, Rev. Martin Luther King Jr. King had the advantage of being so much a newcomer in town that he had made no enemies yet; he had the additional advantage (and prestige) of being a candidate for a doctoral degree at Boston University. Still, by the time King addressed the Black community that night, the movement already existed—brilliantly planned and executed by Rosa Parks, and her allies, E. D. Nixon, Jo Ann Robinson, and Virginia and Clifford Durr. King's audience had already been mobilized. Contrary to subsequent popular history, Martin Luther King Jr. did not create the Montgomery movement. Rather, he became a *symbol* for a movement that was already in existence.

The church service that evening helped create the occasion for King's rise to fame—his pivotal leadership from that point forward as a charismatic leader of the civil rights crusade. But because of all the subsequent focus on King and his leadership, the story of Parks and her colleagues from the 1940s has largely been downplayed in textbooks, with the focus primarily on King. Yet in truth, it was the work of people like Parks, the Durrs, E. D. Nixon, and Jo Ann Robinson for well over a decade prior to the Montgomery bus boycott that the mass movement of the 1950s and 1960s became a reality.[29]

Significantly, Montgomery was not alone as a site of protest. In Tallahassee, Florida, there was a similar bus boycott in 1956. Here, too, the protest movement built on a freedom struggle by local Blacks that had been flourishing for years. Laura Dixie, born in 1925, had long led a group of working-class Black women who pursued voter registration efforts in the community, as well as triggering worker protests at the hospital where Dixie worked—including wildcat strikes led by the union of which she would eventually become president. Dixie learned her activism from her mother and father. "My mother always told us," she said in an interview, "that we were just as good as anybody else . . . [and you did] not have to go to anybody's back door." Her father, in turn, used his job as a janitor at a local bank to look at the records and correspondence of the executive vice president, who also happened to be the mayor of Tallahassee. "You know," he said, "a janitor sees a *whole* lot of things that they normally don't think he would see, on a [person's] desk."

Dixie and her husband attended Bethel Baptist Church, whose pastor, Reverend C. K. Steele, had long been recognized for his devotion to the freedom struggle. Less well known is that Steele, and the Dixies, had to fight the board of deacons at the church who sought to restrict church activism in the civil rights movement. But with the leadership of Dixie and her husband, the congregation rejected the deacons' resolution. With her parents as role models, Dixie had carried on the struggle, now passing it down to her own children. "I was just determined for them not to have to go through . . . the stuff that I had to go through," she remembered, "and so that's [why] I got involved . . . working for civil rights."

With her husband and Reverend Steele, she and her fellow church members spearheaded the Tallahassee bus boycott. For years, there had been intermittent protests against the Jim Crow bus system. Now, they mobilized the entire community to do what Montgomery was doing—and success greeted their efforts, just as it had those of Rosa Parks and her colleagues in Montgomery.[30]

The Movement Grows

First in Montgomery, and soon throughout the South, Martin Luther King rose to the challenge before him. With virtually every Black person in Montgomery persuaded by Jo Ann Robinson's mimeographed bulletins not to ride the buses, King provided a new intellectual and spiritual framework for other Americans to understand the courage and motivation that inspired Montgomery's Black citizens to refuse to countenance Jim Crow any longer. "There comes a time," King told his audience of five thousand that Monday night, "when people get tired. We are here this evening to say to those who have mistreated us so long that we are tired—tired of being segregated and humiliated, tired of being kicked about by the brutal feet of oppression." No longer, King declared, would Blacks "be patient with anything less than freedom and justice." Christian love and nonviolent resistance would triumph over the evil of racism. Those Black Americans who believed in the redemptive love of the Christian Savior would now set forth—with a new credo to inspire them—to achieve the justice that had been denied them for more than two centuries.

It would not be an easy fight. The Montgomery boycott went on for 381 days. Blacks in Montgomery had to create their own informal transportation system, a car pool of Black drivers willing to give up their mornings to help the cause. Thousands made phone calls, organized cadres of supporters, created phalanxes of people who every day walked to work to demonstrate their conviction. As one famously quoted older woman told a reporter, "my feets is tired, but my soul is rested." When the white-robed Ku Klux Klan drove through Black Montgomery to splinter and intimidate the community, no one ran away. Instead, the Black residents of Montgomery jeered and laughed at the Klan members. Despite the manipulation and duplicity of white authorities, Blacks would not give up. And a year and two weeks after the boycott began, the Supreme Court ruled that segregation on Montgomery's bus system—and elsewhere—was unconstitutional. It deprived all Black citizens of equal protection under the laws. Rosa Parks, the NAACP, the Brotherhood of Sleeping Car Porters, and the Women's Political Council—together with the philosophy of nonviolence now being preached by Dr. King—had finally scored a victory for direct action. It was not the end of massive collective resistance. But it was a beginning.

Chapter 10

A New Language of Protest, a New Generation of Activists

Despite creating a precedent for mass protest, the Montgomery bus boycott was not enough to ensure more far-reaching change. The brilliance of the boycott also represented its major weakness. It was a passive act. Blacks in Montgomery made themselves heard by refusing to ride the bus. Although the bus boycott represented a brilliant way to protest the system of Jim Crow public transport, it did not constitute a frontal assault on the system of segregation. That would require explicit confrontation, a willingness to place life and limb at risk by challenging physically the system of refusing Blacks equal service at hotels, lunch counters, theaters, and voting booths. To counter this kind of segregation, a new form of collective action would be necessary—one that would provide Blacks a vehicle to assault, directly and frontally, the entire structure of Jim Crow racism.

Sit-Ins

The sit-in movement accomplished what a bus boycott could never do. In a series of dramatic confrontations, Black young people—acting consciously in a nonviolent manner—put their lives on the line to demand that they be treated as equal citizens and customers at lunch counters, movie theaters, restaurants, and hotels. Their ranks swelled daily, and as protests multiplied exponentially across the entire South, the federal government was forced—finally—to take action.

The conventional view of the sit-in movement is to treat it almost as "an immaculate conception"—something totally new, without precedent, a near miracle that soon transformed the nation. Suddenly, one winter day—February 1, 1960—four Black freshmen at the all-Black North Carolina A&T College in Greensboro decided on the spur of the moment to go to Woolworth's, a local variety store, and demand to be served food at the store's lunch counter. When they were refused service—"We don't serve colored people here," the Black waitress behind the counter told them—they opened their schoolbooks, started to study, and did not leave until the store closed.

Word quickly spread around campus about what they had done. The second day the four became twenty-three; the next day, sixty-six; then the day after that, one hundred; until on day five, one thousand Blacks—adults as well as students—surrounded stores in downtown Greensboro. Over the next eight weeks, similar demonstrations broke out in fifty-four cities in nine different states. From the point of view of many observers, this was a brand new, dramatically different social movement—a complete departure from the past.[1]

The truth was very different. Yes, the method—and the language—of protest represented a dramatic departure. But the decision to act was rooted in the decades-old commitment to fight racism embodied in people like Rosa Parks, J. S. DeLaine, and Amzie Moore. The Greensboro students did not miraculously discover the politics of direct-action protest. Rather, they found a new way to express a commitment to fight Jim Crow that had been part of their entire process of growing up. These lessons of resistance had been taught to them by their parents, their teachers, their ministers. Their decision to act—and the method they chose—grew directly from an opposition to racial injustice that was embedded in the Black community. Yes, the sit-ins mobilized a new generation of activists; yes, the tactic of sitting in constituted a dramatic new language for expressing Black protest. But the decisions of the students to sit-in represented a continuation of a struggle they had been told about throughout their lives, and which their parents and teachers trained them to carry forward. It was not an immaculate conception—rather, it was a new way of expressing a lesson the students had been taught for years.

Three of the four first-year students who sat in at Woolworth's on February 1 had been raised in Greensboro. They had just entered adolescence when the *Brown* decision was handed down in 1954. In the aftermath of *Brown*, they had seen little progress occur in race relations—notwithstanding Greensboro's vaunted reputation as a "progressive" city, with good race relations. Having reached the age of eighteen or nineteen, they recognized that they were now responsible for what would happen next in the struggle for racial equality. No longer could they simply be bystanders. Now, the task was theirs to carry forward.

The early years of the Greensboro Four had prepared them for this moment. Their parents were activists, some of them prominent members of the local NAACP—the largest NAACP chapter in the state. Discussions of racial inequality were a frequent occurrence in their homes. Three of the four went to Dudley High School. Like Dunbar High School in Washington, DC, Dudley was a source of pride for the entire Black community.

One reason for that pride was that the teachers there instilled in their students the importance of standing up for their rights. Vance Chavis was a science instructor at Dudley. When he talked to his homeroom students, he conveyed his own anger at the system of Jim Crow. He told his pupils that he had never in his life sat in the back of the public buses that provided transportation in the city; nor, he emphasized, had he ever sat in the balcony of Greensboro's movie theaters—the places reserved for Blacks under the Jim Crow system. If that message were not sufficiently clear, Chavis had the students in his homeroom address envelopes urging Black citizens of Greensboro to register to vote.

Their English teacher was a woman named Nell Coley. She insisted that her students aspire to be the best that they could be. She used her reading assignments in poetry and literature to underscore her message. "We were always talking about the issues," she said. "We might read [a poem or a novel] as a kind of pivot," but she always related the words of Langston Hughes or Thomas Hardy to the inalienable rights of human beings to respect and freedom. "I had to tell youngsters," she said, "that the way you find things need not happen. . . . I don't care if they push and shove you, you must not accept [discrimination]. . . .You are who you are." The world as they found it, she insisted, need not be the world they accepted.

That message was reinforced, daily, at home and in the church. Some of the students leading the sit-in protests attended Shiloh Baptist Church—the largest Black church in Greensboro. The pastor, Otis Hairston, had led civil rights protests at Shaw University in Raleigh, his alma mater, in the late 1940s. He preached about freedom, and under his leadership, the local NAACP had almost doubled its membership in 1959. Significantly, when the students started the sit-in movement, they immediately went to Hairston to seek help with supplies and the means for mimeographing pamphlets. Two of the students also had participated in the local NAACP Youth Group that Ella Baker had started in 1943. There, they discussed each week local and national protest activities. The students who integrated Little Rock's Central High School came to talk to them. They especially concentrated on the Montgomery bus boycott. "It was like a catalyst," one of the four original demonstrators recalled. "It started a whole lot of things rolling." Soon thereafter, Martin Luther King Jr. came to Greensboro to preach about Christ's message for America. At that point, things started to fall into place. Dr. King's sermon was "so strong," one demonstrator recalled, "that I could feel my heart palpitating. It brought tears to my eyes."[2]

It was hardly surprising, therefore, that when they enrolled in college in the fall of 1959, the four sit-in demonstrators started talking immediately—and nightly—about how they should act to advance the struggle for freedom. They had witnessed a bewildering set of tactics by white leaders in Greensboro. Although on the night after the *Brown* decision, the school board had voted 5–1 to comply with the decision, Eisenhower's failure to enforce *Brown* set up a situation where North Carolina governor Luther Hodges could establish the Pearsall Plan, essentially guaranteeing that any white student who did not wish to attend school with Blacks could get state funds to pay for private school tuition. Greensboro had agreed to the token integration of six Black high school students in 1957, but it had done so at the instruction of the governor to "hold an umbrella" over the rest of North Carolina and prevent a class action lawsuit by the NAACP against the entire state.

Indeed, duplicity characterized Greensboro's entire response to civil rights protests, even if cloaked in the guise of "civility." When Blacks attempted to integrate the local public golf course, they were arrested. Then, mysteriously, the clubhouse burned down and the golf course was closed. Black college graduates from A&T and nearby Bennett College were told by local employers that they could apply for jobs as janitors and maids, but not as salesclerks. Throughout, good manners prevailed. "No one ever called me nigger here," one local Black said; and whites boasted of their paternalism—how they looked out for "their" Negroes. But beneath the surface display of gentility, the underlying structure of racism remained. The bottom line, one Black leader observed, was that Greensboro was a "nice-nasty town."[3]

It was against this background that the Greensboro Four initiated their nightly discussions "We challenged each other, really," one of them recalled. "We constantly heard about all the evils that are occurring and how blacks are mistreated and nobody was doing anything about it. . . . We used to question, 'Why is it that you have to sit in the balcony? Why do you have to ride in the back of the bus?'" Acutely aware that they were about to reach voting age, they asked each other how long they would have to wait before they could be treated as equal members of American society, especially when the Supreme Court had ruled in their favor. "I don't know how many Black babies had been born eighteen years ago," one student remembered, "but I guess everybody was pretty well fed up at the same time." If whites had not responded to the peaceful petitions of an older generation, perhaps they would listen if a younger generation found a different way to express their anger, discontent, and impatience.

As the four students talked at night trying to discern the best course of action, they drew strength from each other. "The thing that precipitated the sit-ins," one of the students recalled, "was that little bit of incentive and that little bit of courage that each of us instilled in each other." Then, on a day in January, one of the four—returning from a trip to Richmond—became furious at the personal disrespect he experienced at the hands of a white employee at the Richmond bus station. He was not allowed to use the only working restroom at the station. The incident provided the final trigger. The students had to act, and they had to act now. One of them went home on a Sunday evening and asked his parents if they would be embarrassed if he got into trouble. "Why?" his parents asked. "Because," he responded, "we're going to do something that will shake up this town." In fact, his parents were proud of their son. He was acting on the values they had imparted. And so the students proceeded. Scared, fearful, not knowing what might happen, the four friends shored up each other's confidence until the next afternoon. "All of us were afraid," one of them remembered, "but we went and did it."

"We had the confidence . . . of a Mack truck," one of the students recalled. "I felt better that day than I had ever felt in my life. I felt as though I had gained my manhood."[4]

Within days it became clear that a well-planned, but new kind of demonstration had mobilized the entire community. When nearly one thousand students and teachers, including the A&T football team, gathered in downtown Greensboro that fifth day of the protests, white gangs surrounded them, waving Confederate flags. Carrying their own recently purchased American flags, the Black football players intervened, creating a wedge through which the demonstrators could move to the lunch counters. "Who do you think you are?" the whites asked. "We're the Union Army," the players responded. Nell Coley, the Dudley High School English teacher, looked on, excited and proud.

"You are never going to see this kind of thing again," she said, "and I'm always happy that I [was there] because here were these Black kids lined [up] around this counter with books in their hands . . . and I was right there when the store was closed and when those Black youngsters formed lines and yelled 'We won.'" In one town, in one week, these four young people had decided to express something that had been in their minds for a long time. They did not know it, but by acting as they did, these four young men had found a new way to generate and accelerate change. By their actions, the Greensboro "coffee party" would take its place alongside the Boston Tea Party as a moment symbolizing the beginning of a new era.[5]

Within a week, sit-ins started to occur elsewhere. Soon, students in Charlotte, Winston-Salem, Durham, and Raleigh had joined their compatriots in other Piedmont North Carolina cities. The next week, young people in Nashville joined the crusade, led by people like John Lewis and Diane Nash, whose names soon became synonymous with the civil rights revolution of the 1960s. The Greensboro Four had been the spark that set off fires of protest across the country, but the kindling and fuel had been gathering for decades. Indeed, students in Nashville had been talking about starting their own demonstrations, akin to the sit-ins, even before February 1. Ever since *Brown*, the stage had been set for action. Now, it had happened.

From the point of view of those committed to a new era of racial activism, it was fortuitous that the student sit-in movement began in North Carolina and Tennessee. Both states had opted for using the "politics of moderation" to sustain racial segregation. Violent repression of Blacks who protested was not customary in either state. Hence, the risks of initiating new tactics of protest were lower. Had the sit-ins started in places like Mississippi or southwest Georgia, they would have immediately been snuffed out by violent whites. But by starting in more moderate states, the sit-ins had the opportunity to take off, gaining ever more momentum as they spread into other parts of the South, until eventually, they could not—and would not—be stopped.

Success of the student protests in one place led to emulation of the sit-in tactic elsewhere. Although representatives of CORE, the NAACP, and SCLC traveled from one flash point to another, there was no collective planning involved. Instead, each group, hearing about the protests of students elsewhere, drew on the Greensboro example and proceeded to act. People such as Julian Bond in Atlanta, John Lewis in Nashville, and Cleveland Sellers in Denmark, South Carolina, all heard the news and were inspired to start their own crusade. "My identification with the demonstrating students was so thorough," Cleveland Sellers recalled, "that I would flinch every time one of the [white] students taunted them. . . . I had a burning desire to get involved." So did thousands of others—hence the eruption of sit-ins in nine Southern states during the eight weeks immediately following February 1.[6]

But a feature of the sit-ins too often ignored by historians was the degree to which they represented a continuity of protest within the Black community. The students may have found a new language and a new tactic to express their commitment to protest, but they did so by carrying forward the tradition of resistance to discrimination that they had been taught by their parents, their teachers, their ministers, and groups like the NAACP Youth Chapter.

No one symbolized that continuity more than Ella Baker. As the person in charge of NAACP field work in the South during the 1940s, Baker had organized hundreds of local NAACP groups, including the Youth Chapter in Greensboro where the Greensboro Four discussed repeatedly how to make change happen.

Now, Miss Baker was ready to carry over to the 1960s that same leadership of creating and sustaining Black activism. She had recently been appointed acting executive secretary of Martin Luther King Jr.'s Southern Christian Leadership Conference (SCLC). And when she learned of the sit-ins, she immediately sensed the importance of the new student protest movement. Using $800 of SCLC money, she invited all the student protestors she could identify to meet at her alma mater, Shaw University, in early April 1960. Greeting the students, she set forth her own bold agenda. It was "more than a hamburger" that the students sought when they staged their lunch-counter sit-ins, she declared, and more than a seat at a theater. Rather, it was freedom they were after—freedom from economic squalor, from educational deprivation, from political disenfranchisement. Rev. James Lawson of Vanderbilt Theological Seminary galvanized the students with his call for a movement of nonviolence. "Love is the central motif of nonviolence," he declared. "Such love goes to the extreme; it remains loving and forgiving even in the midst of hostility." Martin Luther King Jr. also addressed the crowd, affirming the importance of "revolt against the apathy and complacency of adults."[7]

While most followers of SCLC expected the student demonstrators simply to become a new appendage of their organization, Ella Baker had other ideas. She understood the importance of the student movement being *independent*, able to determine its own course of action. The students themselves were fearful that the top-down approach of ministers in SCLC would destroy their autonomy. They preferred to have local self-governance, the freedom to go where the spirit moved them. At *the* critical moment of decision, Baker sided with the students, affirming the importance of their having their own organization—the Student Non-Violent Coordinating Committee (SNCC)—and charting their own course of action, independent of Dr. King and the SCLC.

The next four years highlighted the importance of that decision. SNCC became the cutting edge of the movement. It challenged the racist practices of America where the most virulent white supremacists held power: Mississippi and southwest Georgia. It confronted the most vicious forms of white violence; dared to challenge white officials directly; mobilized large segments of Black adults to go to seek the right to vote; and joined together as one the individual right of citizens to be treated equally and the collective need of Black Americans to battle poverty, refuse to accept economic intimidation, and create school systems—pre-kindergarten as well as elementary and secondary—that would break the vicious cycle of intimidation that for generations had kept Black people oppressed. Only SNCC could begin to demonstrate, on a daily basis, the kind of courage, imagination, persistence, and heroism that became the hallmark of this new student movement. While the NAACP and the SCLC were hierarchical, top-down organizations that took a long time to make decisions, SNCC students operated from the bottom up, and in each community they visited, their determination to organize protests occurred in the homes and churches where the students gathered with their community allies.

Robert (Bob) Moses, a Harvard-educated teacher from New York—who became the spiritual model for SNCC workers everywhere—embodied SNCC's approach. Moses always sought guidance from local Blacks and their community institutions, encouraging grassroots citizens to chart the objectives of the movement, rather than telling them from above what they should be doing.

Moses came South in the summer of 1960, and after working in the SNCC office in Atlanta for a few weeks, accepted an assignment to explore the possibilities of building a movement in Cleveland, Mississippi. Upon arriving, Moses immediately sought out Amzie Moore, by then well known throughout Cleveland—and the state—as a quiet but assertive leader, strong but calm. Moore was universally respected by the African American community. Moses stayed in Moore's home, met a cross section of the Black community, and then, with Moore's encouragement, organized local Black citizens to go down to the county clerk's office and register to vote.

As anticipated, the Black citizens were immediately turned away, and Moses was attacked and bloodied by a Cleveland policeman. But Moses had just begun. He lodged a charge against the policeman who had beaten him, forcing a court hearing to have his allegations heard. Again, as anticipated, a judge found the officer not guilty. The contest was joined now in earnest, and the police retaliated by trailing Moses everywhere and harassing his every move. But the community had seen Moses's courage. The inspiration of the Greensboro Four that had launched SNCC, and that motivated Moses to go to Mississippi, now swept through the entire community of Blacks in Cleveland. They began to meet, collectively, at a local Black church. Something was happening.[8]

For every step forward, there was always a step back. Herbert Lee, an NAACP member and a Black farmer with wife and children, had dared to try to register to vote in Liberty, Mississippi. Soon thereafter, his white neighbor, brandishing a gun, stopped Lee in his truck near the center of the city. He demanded that Lee get out of his truck. Lee refused until the white neighbor put away his pistol. The white neighbor then put the gun in his pocket. When Lee got out of his truck, the white neighbor then pulled out his pistol and shot Lee dead. For two hours, Lee's body lay on the street, unattended. When charges were brought against the killer by Moses and other Black activists, he was immediately acquitted by an all-white jury. The same story would occur multiple times in Mississippi during 1961, 1962, and 1963. But Moses would not retreat, nor would his allies in the Black community. Moses brought suit against white racists who attacked him, and although his lawsuits failed, his courage reverberated through the community. SNCC was making a difference, imbedding itself in every local Black community it visited, relying on group meetings to plot the next stage of protest. SNCC would not be intimidated, nor would the local communities of Blacks that it mobilized.[9]

The nation as a whole became more aware of the pervasiveness of white violence against Black protestors in the spring of 1961 when national television news started focusing each night on civil rights protests. Black activists—and some whites who now joined them—decided to test a recent court ruling against segregated seating on interstate buses. Boarding both a Greyhound bus and a Trailways bus in Washington, DC, headed to New Orleans, James Farmer from CORE and others set out on their journey through Virginia and North Carolina. But then, in Rock Hill, South Carolina, a mob of twenty whites brutally beat John Lewis, a Freedom Rider and a veteran of the Nashville sit-ins. Shortly thereafter—on Mother's Day in Anniston, Alabama—a huge white mob surrounded the Greyhound bus, cut its tires, and then threw a firebomb through a window, driving the passengers out onto the road. The Freedom Riders were pummeled. The same thing happened when the Trailways bus arrived an hour later. Throughout, as the Southern Regional Council later noted, "police were either inactive, or not present, or strangely late in arrival," even though they knew exactly when the buses would arrive.[10] As the nation watched each evening, word spread of the movement's growing presence, with the TV viewers astonished by the cruelty of white racists, and the failure of Southern police to do anything to protect the bus riders.

In response, most of the adults who had embarked on the Freedom Ride chose to complete their journey to New Orleans by air. But not SNCC activists. Diane Nash, Ruby Doris Smith, John Lewis, and others determined to continue, *by bus*, on the ride. Birmingham's police commissioner "Bull" Connor met the SNCC workers when they arrived in Alabama, and immediately transported them back to the Tennessee border. But they refused to take no for an answer. The students got back on the bus and returned to Birmingham. They were beaten again by an uncontrolled mob that also pummeled John Siegenthaler, Attorney General Robert F. Kennedy's right-hand man in the Justice Department, whom he had sent to Alabama to observe the movement. Still, the students would not stop, journeying on to Jackson, Mississippi. There they were immediately arrested and thrown into Parchman Prison, one of the most infamous prisons in the world. Soon they were joined by three hundred other young activists arrested on Freedom Ride buses. But they would not give in either; they refused to pay bail; and even though their mattresses, then their sheets, then their toothbrushes and towels were taken away, they persisted, sleeping on steel. That was the kind of courage that made SNCC different—and put it in a category by itself in the growing youth movement for civil rights. Even if Black adults in local communities had demonstrated before, the SNCC pioneers created a whole new world of activism.[11]

Howard Zinn, a historian as well as a youthful demonstrator with SNCC, has given us some sense of the interaction between bold

SNCC activists and committed local citizens who rallied to the cause of racial justice. One night, in Hattiesburg, Mississippi, Zinn and his fellow civil rights workers arrived in the middle of the night at a Black family's house where they were to stay prior to a massive demonstration scheduled for the next day. The man and his wife greeted the SNCC activists, then dragged a mattress into the living room, where the SNCC workers would sleep. Zinn woke at dawn, hearing a sound. "At first," he wrote, "I thought it was part of a dream. . . . But it [was] a woman's voice, . . . chanting softly. . . and it was his wife, praying, intoning, 'oh Lord, Jesus . . . let things go well today Jesus. . . . Oh make them see, Jesus." As the lights came on, Zinn could see through an open doorway that there was no mattress on the bed of the Black couple—because they had given it to the civil right workers.[12]

Thousands of such stories—of brutal racist violence, community solidarity, church congregations rallying to the cause while singing "Oh Freedom"—spread across the nation. By 1962, the *New York Times* was devoting three to four pages each day to civil rights demonstrations. Nightly TV broadcasts alerted the country that a war for America's soul was taking place. Civil rights issues had become part of the daily agenda of life for Americans, whatever their background, and as more and more young people, some white as well as Black, joined the Southern struggle, racial equality became a focal point for the entire nation. More than any other issue, it provided the moral challenge that would galvanize a generation. And it came, not from above, but from below—from the people themselves who had fought back against racist tyranny for generations, but now declared, in voices of collective determination, "We will take this no more."

Washington's Response

The Kennedy administration responded with only partial support. As had happened time and time again, politics trumped principle, and the Kennedy administration responded with only partial, and tepid, support. Although historians now know that Kennedy's margin of victory in 1960 came directly from the Black community in the North, in large part because of JFK's impromptu phone call to Coretta Scott King after her husband had been arrested, then sentenced to hard labor in an Alabama prison, Kennedy did not follow through with active engagement on behalf of civil rights activists.

His brother, Attorney General Robert F. Kennedy, represented the more aggressive response of the Kennedy administration toward civil rights. RFK was outraged at the failure of the Justice Department to implement existing legislation on voting rights. In his first year as attorney general, he initiated fourteen new voting rights lawsuits, increased the number of Black staff members in his office from ten to fifty, and petitioned the Interstate Commerce Commission to desegregate all public accommodations involving travel across state lines. By 1963, the Justice Department had become involved in voting rights cases in 145 Southern counties, nearly a 500 percent increase over the figure at the end of the Eisenhower administration. Intentionally, the attorney general surrounded himself with close advisors like John Siegenthaler and John Doar, who passionately believed in the Justice Department's intervention in cases of voter suppression and police brutality in the South. When Siegenthaler was beaten unconscious by racist extremists during the Freedom Rides, Robert Kennedy was finally persuaded that the word of Southern law enforcement officers could not be trusted and that the Justice Department must send in federal marshals.[13]

But President Kennedy himself refused to act boldly. The president's approach was basically controlled by Southern Democrats who chaired key congressional committees. He would not act until he was forced to—which put the burden, again, on Black activists.

JFK never mentioned civil rights in his inaugural address in January 1961. Although the federal government offered some assistance during the Freedom Rides, it rarely if ever intervened to act against the beatings inflicted on Blacks by whites; moreover, it looked the other way when Mississippi jailed hundreds of Black student activists who had joined the Freedom Rides.

But now, the nightly TV broadcasts of white violence against SNCC workers forced the administration to respond. Robert Kennedy had pushed hard for SNCC members to focus their efforts on voter registration. He may have thought that by emphasizing a legal right—the franchise—rather than confrontational demonstrations in restaurants and movie theaters, he could tone down violence. But he was wrong. SNCC activists like Robert Moses knew in their gut that petitioning for the franchise would unleash just as much violent opposition as the demand for equal access to good seats in the movie theater.

When SNCC workers put their lives on the line by seeking to register voters in southwest Georgia and the Delta counties of Alabama and Mississippi, they were met by brutality and violence. In Georgia, four Black churches were firebombed after they had become centers of voter registration work. Fannie Lou Hamer, a sharecropper in Mississippi, decided to go and register to vote after a SNCC worker visited her home—only to be immediately fired by her plantation landlord and evicted from her home. But in this instance, Hamer responded by immediately becoming one of SNCC's most effective civil rights activists, soon to become a national heroine. When civil rights workers journeyed back to their headquarters at night, they were constantly followed by white racists, and often physically attacked. Local law enforcement officials not only failed to protect the activists; they often took the lead in harassing them, including shooting at them. In the meantime, federal officials did nothing. Instead of intervening to protect SNCC workers, FBI officers stood by, simply taking notes as the violent attacks escalated.

Whatever promises Kennedy had made during his presidential campaign were now broken—consistently—causing liberal campaign aides, and especially Blacks in the administration, to feel abandoned. When JFK's personal aide Ted Sorenson told Black staff members that the time was not ripe for a civil rights battle, Black staff member Louis Martin responded, "The time has *never* been ripe." Kennedy's stance left Blacks on their own. Although the government might mobilize federal forces to ensure the admission of James Meredith to the previously all-white University of Mississippi, it did little to respond to the demands of local Black activists for racial justice. As Martin Luther King Jr. observed in 1962, "If tokenism were the goal, the administration [has moved] us adroitly toward it." Black Americans were once again bearing almost the entire burden of change, advancing toward justice on their own.[14]

Yet by 1963, inaction was no longer a viable option. The young people of SNCC, joined by every other civil rights organization in the nation, created a mass movement hitherto unknown in American history. Daily, in Albany, Georgia; in McComb, Mississippi; and in Birmingham, Alabama; Black protestors—joined by some whites—took to the streets demanding desegregation of all public facilities, and recognition of the right of every citizen to vote. Each night the evening television news was dominated by the demonstrations. Depictions of racial violence blazoned across newspapers and movie screens. No one—not even the most complacent and indifferent Northern white suburbanite—could avoid facing directly the insistence of Black Americans, led by young people, on receiving racial justice.

The smoldering fire began in Albany, Georgia. In traditional SNCC fashion, SNCC workers—led by Charles Sherrod, Cordell Reagon, and Charles Jones—came to Albany in the fall of 1961. They made contact with the local NAACP, Albany State College students, and neighborhood ministers. Although viewed with suspicion by some older, more established Blacks, they soon had won sufficient support to start a new Albany Movement, headed by a local Black doctor. Albany had its own long history of Black activism. As far back as Reconstruction, thousands of local Blacks had elected fellow African Americans to local and state offices. Despite the subsequent defeats of Reconstruction in 1877 and the onset of legalized Jim Crow with the *Plessy* decision, resistance persisted. A local NAACP chapter was initiated after World War I, and was re-energized in the 1940s and

1950s. Now, the new Albany Movement, infused with the energy that SNCC workers brought, set out to demand desegregation of the bus terminal and mobilize local Blacks to register to vote. After successive mass meetings and protest marches, more than five hundred demonstrators had been jailed. Although the Kennedy administration pledged to watch developments in Albany carefully, it ultimately did nothing, only exacerbating the frustration of Black activists with the federal government.[15]

Contributing to the Kennedy administration's inaction were the politically astute tactics of Albany police chief Loren Pritchett. From day one, Pritchett sought to avoid using violence against Black demonstrators. His police officers were instructed to arrest the protestors peacefully—no beatings, no brutality. Then, he arranged to distribute those arrested into a series of rural jails miles away from Albany itself, thereby avoiding additional local confrontations of movement activists rallying around overcrowded jail cells.

Pritchett's cleverness then helped to trigger the next blow to the local movement. Against the wishes of SNCC students, who already were suspicious of the top-down tactics of SCLC, leaders of the Albany Movement asked Martin Luther King Jr. to come to Albany in the hopes that his fame would generate more Black fervor and maximize national publicity. After addressing a mass meeting, King marched with demonstrators the next day and was arrested. But after he had been led to believe by Albany officials that they would concede to several demands of the Albany Movement, he posted bail and was released. The officials then repudiated the alleged "settlement," tarnishing King's reputation among the uncompromising activists in SNCC. King's visit to Albany—and then his departure after Albany officials refused to compromise—exacerbated dramatically the tensions between SCLC and SNCC. King himself stayed up all night to try to talk through his differences with SNCC students, but the seeds of division within the movement would never be fully healed.

Students sarcastically started to refer to King as "de Lawd," mocking the minister's theological preeminence. And though King eventually returned to Albany with SCLC staff in the spring and summer of 1962 seeking to rejuvenate the movement, once again Pritchett and his allies proved too shrewd. After King was arrested again and refused bail, Pritchett arranged for an anonymous citizen to post King's bond and release him.[16]

The national media—and many local activists—considered the Albany Movement a complete failure. Many civil rights workers were despondent, feeling that for the first time, clever whites—Loren Pritchett and his colleagues—had outsmarted them with sophisticated tactics and political finesse.

In fact, it could be argued that ultimately the Albany Movement was as much a success as a failure. As SNCC's Charles Sherrod observed, "I can't help how Dr. King might have felt . . . but as far as we were concerned things moved on. We didn't skip one beat." Voter registration efforts continued, a Black candidate for the city commission forced a run-off, and in the spring of 1963, the city commission removed all segregation statutes from Albany. The movement soon spread to other Georgia cities, such as Americus. Perhaps most important, a musical group called the SNCC Freedom Singers, led by Albany's Bernice Johnson Reagon, became a new rallying point for the entire movement. The Freedom Songs of Reagon and her peers quickly became a new musical inspiration for thousands of freedom fighters.[17]

From a media perspective, the Albany campaign seemed a failure. But whatever the opinion of journalists, the primary significance of Albany was to set the stage for a dramatic revival of the civil rights revolution the following spring in Birmingham, Alabama. King was desperate to reclaim the initiative. On this occasion, he and his staff devoted more time to planning the mobilization of Black protestors than ever before. His efforts were enhanced by the on-the-ground heroics of Rev. Fred Shuttlesworth, the head of the Alabama Coalition for Human Rights. Now, together, King and Shuttlesworth sought to make Birmingham, which Blacks frequently called "Bombingham," the Gettysburg of the new civil war. For King, it was a now or never moment, the testing site for whether the civil rights movement could survive, grow, and force a national reckoning with racial injustice.

In truth, Birmingham proved pivotal not just because of King's planning, but because of the blatant cruelty of Birmingham's police commissioner, Bull Connor. No law enforcement official had a reputation for being as brutal, aggressive, and rapacious as Connor. In fact, he was the total opposite of Loren Pritchett.

King's initial recruitment of Black protestors from Birmingham proved less productive than he had anticipated. The movement in Birmingham was demanding desegregation of hotels, department stores, and public schools. But despite the planning done by SCLC staff, fewer activists came out to march. The initial confrontations of civil rights demonstrators with police proved less brutal than anticipated. Indeed, some within the movement began to question whether Birmingham might become another Albany.

But then everything changed—literally overnight. Starting in late April, young people, on their own, flocked to the demonstrations. Some were middle school students—aged nine to thirteen. Others came from high schools that they were boycotting in solidarity with the movement, and in protest against Birmingham's Jim Crow establishment. Most dramatically, Bull Connor consciously decided to pummel the young people. Rejecting Laurie Pritchett's example of meeting nonviolent protest with nonviolent police arrests, Connor unleashed vicious reprisals against the demonstrators. Connor sicced police dogs on children, knocking them to the ground and attacking them. He called out fire trucks and had them crush protestors with searing blasts of water, aimed with such pressure and force that even the largest, healthiest adults were thrown to the pavement. Television cameras recorded it all—with children hurled through the air by the fire hoses, and sixth graders viciously attacked by police dogs. Every evening, network news broadcasts scandalized Americans—and people watching around the world—as peaceful young people were brutalized. The entire nation was transfixed. Even the most complacent Northerners living in all-white suburbs, who never in their lives had experienced the remotest sympathy for civil rights demonstrators, were repulsed. "A newspaper or television picture of a snarling police dog set upon a human being," wrote the CBS news commentator Eric Sevareid, "is recorded in the permanent photoelectric file of every human being."[18]

No longer could the Kennedy establishment remain silent. At the White House and Justice Department, staff members at every level brought pressure to bear on Birmingham's political and economic leadership. Working behind the scenes, Justice Department officials carried on delicate negotiations between civil rights leaders and business executives seeking a comprehensive. agreement. Yet the crisis continued to intensify, with Birmingham's mayor denouncing whites who negotiated with Blacks as "a bunch of gutless traitors." At the same time, Birmingham's white extremists, encouraged by Connor, resorted to bombings, fire, and riots to block any possibility of compromise. As the protests escalated and grew more violent, the Kennedy administration—despite its lobbying efforts—recognized that direct action was necessary. When Alabama governor George Wallace pledged to "stand in the door" to block the admission of Black students to the University of Alabama, Kennedy ordered the mobilization of federal troops at Tuscaloosa, while intensively lobbying Alabama's business leaders to work for compliance with federal judicial decrees on desegregation.[19]

The confrontation between Birmingham officials, civil rights leaders, and the Kennedy administration had now reached fever pitch. King had been arrested and was being castigated by moderate white church leaders for being too militant. In response, King wrote, in longhand, his *Letter from a Birmingham Jail*, perhaps the most passionate and eloquent denunciation of white moderates ever issued by a protest leader. What would Jesus do in this situation?, King pointedly asked. With excoriating precision, King declared that the "Negro's great stumbling block in the stride toward freedom is not the White Citizens Counciler or the KKKer, but the white moderate who is more devoted to 'order' than to justice, . . . who paternalistically feels that he can set the timetable for another man's freedom." Every day, more and more, events drove all sides toward crisis and confrontation.[20]

By the end of May, events came to a head. The Kennedy brothers met nearly every day with leaders of national chain stores, hotel executives, and restaurant conglomerates to pressure them to desegregate their Southern outlets. Slowly they began to comply, fearing even greater disruptions if they failed to compromise. JFK kept up the pressure, sending letters of thanks to those who cooperated while ratcheting up his campaign against those who resisted.

Now in a new mode, the president chose to go public, addressing the nation on national television and placing himself, for the first time, solidly and *personally* behind the civil rights movement. Kennedy did so against the advice of virtually his entire cabinet. But he was emboldened by the success the young Birmingham demonstrators had achieved in rallying the entire country in protest against Bull Connor's brutality. Kennedy's speechwriters had not even finished a draft of his presentation when he went on the air, so his words were all the more dramatic because they were largely extemporaneous.

Civil rights, JFK began, was above all "a moral issue, . . . as old as the Scriptures . . . and as clear as the Constitution." The foundation of America, he continued, was "the principle that all men are created equal, and that the rights of every man are diminished when the rights of one man are threatened." Kennedy went on to itemize the steps necessary to be true to that national ideal: to have schools open to students of any color; to provide equal access to food in restaurants, rooms in hotels, seats in theaters; and to ensure the right to vote in all elections without fear of reprisal. But today, Kennedy declared, "this is not the case. . . . We preach freedom around the world and we mean it . . . but are we to say to the world, and much more important to each other, that this is the land of the free, *except* for Negroes; that we have no second class citizens, *except* Negroes; that we have no class or caste system, no ghettoes, no master race *except* with respect to Negroes?" It was as if Frederick Douglass were alive, and speaking from the Oval Office.

Then, with a passionate plea, Kennedy concluded his address. "Who among us," he asked, "would be content to have the color of his skin changed and stand in [the Negro's] place? Who among us would then be content with the counsels of patience and delay?" Reversing his own rhetorical position of the previous thirty months, Kennedy declared that the time had come for "the nation to fulfill its promise. . . . A great change is at hand, and our task, our obligation, is to make that *revolution*, that change, peaceful and constructive for all."[21]

The shift in Kennedy's position was enormous. For the first time, a president had embraced almost all of the demands of civil right demonstrators. The legislation he then proposed—to end discrimination in employment, to guarantee equal access to public accommodations, to support Justice Department initiatives on school desegregation—would still need to be strengthened over the next year of debate. But the most important reality was that—finally—the civil rights movement had compelled a president to make a commitment neither he nor any previous president had been willing to make. Over the next six weeks, Kennedy met with nearly 1,600 leaders from religious, labor, business and women's groups, enlisting their support for his proposed legislation and their cooperation in establishing biracial committees in their own communities in support of desegregation. For a person who had for so long avoided taking sides, it was a decisive moment—first because it was right, and second, because Kennedy no longer had the option of avoiding a choice. The civil rights movement had forced JFK to act, and—finally—he had responded.[22]

Significantly, in the next two days Kennedy undertook other dramatic initiatives. Ever since the Cuban Missile Crisis, when against the advice of most of his cabinet and military he had refused to bomb or invade Cuba, and instead had sought a peaceful solution in collaboration with Russia, Kennedy had become less a cold warrior and more an ambassador for peace. Now, at American University in Washington, he totally reversed the hawkishness of his inaugural address in which he railed against the Soviet Union—"We will fight any war, at any time, to preserve freedom." Instead, he told the students at the university, there was "no nation without virtue." The time had come for peace, he declared, launching a campaign for a nuclear test ban treaty, and a new era of accommodation. The next day Kennedy announced his support for a war on poverty, for the first time acknowledging that income inequality and class restrictions were a direct threat to the American Dream.

But on no issue was Kennedy's change more dramatic or bold than on civil rights. Black activists had forced him to move dramatically forward, and now, it seemed, a new presidency had begun.

Reflections

There remained miles to go, and countless obstacles to be overcome. Six months after the start of the Birmingham campaign, and two and a half months after Kennedy's televised embrace of civil rights reform speech, the March on Washington on August 28, 1963, brought over a quarter of a million whites and Blacks together to dramatize the demand for racial equality. "We shall overcome" became the new byword of activists, Black and white, old and young, women and men.

A new era had begun. As had happened repeatedly in the past, the threat of that new era energized reactionary conservative interests. The same night as Kennedy's speech to the nation on civil rights, civil rights leader Medgar Evers was gunned down in his driveway in Jackson, Mississippi. And President Kennedy's embrace of new possibilities on racial justice, world peace, and income equality was cut short by an assassin's bullet in November 1963.

But a dramatic breakthrough had occurred. It was the direct product of decades of grassroots activism among Black Americans. To be sure, the tactics were new, the slogans and movement singing a departure from the past. But the struggle for racial equality that had been waged for years by Blacks, now supplemented by young activists from SNCC—and their compatriots in struggle from the

NAACP, CORE, and SCLC—had given the president no choice but to embrace, for the first time, the cause of racial equality. What would happen in the future remained uncertain. But finally, after generations of protest, Black activists had finally forced the struggle into a new stage of engagement.

Chapter 11

Winning the Right to Vote, Coming Apart in the Process

The March on Washington in August 1963 was an iconic moment in the struggle for racial equality in America. A quarter million people gathered on the Washington Mall. They were white and Black, they carried American flags, they sang Freedom Songs, and they were entertained by renowned singers like Pete Seeger and Joan Baez. At the end, they heard a powerful exhortation by Martin Luther King Jr., soon to be immortalized as his "I Have a Dream" speech. Then, having finished the afternoon with a resounding chorus of "We Shall Overcome," most marchers left the nation's capital to return to their homes, hundreds, if not thousands, of miles away. The leaders of the March, in turn, went to the White House to have teas with President Kennedy.

That is one version of what occurred that summer afternoon.

Another, behind the scenes, proved to be less iconic, more real, and powerfully suggestive of ongoing tensions within the movement itself, and between Black activists and the Kennedy administration. The March had initially been planned as a multi-day occupation of Washington, including sit-ins at the Capitol. The administration insisted, instead, that the March be limited to a one-day affair. People would arrive in the morning and leave by sunset. All liquor stores were closed, suggesting to many a deep suspicion on the part of the executive branch that civil rights activists could not be trusted to act with discipline. Deep fissures split people organizing the March, with more conservative civil rights groups forcing SNCC leader John Lewis to delete from his speech any criticism of Washington's politicians, Democrats or Republicans. More radical leftists in the movement—and nearly all women—were kept from assuming any significant role, lest they challenge more cautious moderates.

Even King's resounding speech was almost an accident. The SCLC leader resorted to the sermon he had given many times before when his original speech fell flat, and Mahalia Jackson, one of his followers on stage, yelled to him, "Tell them about your *dream*, Martin." Divisions within the movement were rife, and the Washington administration's insistence on controlling every aspect of the day, even the culminating event of a White House tea—all suggested a very different interpretation of what was actually taking place that warm summer afternoon.

Those tensions would remain. Even as the sanitized picture of the March became pivotal to the eventual enactment of the Civil Rights Act of 1964 and the Voting Rights Act of 1965, the divisions within the movement, and between civil rights activists and the government, spoke to larger realities that would persist for generations to come. Far from representing the highlight of a movement approaching its culmination, the March spoke just as powerfully to ongoing tensions inside the struggle—tensions between Northern and Western Blacks and Southern Blacks, between advocates who sought Black autonomy and those who focused on working with the white "establishment," and, above all, between those who sought a transformation of the social and economic system and those who sought simply to become *part* of "the system."

The comments of various Black leaders highlighted the different opinions of the March. Roy Wilkins, head of the NAACP for decades, referenced the 100th anniversary of the Emancipation Proclamation as he spoke about Black successes. Negro Americans, he said, had "amassed billions of dollars of property" and contributed "immeasurably to the economic growth of [America]." By contrast, James Baldwin, prophetic Black critic and author of the sensational polemic

The Fire Next Time, decried the platitudes of white liberals, while warning of impending riots in Harlem. "We talk endlessly about progress and chatter about the future," he noted, "because we are afraid to pay the price of change in the present." Laying bare the differences, Malcolm X, the young insurgent leader of the Nation of Islam, in a subsequent article called the March on Washington a "circus." The next few years would highlight the dramatic contrast between these different points of view.[1]

Divisions within the Movement

The schism between SNCC and SCLC was there from the beginning. When SNCC was formed in April 1960, Ella Baker already had a shrewd understanding of the differences. "Black ministers," she later recalled, "always like to be at the center of things, but they tend to be conservative and have to be prodded." Despite Baker's brilliance as an organizer, SCLC's executive leadership always kept her on the margins, never giving her the authority or independence normally expected from an executive officer. Male preachers did not wish to be told what to do, especially by a woman who pushed back when ministers tried to order her around. Reflecting on the birth of SNCC one month after the conference organized by Ella Baker at Shaw University in April 1960, Baker noted that the students had made it "crystal clear" from the beginning "that the current sit-ins . . . are concerned with something much bigger than a hamburger or even a giant-sized Coke." Hence, Baker wrote, they opted for a "group-centered leadership, rather than a leader-centered pattern of organization." Pledging to "keep the movement democratic," they feared that "adults might try to 'capture' the student movement." Thus they "were intolerant of anything that smacked of manipulation or domination." In a not too veiled reference to Dr. King, Baker even warned that frustration and disillusionment could occur "when the prophetic leader turns out to have heavy feet of clay."[2]

In fact, Dr. King and the students of SNCC started out with very different perspectives. King sought to use his brilliance as a preacher to reach out to whites—and especially white Christians—across the country, threading the needle to bring them into a multiracial coalition, united by a common faith and a desire to reform the country according to the American Dream and the Gospel of Jesus. Later, of course, he became more outspokenly radical, especially when, in the late 1960s, he openly turned against the Vietnam War and endorsed a radical redistribution of income. But in the early 1960s, he sought reform and conciliation above all else, believing that only a coalition with middle-class whites could secure change from the powers that ruled the nation. Moreover, by definition, SCLC, the Southern Christian *Leadership* Conference, operated as a top-down organization, controlled by a circle of pastoral leaders.

SNCC, by contrast, focused on mobilizing Black citizens to confront white authorities directly, and fight from the bottom up. Courtland Cox, an early SNCC activist who had joined the movement as a Howard University student, zeroed in on the difference. "SNCC did not particularly like authority," he noted, "we loved conversation [and] did not like hierarchical decisions. . . . It was the culture. We wanted bottom-up decisions . . . with people being in conversation until consensus was reached." Instead of seeking to work *with* the establishment, SNCC sought to *transform* it, to make the people in power listen to those without power, and to use those voices to create a more just and racially equal society.

The SNCC mode of action was quickly established. After working for a few months in SNCC's Atlanta office, Bob Moses—a New Yorker who had been teaching in a prep school before joining SNCC—headed off to Cleveland, Mississippi. He immediately contacted Amzie Moore, the Black storekeeper who was a leader in the community. With Moore's assistance, Moses contacted Black families throughout the community, and soon mobilized a group of Black citizens to go to the courthouse and try to register to vote. When Moses himself was beaten up by an angry white man, he had the courage to bring charges against the individual. Although there was no chance of winning a conviction, Moses had demonstrated his courage and steadfastness. Moses continued his grass roots organizing in the community—from the ground up—and soon was joined by SNCC workers in similar small towns throughout Mississippi. It was a different kind of organizing than that of SCLC.

Early on, SNCC learned to distrust the law enforcement in local Southern communities. In small towns all across the Delta counties of Mississippi and Southwest Georgia, SNCC workers had experienced the cruelty, barbarity, and racial intolerance of whites who wielded power. They also became increasingly angry at the refusal of the federal government to intervene on their behalf. In Walthall County, Mississippi, not a single Black out of three thousand eligible Black citizens could cast a ballot. When a SNCC worker took two Blacks to register to vote, the registrar declared that SNCC had "no right to mess in the 'nigger's' business," then cracked the worker over the head with his pistol and arrested him. When Hartman Turnbow, a legendary SNCC figure, tried to register in Milestone, Mississippi, whites threw a Molotov cocktail into his house. Then, when the family fled, the whites fired their guns at those who were fleeing. How did local law enforcement officials respond? Sheriff's deputies proceeded to arrest SNCC workers for arson.

In Ruleville, Mississippi, Fannie Lou Hamer, having worked and lived on a white-owned plantation for decades, was inspired by SNCC organizers to go and register to vote. That night, she later noted, the owner of the plantation "asked me why I went to register. I told him I did it for myself, not for him." Immediately, the owner evicted Hamer from her home and told her never "to be seen near it again." Shortly thereafter, Hamer was forced off a bus, taken to jail, and viciously beaten by police, who inflicted injuries so severe that she never fully recovered. From that point forward, Hamer became a legendary leader of the movement, speaking for the masses of Black people who constituted its base.[3]

As poverty became ever more oppressive, Black America's struggle for racial justice became more and more entwined with the struggle for social and economic justice. When Lyndon Johnson took office after JFK's assassination, 55 percent of Blacks lived below the poverty line. SNCC workers soon recognized that ending poverty was just as important as obtaining the right to vote. True racial justice would come only with a redistribution of wealth and income. As SNCC workers came into daily contact with people earning under $500 a year, they recognized—as did Ella Baker—that just as important as having the right to buy a hamburger was having the money to afford one.[4]

All during these years, SNCC activists were deeply cynical about the good faith of America's white leaders. President Kennedy may have finally come through with a passionate commitment to civil rights after Bull Connor brutalized young Black demonstrators in Birmingham. But no matter how many times SNCC activists filed affidavits with the Department of Justice, only rarely was there any response—a pattern that, to SNCC workers, conveyed a message of callous neglect of Black rights from those theoretically committed to protecting those rights. They lived day to day in situations that amounted to brutal combat with a mortal enemy. The assurance that federal authorities would take action *later* meant to SNCC activists that the American government had no intention of confronting *now* the brutality being meted out by white racists. It was hardly surprising, then, that even as Dr. King was trying to cultivate support from white liberals and moderates, SNCC workers perceived *confrontation* with whites as the only way to make change happen. As King sought to cultivate the nation as a whole, SNCC activists struggled to simply survive the brutality of local whites, even as federal officials silently stood by. Caught in this seemingly unresolvable dilemma, SNCC searched for a way to force a change in the federal government's stance. No matter how many Blacks were brutally beaten—or killed—in small Mississippi towns, federal agents seemed totally indifferent.

In the fall of 1963, SNCC activists saw a glimmer of hope. In order to dramatize the desire of Blacks to vote in Mississippi, SNCC conducted a "Freedom Vote" in November. Even though they were not registered, more than eighty thousand Negroes turned out at polling places in churches and community centers throughout Mississippi to demonstrate that—contrary to white claims that Blacks did not care about politics—in fact they wanted fervently to be full and equal citizens. Allard Lowenstein, a white liberal activist, helped develop the idea. In response to his effort to rally collegiate student support, scores of white volunteers from non-Southern elite colleges like Yale and Stanford journeyed to Mississippi to help facilitate the "Freedom Vote." Their presence appeared to generate greater press coverage. Reflecting on that experience, Lowenstein proposed that hundreds more white volunteers come to Mississippi after school was out to create a "Freedom Summer" in 1964 that would help further the cause of racial justice.[5]

SNCC members were deeply divided over the idea. People like Bob Moses, Stokely Carmichael, and Hartman Turnbow were concerned that Northern whites would be insensitive to Southern Blacks and try to take charge of the movement. On the other hand, they were keenly aware that a white presence in the Mississippi movement might increase dramatically the likelihood of the federal government becoming more involved. Bob Moses pondered the dilemma intensely, consumed by personal doubt. He understood that if a white Harvard student were killed by white racists, it could make a huge impact on the nation—both in terms of publicity and in terms of White House reaction. On the other hand, he felt deeply the personal responsibility of inviting white volunteers into a brutal and threatening environment, where violence and death were inevitable.

In the end, Moses and his fellow SNCC activists took the path that made the most sense politically. Blacks had suffered for years in Mississippi without triggering *any* federal intervention. If it took violence—even the murder of a Northern white—to provoke that intervention, Moses and his brethren concluded that the risk was worth taking.[6]

As a result, in the spring of 1964, SNCC and the Council of Federated Organizations, their partners in Mississippi, sent out a call for white volunteers from the North and West to join them for Freedom Summer. More than a thousand white students responded—women as well as men. Most came from elite campuses—the Ivy League, Smith, Bryn Mawr, Wisconsin, Stanford, Berkeley. Lowenstein eventually abandoned the task of recruiting volunteers. Always suspicious of left-wing influences, he worried that people who were Marxists would play too large a role in Freedom Summer. But an amazing assemblage of volunteers did sign up. While many brought with them a dangerous (and usually unconscious) assumption that, as bright Northerners, they knew best how to run the movement, many others understood that they should look to local Blacks—those who understood the situation from the inside out—for leadership and direction. By early June, the white students were ready to journey south to Mississippi. Some would teach in day care centers; others would organize Freedom Schools; but the project that garnered the most attention was the creation of the Mississippi Freedom Democratic Party (MFDP). Through statewide recruitment of Blacks and some whites, the MFDP planned to develop an alternative to the existing Democratic establishment. It would challenge the legitimacy of an all-white delegation to represent Mississippi Democrats at the Democratic National Convention in Atlantic City in August 1964.[7]

It took only a few days for the strategic rationale for Freedom Summer to become a reality. While scores of white volunteers were going through orientation and instruction at Miami University in Oxford, Ohio, word reached the gathering that three SNCC workers had disappeared in Philadelphia, Mississippi. One, James Chaney, was a Black SNCC worker from Mississippi. The other two were white volunteers from New York. Michael Schwerner and Andrew Goodman had gone to progressive private schools all their lives. They exemplified the idealism, commitment, and elite background of those who had volunteered for Freedom Summer.

Chaney, Schwerner, and Goodman had journeyed to Philadelphia to work on voter registration. They were quickly arrested and taken to jail. After hours of intense questioning, they were released. But immediately—and in collaboration with Philadelphia's law enforcement officials—a carload of whites followed their car as they drove away. The SNCC volunteers were never heard from again. Many weeks later, their bodies were found near the Tallahatchee River, brutally ravaged, body parts missing.[8] It had taken mere days for Bob Moses's fears, and the political gamble they reflected, to become a reality.

As Moses had understood from the beginning, the killing of white students from elite Northern environments immediately made a difference. Federal officials crowded into the state. No longer were KKK members absolutely free to do as they wished; the country now learned from newspapers and television what was taking place in Mississippi on a daily basis. Violence against Blacks was still rampant, but now an FBI agent was nearby, and at least on occasion, did more than simply take notes.[9]

In Washington, too, there was a turn. Whatever else one might say about Lyndon Johnson's topsy-turvy political career—the press joked about his eighty-seven-vote "mandate" when he won his Senate election in 1948 after a late, Johnson-controlled county suddenly turned in his near unanimous plurality—no one could dispute his consummate abilities as a political wheeler-dealer. Elected majority leader of the Senate in 1954, he brilliantly played his strengths against his enemy's weaknesses. Sometimes placating potential allies, at other times acting as a bully, he almost always got his way.

Now, in the summer of 1964 and from the Oval Office in the White House, he displayed all his talents in putting together a bipartisan coalition to enact the 1964 Civil Rights Act. First introduced by Kennedy five months before his assassination, the bill initially encountered fierce partisan opposition. But LBJ knew how to woo as well as chastise his opponents. On an almost nightly basis, he brought Republican leader Everett Dirksen to the White House for a glass (or two) of his favorite Scotch whiskey. Brilliantly, he played up the importance of seeking bipartisan unity on a measure that spoke to the very identity—and survival—of the American republic. At the same time, he worked with Republican allies of the civil rights movement such as Jacob Javits of New York to put pressure on Dirksen from within his own party. Southern segregationist and Johnson's close friend Richard Russell marveled at the president's shrewdness, his ability to know just what to say to persuade a fence-sitter to move to his side. Even as Mississippi was imploding during Freedom Summer, LBJ delivered the biggest political victory that the civil rights movement had ever won. In July 1964, by a decisive majority, Congress passed a comprehensive Civil Rights Act. It ended all discrimination in hiring for jobs, barring discrimination based on gender as well as race; it opened all public accommodations—restaurants, toilets, movie theaters—to Blacks on an equal basis with whites; and it significantly enhanced the powers of the federal Equal Employment Opportunity division.

Now, there would be a pivotal federal presence in Southern states around issues of race, mandated by congressional legislation. No longer were civil rights advocates limited to petitioning for help. A former senator from a Southern state, Johnson had accomplished—brilliantly—what perhaps no other white politician could have done.[10]

Yet, as in all things political—especially at a time of unprecedented volatility—poor judgment could also follow quickly after wisdom, especially if one's ego and obsession about control took precedence over the substantive merits of an issue. That, in effect, is what occurred when Lyndon Johnson set out to derail the MFDP initiative.

With increasing intensity through the summer, SNCC had focused most of its energies on building the Mississippi Freedom Democratic Party. Volunteers, white and Black, scoured the state. They held rallies, signed up volunteers, built their own Black political infrastructure. They collected affidavits from Black citizens who had repeatedly been denied the right to register. Each district elected delegates who would go to Atlantic City to represent the MFDP at the Democratic National Convention. They documented the near-unanimous sentiment of the white Democratic delegation to Atlantic City to support Barry Goldwater, the right-wing Republican nominee, over the presumed Democratic nominee, Lyndon Johnson, in the November election. The white Mississippi delegation was headed by a former governor who had described the NAACP as "niggers, alligators, apes, coons and possums." How could the Democratic convention seat delegates pledged to Goldwater who used such language?

People working for SNCC and the MFDP had already contacted numerous delegates who would serve on the credentials committee at the Democratic convention. They were assured that they had more than enough votes to bring the issue to the floor of the convention. When that happened, they believed, the MFDP would carry the day and would be able to seat the MFDP delegates as the *true* representatives of the state of Mississippi.

But LBJ was not about to let that happen. If one side of Johnson exemplified political brilliance, the other side exuded profound insecurity. Johnson felt an almost pathological need to be in total control, never to allow others—especially those who might seek to take power away from him—to ever be granted any legitimacy. Johnson deeply feared competition from those he felt inferior to—the Kennedy brothers, for example, their close aides, those who might get in the way of his having everything his way—which is why he made sure that Bobby Kennedy's speech to the convention would occur *after* LBJ had been selected as the party's candidate, so that there could be no chance of a spontaneous clamor for Bobby to be the nominee in the aftermath of his speech. Johnson wanted the presidential nomination by acclamation. He was terrified of any controversy that might get in the way, distract delegate attention, or harness energies that might interfere with his hope for a convention that totally focused on celebrating his presidency. As a result, LBJ was "almost hysterical" over the threat posed by the MFDP, according to LBJ biographer Robert Dallek.[11]

The MFDP fight, Johnson believed, would direct attention to an issue of profound ethical as well as political import. It might well attract support from people who, Johnson feared, could be susceptible to a last-minute presidential challenge from Robert F. Kennedy, the person he feared most among the Kennedys, but also the person who carried the charisma and the moral commitment to racial justice that might trigger a spontaneous ground-floor campaign to make *him* the presidential nominee. Hence, from day one, Johnson was intent on denying the MFDP a chance to have its issues even debated on the floor. LBJ was willing to assure the MFDP that four years later, it would be fully represented at the Democratic convention. But he was convinced that "giving in" to civil rights activists now would alienate the white South, cause the loss of several states to Goldwater, and—in the long run—do more harm to the struggle for racial justice than good. In short, the same man who proved indispensable to enactment of the Civil Rights Act of 1964 did everything in his power a month later to prevent recognition of the MFDP, or even to have an open discussion of the right of Mississippi Blacks to be recognized and represented at his convention.

LBJ's response was excessive. On the pretense that some MFDP activists might be subversives, Johnson ordered the FBI to put listening devices in the hotel rooms that SNCC people occupied. At the same time, he had all of their phones wiretapped. To prevent delegates to the credentials committee from voting to bring the MFDP to the floor for debate, he had his aides call pro-MFDP delegates and threaten to have their friends and relatives who worked for federal agencies fired from their jobs. Indeed, leaders of the credentials committee were told that voting against the MFDP petition was *the* litmus test of loyalty to the president.[12]

Two interventions, in particular, underscored the extent of Johnson's obsession. The first occurred when Fannie Lou Hamer, already a legend in the Mississippi civil rights movement, was testifying before the credentials committee in a proceeding that was broadcast on national television. Hamer was passionate, eloquent, and spellbinding. When he saw her live on television, Johnson called an emergency press conference on a matter of national urgency to force the networks to drop coverage of Hamer's testimony and shift to the White House press room. In fact, all LBJ talked about in his press conference was a prospective international treaty. The issue was neither urgent nor important, but Hamer's televised testimony had been taken off the air. LBJ had successfully—and deceitfully—removed from the TV networks someone who might have generated significant support for the MFDP challenge.

The second intervention was even more eerie. Johnson called Hubert Humphrey. He told Humphrey he wanted him to be his vice-presidential running mate—but only on the condition that Humphrey persuade his liberal followers on the credentials committee to vote against bringing the MFDP issue to the floor of the convention for debate. Caught between his personal convictions and his political aspirations, Humphrey did as he was told. His entire political future depended on it. And he reasoned to himself that he could repay the civil rights movement in other ways, later on. In the end, he delivered the votes. Previously confident, with good reason, that they had more than enough support to force a floor debate, MFDP supporters now discovered that Johnson, through intimidation and wheeling and dealing, had crushed their hopes. The credentials committee now passed a resolution recommending that the MFDP be given two delegate slots—to be named by the party, not the MFDP—and that the previously selected all-white Mississippi delegation should be seated.[13]

SNCC and the leaders of the MFDP were furious. They had been scammed. All their hard work—securing affidavits, documenting their town-by-town efforts to register voters and become part of the Democratic Party—had been discarded, ignored, buried. Above all they felt totally disrespected—scorned. And who made it all happen? Lyndon Johnson, the hero who had brought to final fruition the 1964 Civil Rights Act.

At the heart of the matter was the issue that ran through the entire history of Blacks confronting white supremacy, Jim Crow, and the denial of equal rights. It was the issue of agency. Who was in control of the civil rights movement? Who started it, suffered for it, died for it, and succeeded in bringing it to the forefront of America's agenda? What did equal rights mean if a president could intervene, take over, and undercut everything the movement was about? While from Lyndon Johnson's long-range "white" political perspective, it made sense to defer equal representation for the MFDP in the Democratic convention—after all, hadn't he, a white president from the South, delivered on the Civil Rights Act?—from the perspective of SNCC and other Black activists, Johnson's behavior was a classic example of white hegemony, an insistence, that, once again, white power and privilege were all that mattered. White leaders—not Blacks—would make the final decisions on Black autonomy and racial justice.

There was never any chance that SNCC and the MFDP would play Johnson's game. Churches were still being bombed, young demonstrators still being brutalized. Even as the convention met, MFDP headquarters in Tupelo, Mississippi, burned to the ground, set afire by whites carrying cans of gasoline. Yet in the midst of this, some white liberals, led by Hubert Humphrey, were claiming that their MFDP "compromise" of securing two delegate votes was the best thing since the emancipation proclamation. Martin Luther King Jr. assured SNCC that he had talked to Humphrey and that the prospective vice-presidential nominee had "promised me there would be a new day in Mississippi if you accepted the proposal." Others, like Bayard Rustin, urged SNCC to "go along." It was the politically smart thing to do. It would lead, later on, to white liberal support.

But SNCC was tired of "going along," of permitting white politicians, however liberal, from controlling their destiny. Angrily, one black MFDP delegate declared, "[This] compromise would let Jim Crow be. . . . Ain't no Democratic Party worth *that*. We've been treated like beasts. . . . They shot us down like animals. We risked our lives coming here. . . . Politics must be corrupt if it don't care about people [like us]." Fannie Lou Hamer—forced off the air by LBJ, and now told that she needed to go back home since she had made her point, summed it all up. "We didn't come all this way for no two votes."[14]

In its usual democratic way, SNCC convened a meeting to discuss the "compromise" and take a vote. Some more established civil rights groups argued for accepting the Humphrey proposal, pointing to the benefits of a long-term coalition with liberal white Democrats. MFDP delegates were not convinced. *They* had endured brutality that Northerners from Michigan and New York had never known. They had proceeded to do what they were supposed to do—collecting all the affidavits, organizing their own ranks, petitioning the appropriate committees, playing by the rules—only to be betrayed, not by white racists in Mississippi, but by supposed white liberal allies who presumed to speak for them.

In the end, these white liberal allies had marched to a different drummer. If politics meant forgoing protest and allowing someone else to tell you what course you should follow, SNCC would say no. Rejecting the compromise nearly unanimously, the entire MFDP delegation left Atlantic City, returning to Mississippi, riven by anger and confusion over whether ever again to trust white liberals in their struggle for freedom.[15]

The Aftermath

Disillusionment and anger spread quickly among SNCC activists in the months following Atlantic City. A number of SNCC's most thoughtful activists, including Bob Moses, decided to travel to Africa in the fall of 1964. They wanted time to think through, in a different political and cultural environment, the options they might pursue in the future. Many were attracted by the ideas of Pan-Africanism, variations of which had been present in America from the post–Civil War period through the Garvey movement of the 1920s, 1930s, and 1940s. What was most clear was that Atlantic

City had caused them to question their previous assumptions about working closely with white liberals, especially politicians. Some SNCC members remained in Africa for a lengthy period. Others, including Bob Moses, changed their names, taking on African names, as if, symbolically, to become a person different from who they had been in the past.[16]

Back at home, SNCC supporters in Mississippi reflected the same sense of uncertainty and disarray. Some members of the MFDP continued to work for change within the Mississippi Democratic Party, and in cooperation with white liberals, wherever they could be found. Others moved more toward separatism. In part, the tensions reflected the conflicts that developed during Freedom Summer between white volunteers for Freedom Summer and long-standing Black activists. In most cases, white students and Blacks had worked together, part of the "beloved community" that found, in their common struggle, powerful bonds of solidarity, affection, and communion.

Yet problems were also present. Without necessarily being aware of it, many whites from elite Northern colleges thought it natural to use all the skills they brought with them to "show" their less-educated brothers and sisters how to do a better job of writing press releases, or teaching in Freedom Schools. But whereas whites were there only for the summer and could leave at any time, Blacks had worked tirelessly for years, and were there for the duration.[17]

Conflict also developed within the movement over issues of interracial sex. Many white women were ready to sleep with their Black comrades—a sign of their solidarity and commitment to overcome racial differences. Yet many Black women found such interracial affairs problematic, to say the least.

Lying beneath all these tensions was a fear that because of differences in background, experience, and expertise, whites—even the "good, activist" whites from Freedom Summer—might try to take over their Black movement. As SNCC activist Courtland Cox noted, "After Atlantic City, it was clear to us that we were no longer . . . going to move the Democratic Party to do the right thing. We felt the need to rethink what we were doing and where we were going. Clearly, [after Atlantic City] we needed to find another direction." Echoing the same reaction, Charlie Cobb declared that in the aftermath of Atlantic City, "SNCC was struggling with its own sense of direction and its sense of what its mission should be."[18]

In the end, therefore, Freedom Summer exemplified both the extraordinary achievements that grassroots activists could achieve by coming together to fight for racial justice, and the underlying divisions of power and race that had been part of the fabric of America from the beginning. Nothing epitomized the ideal of American democracy—equal opportunity for all—more than Black and white students together, working with World War II veterans like Amzie Moore, to enroll all voters, white and Black, rich and poor, to vote in a fair election. On the other hand, nothing epitomized the difficulty of achieving that ideal more than the assertion of privilege and status that whites refused to give up, either within the movement, or in the halls of government. Whether the battle for a true democratic republic committed to racial justice could ever be won remained an open question.

The Future

In the meantime, more and more Blacks in the North and Midwest were calling into question the whole idea of an integrated society in which Blacks and whites could work together in harmony. Was that a good idea in the first place? In the 1950s, Elijah Muhammad had begun an organization called the Nation of Islam (NOI). Composed of Blacks who pledged themselves to the Muslim faith, it spread rapidly through the Midwest and Northeast, galvanizing hundreds of thousands of Black followers who believed that racial separatism, not integration, represented the path that Blacks should pursue, with Black Muslims building their own structures of faith, community, and political advocacy.

Central to the burgeoning success of the NOI was the leadership of Malcolm X. The son of parents who had been staunch followers of Marcus Garvey's United Negro Improvement Association, Malcolm had experienced a troubled childhood. Both his parents died when he was young, and although Malcolm quickly became a popular leader in high school, he then got caught up in an urban gang. In 1946, when he was just twenty-one years of age, he was arrested for burglary, and sentenced to serve six years in jail.

By the time he was released from prison in 1952, Malcolm had already become inspired by the teachings of Elijah Muhammad and the NOI. Within months, he had become the leading lieutenant of Elijah's rapidly expanding movement. Charismatic, shrewd, and inspiring, he attracted a myriad of followers—first in Detroit, then in Philadelphia, and finally in New York. Blacks should take pride in themselves, he preached, not petition to join whites in biracial coalitions. Whites would always lord it over Blacks, he insisted, and would never give up power. In the face of racism that knew no bounds, Malcolm and his fellow Black Muslims declared, only those Blacks who took pride in their race, proclaimed their separate religion, and advanced their own cause had any chance of achieving equality.

On numerous occasions, Malcolm went to Africa, joining his fellow Muslims in Ghana and Ethiopia to attend conferences that emphasized the importance of racial autonomy and independence. Wherever he went, the number of his followers grew; his activities generated widespread publicity and controversy. Here was an urban, politically shrewd leader who inspired all who came into his presence to embrace his doctrine of separatism and strength. Malcolm's message seemed directly opposed to that of Martin Luther King Jr. Malcolm avoided direct confrontation with King, and in 1963, when the two met at the March on Washington, each sought to be supportive of the other, and not to tear each other apart. But there could be little question that the fundamental messages of the two movements went in opposite directions.

Eventually, Malcolm became so popular that Elijah Muhammad saw him as a direct threat to his own prestige and power. Malcolm had converted to Sunni Islam after his trip to Mecca. Now, Muhammad removed Malcolm from the leadership of his mosque in December 1964, and then ordered his lieutenants to sabotage Malcolm's organizing efforts. The two became archenemies, each threatening the other's well-being and sustainability. On more than one occasion, Malcolm barely avoided overt, physical confrontations with Elijah's troops. Then, at a rally at the Audubon Ballroom in New York City on February 21, 1965, a gang of Elijah's supporters disrupted Malcolm's speech with a smoke bomb, and as Malcolm struggled to bring the crowd to order, three of Elijah's gang crept toward the stage and sent a bullet through his chest.[19]

Thus by the spring of 1965, greater tensions fragmented the Black struggle for freedom than ever before. The grassroots activism of SNCC workers had helped inundate Mississippi, the most racist state in the nation. With acute sensitivity and ambivalence, Bob Moses had agreed to bring white Northerners into the state for Freedom Summer. The murder of whites, and Blacks, by Mississippi racists had brought the kind of federal intervention that was pivotal for any forward progress to occur. But Lyndon Johnson's almost paranoid fear of losing control of his party and his future caused him to alienate Mississippi's freedom workers over the MFDP in Atlantic City, and inspire renewed fears among SNCC activists about white influence over the movement. At the same time, a renewed and vibrant Black Muslim movement, led by the charismatic Malcolm X, called into question the whole idea of the value of integration as a movement goal.

After a year of unprecedented successes in galvanizing the nation's attention to the issue of racial justice, the question now became whether the movement could withstand and triumph over the divisions that threatened its ranks.

Chapter 12

Triumph and Division

"[Our] people felt that they could do anything," SNCC activist Worth Long declared. In 1963 he went to Selma, Alabama, to head SNCC efforts there. But Selma proved to be a difficult terrain for the movement. By 1965, many of the deep divisions within the civil rights movement came to a head during the voting rights campaign there. As weeks went by, SNCC began to share their effort to secure voting rights with SCLC. Martin Luther King Jr. hoped to attract the same kind of national publicity to Selma that had proved so transformative in Birmingham during the spring of 1963. Although SNCC's leaders wanted to pursue a more grassroots approach than King, they reluctantly agreed to have their supporters join King's followers in a proposed march from Selma to Montgomery in March 1965.

In most respects, King's plan for a larger movement on voting rights proved to be on target. As Black activists crossed the Edmund Pettus Bridge outside of Selma, police on horseback who were gathered on the other side plowed into the line of marchers, knocking them to the ground. Police beat the marchers brutally with batons, and trampled their bodies. Their response was even crueler than Bull Connor's brutality in Birmingham. Bleeding, limping, and with terror in their eyes, the marchers retreated to the Black church they had left just minutes earlier All of this was captured by the national media. On first glance, at least, it looked as though King were in the process of creating exactly the same confrontation with white racists that had happened two years earlier.[1]

But before long, the difference between SNCC's grassroots approach and King's focus on building a national biracial coalition came into profound conflict. SNCC followers wanted to challenge the Alabama police immediately by marching across the bridge again. State authorities announced that they would once again block such a march. At this critical moment, a federal court handed down an injunction against a renewed march. The federal government—as might have been expected—supported the court's action.

What would King and SCLC do? It was here that the recurrent conflict between King's desire to stay on the side of the federal court system and SNCC's determination to confront police brutality directly came into conflict. King hoped to enlist LBJ on his side, which meant *not* challenging the federal courts. Given King's experience—and his success in Birmingham—his approach made sense. But SNCC did not care. Sensitivity to the preferences of the establishment might have proven persuasive in the past, but not after the betrayal of LBJ and his followers at the Democratic convention in Atlantic City. If nothing else, LBJ's oppressive tactics in Atlantic City confirmed that he could not be trusted. In the end, King decided to respond *his* way. He would organize another march, and be in the front ranks as it crossed the first part of the bridge. But this time, when the police ordered the marchers to stop, invoking the court injunction against the march, King turned around, and ordered his fellow marchers to return to Selma. From King's point of view, he was carrying his message as far as he could without further endangering the marchers, or his ongoing relations with LBJ and the federal government. Yet from SNCC's perspective, King had turned his back on the indigenous movement they had helped advance in Selma, and showed that when faced with a federal court order, he would not alienate the white liberal establishment. It was a powerful moment—one that in the end magnified the divisions that were growing inside the movement.

Once civil rights activists returned to Selma from the Pettus Bridge, they continued to build support for their movement. King and other civil rights leaders waited while the courts deliberated on their right to march. Discussions continued on how a march from Selma to Montgomery could be used to focus national attention on federal legislation to guarantee Blacks the right to vote. Eventually, the courts cleared the path for the march to proceed. Yet the tensions between SNCC workers and SCLC continued to fester.

Thus, even as the civil rights movement appeared to be in the process of achieving another great success—at least from the point of view of the national media—its internal relations were crumbling, in greater danger of implosion than ever before. To the national TV audience, the movement still seemed to be one, a model of unity and triumph. Yet those serving in the trenches experienced growing rancor, division, and estrangement. As one Northern white volunteer wrote on returning from Montgomery:

> The major gap between King and SNCC is that [SNCC workers] do the grassroots work, prepare the way, clean up afterwards, and get neither the credit nor the results they seek, because King . . . always compromises. SNCC is the vanguard of a revolution which seeks to transform the system while King seems to be in the middle of an effort to reform it. In the televised proceedings at Montgomery, Ralph Abernathy . . . at no point bothered to thank SNCC for all the organizational dirty work it had done. The liberal smoothly clad visitors from the North dominated the proceedings and [SNCC's] James Forman, in his dungarees, was given one minute [to speak].[2]

Such comments indicated how deep the divisions in the movement had become, rather than highlighting King's complex role in advancing civil rights. In the end, King's strategy of not alienating the powers in Washington produced results. The Selma march took place *after* the court injunction became void. With LBJ's support, Congress subsequently enacted the Voting Rights Act, virtually guaranteeing every Black adult the right to vote. But on the ground, the split between SNCC and SCLC only deepened. Most Northern observers, especially in the news media, remained blind to the festering gap that was growing day by day. But for those who stayed on the ground and continued the war against racism, the divisions were a visceral reality.[2]

Northern volunteers who went to Montgomery to arrange food and lodging for the marchers were struck by the sarcasm of SNCC staff members who sarcastically referred to King as "de Lawd."

By the summer of 1966, what had begun as anger at the betrayal of the MFDP by white liberals at Atlantic City had grown into what became a national headline: "Black Power: Move on over Whitey or We'll Move on over You." SNCC had already taken a step toward increased militancy when it selected Stokely Carmichael, who had denounced the Voting Rights Act as a "white man's bill," to replace John Lewis as its national chairman. At the same meeting, SNCC also decided, after an all-night debate, that henceforth white staff members would play a peripheral role in the movement, concentrating on white communities, and Blacks would exercise primary decision-making power within the organization.

Carmichael was the SNCC staff member who in the winter of 1965–1966 took over directorship of the SNCC movement in Lowndes County, Alabama. There, he worked intensively with local activists to create a base of support for challenging white political rule in the county. More and more, the local movement became convinced that Black interests could best be served by focusing on Black-only constituencies, and not relying on, or even trusting, a coalition of whites and Blacks. Supporters of the Lowndes County movement came to that conclusion only after intense debate and experimentation with the possibility of biracial coalitions. The conversations in Lowndes County replicated discussions that were taking place in SNCC throughout the South—all rooted in the conflicts that had emerged in the aftermath of Atlantic City, and that continued during the campaign for voting rights in the Selma to Montgomery march. Could Blacks trust whites to be allies, or did it make more sense to rely primarily on their own solidarity? These debates continued through the spring of 1966. As the white liberal press persisted in highlighting SNCC's radicalism, the stage was set for confrontation within the movement.

When James Meredith, the Black man who had integrated the University of Mississippi in 1962, started a solo march across Mississippi in the late spring of 1966 to dramatize Black rights, he was severely wounded by a shotgun blast that came from roadside bushes. Immediately, major civil rights groups resolved to complete his march to Jackson.

That set the stage for the first public declaration of the split that now—at least internally—consumed the movement. As the followers of SNCC and SCLC marched across the state to complete the Meredith march, each night King and Carmichael addressed rallies of civil rights supporters. King exhorted the crowds with the traditional movement cry of "Freedom *Now*." But more often than not, the audience response was passive. Carmichael, by contrast, focused on "the betrayal of black dreams by white America." The difference in approach continued to crystallize. One day in Canton, Mississippi, after King had delivered his customary speech, Carmichael zeroed in on the difference. "The only way we are going to stop them from whuppin' us is to take over," he declared. "We've been saying freedom [now] for six years and we ain't got nothin'." Then, using in public for the first time a phrase that had been circulating inside SNCC for months, Carmichael declared: "The time for running has come to an end . . . Black Power. It's time we stand up and take over. Move on over Whitey, or we'll move on over you!" Seized by the moment, the crowd immediately started to chant "Black Power! Black Power! Black Power," in rhythmic response.[3]

A new movement had been born. A new stage in the decades-old struggle for racial justice had commenced. For many who had fought for Black freedom for generations, Dr. King's cry for racial progress—"Black and white together"—had fallen into the background and had been superseded by pride in Black solidarity. During the March on Washington in 1963, King had told his audience of 250,000 that "the Negro dream is rooted in the American dream." According to King's vision, Christian love and the redemptive suffering of nonviolent protest would allow America to transcend its past, experience a new birth, and create a society where Black children from the dusty fields of Georgia and Alabama could walk hand in hand with their white brothers and sisters to the promised land. Now, it seemed to many, America was moving down a different road, one that was rooted in the determination of Black Americans *to insist on their own freedom*, regardless of whether whites chose to join their cause.

Significantly, the shifts occurring within the movement in Mississippi and Georgia reflected a growing militancy within the Black community in the North and West as well. Nearly two million Blacks had moved from the South during the first Great Migration that started during World War I. Then, in response to the growing demand for workers in the North and West during World War II, the second Great Migration occurred, sweeping up even greater numbers. Chicago, New York, Philadelphia, Detroit, Pittsburgh, Los Angeles, and San Francisco swelled with new Black citizens. But while the "new" Black population in the North succeeded in securing better jobs, they also encountered rampant discrimination. Hotels in Northern cities excluded Blacks, including such prominent entertainers as Paul Robeson and Lena Horne. Blacks were forced to live in segregated ghettoes that were in horrible condition, and deteriorating rapidly. And as whites moved to suburbia during the postwar period, they excluded Blacks. Levittowns—the embodiment of the new suburbia—explicitly prohibited Black homeownership. In Philadelphia, where 153,000 Blacks moved in the 1950s, only 347 of 120,000 new homes that were built in the 1950s were available to Blacks.[4]

While 75 percent of American Blacks still resided in the South at the beginning of World War II, that figure had declined to 53 percent thirty years later, with nearly half of all Blacks living in the North, the Midwest, and the West. For the new migrants, it was a different world. In their new neighborhoods, there were bright lights, street-corner singing, rallies in the parks, and a night life that that seemed electric and non-stop. For the most part, the changes were welcome. In many of the industrial centers, the migrants could expect to find steady work, decent pay, a greater chance of joining a union. Black neighborhoods might be ghettoized, but an electric vibrancy went hand in hand with being part of a new Black urban community with its dance halls, theaters, jazz joints, and beauty parlors. Harlem or the South Side of Chicago might feature deteriorating housing—but they also embodied a vibrant community life, with its music and free-style street culture.[5]

On the other hand, most Black migrants were still channeled into decaying urban neighborhoods. While there were plenty of jobs in the 1940s, 1950s, and early to mid-1960s, shortly thereafter factories started to close, or at least move from the inner city. One-third of Black city dwellers lived in poverty. Black unemployment, female-headed households, drug addiction, and dependency on welfare grew steadily. Ironically, Blacks were joining the industrial working class at the same time that many of those jobs were giving way to mechanization. While some were able to join the new Black middle class, an "underclass" of Black men who could not get jobs grew even faster. The positive political outlook of the early 1960s gave way to pessimistic cynicism by the end of the decade.

Partly because of these trends, Northern cities became the sites of Black rioting in the 1960s. When Blacks in Chicago wished to show their opinion of Bull Connor's actions in Birmingham, they threw stones at the police, rather than engage in peaceful protests. In 1963, there were more than a thousand civil rights protest demonstrations in America, many in Northern cities. Reflecting the viewpoint of the protestors, one demonstrator declared: "White folks ain't going to *give* you nothing. . . . You've got to go and take it." From Harlem to Detroit to Chicago, Northern Blacks showed by their militant protests their rejection of "cooperating" with the white establishment as the only course that made sense. Riots broke out in Harlem and Detroit in 1964. Then came the Watts riot in Los Angeles in the summer of 1965, leaving thirty-four dead and four thousand arrested. Disruptions took place daily after the Black Power slogan became a rallying cry. In almost forty cities, it was a new moment. "Burn Baby, Burn," rioters cried. By the time the violence occurred in Watts, the degree to which anger, not accommodation, had come to characterize the response of Northern Blacks to ongoing oppression was evident.[6]

Despite all the publicity about its new prominence, the Black Power slogan was more a direct outgrowth of the civil rights experience than a repudiation of it. Black Power had emerged as the inevitable outcome of Birmingham, disputes about the March on Washington, Freedom Summer, and the experience of MFDP in Atlantic City. It flowed from decades of daily encounters with the intransigence of white institutions and white power-brokers. Many young Black activists had the growing sense that whites never conceded to Black demands unless they were forced to do so. As Roger Wilkins, nephew of the NAACP leader Roy Wilkins, noted at the end of the 1960s, "There is a growing . . . view among some young . . . Negroes that white people have embedded their own personal flaws so deeply in the institutions [of America] that those institutions are beyond redemption. . . . There is also, I believe, a . . . growing Negro skepticism about the commitment and sensitivity of even 'good' white people." Indeed, the Kerner Commission—established by LBJ to explain how and why rioting had swept the country—concluded in its 1968 report that America was becoming "two societies, one black, one white—separate and unequal."[7]

Despite King's optimism and the victories that his idealism had helped create, such as the Civil Rights Act of 1964 and the Voting Rights Act of 1965, multiple forms of white supremacy still existed throughout America's institutions. Nor did the positive feelings that accompanied those legislative victories necessarily translate into radical change in the way race operated in most American institutions. SNCC's experience with the depth—and multiple forms—of American racism had helped to fuel its growing radicalism. For too long, Blacks had practiced good faith, accepting the professed intentions of white Americans to eliminate white racism. But it was not to be, and now, an increasing number of Blacks concluded that they must control their own movement, shape their own agenda, and define their own identity. America, Carmichael declared, "does not function by morality, love and non-violence. . . . [It functions] by power." Except that power required that Blacks—not "good whites"—control their own institutions, their own programs. In the end, that was what Black Power was all about—a recognition, through the day-to-day experience of the civil rights movement, that Blacks must control their own destiny and not cede that authority to white liberals.

In the meantime, large numbers of white Americans reacted with fear and concern to the radical changes happening around them. In the early 1960s, television showed Blacks being victimized by police dogs and fire hoses in Birmingham. At that time, many whites sympathized with the Black victims. Now, many felt as though *they* were the ones under attack. There was a growing generational divide. The student movement, once peaceful, now appeared on camera attacking elite institutions like Harvard and Columbia Universities. The anti–Vietnam War movement had moved from peaceful "teach-ins" to rowdy marches denouncing all civic authority. The women's movement, once focused on securing an Equal Rights Amendment, now demanded women's liberation, even if that meant a revolt against the traditional American family.

In the midst of all this, the Black struggle took center stage, with Black Power as its incendiary fuse. The entire country seemed about to be broken into pieces. Many of those who endorsed radical change had forgotten Newton's third law of motion—that for every action there is an equal and opposite reaction. Millions of citizens believed that they had devoted their lives to playing by the rules of the game, accepting the status quo of intergroup relations, however unequal and oppressive they might be. Now, Blacks and others were seeking to change those rules, even reverse them. These white Americans rebelled at the way their world—a world of middle-class respectability and good manners—was suddenly being torn apart. As the plea for equal rights turned into a clamor for Black Power, these whites reacted, first with impatience, then with outrage. Many of them had spent years struggling to buy a decent house, achieve job security, and give their children a good education. Now, Blacks seemed to be demanding all of these things—immediately.

In the early 1960s, a majority of white Americans had approved of the Black quest for equal rights under the law; only 34 percent thought that Blacks were seeking too much, too fast. By 1967, that 34 percent with a negative view of civil rights had climbed to 85 percent. A majority of "middle Americans"—those earning between $5,000 and $15,000 a year—felt threatened by activists who seemed to question the cultural values of "America the great." From the perspective of these people, the radicalism of Blacks, poor people, antiwar demonstrators, and "women's libbers" represented an attack on the very foundations of what they defined as the American way of life.[8]

At the same time, Lyndon Johnson and his administration moved away from embracing the cause of Black protest. Increasingly, they went on the defensive. Two "wars" now claimed the administration's attention. The first was the War on Poverty that Johnson succeeded in getting passed by Congress in 1965. Very much a complement to the civil rights movement, the War on Poverty sought to reduce radically the number of American citizens who lived below the poverty level. Blacks were ready to be supportive of that effort. But the second war was the battle against "communism" in Vietnam. The American military—and Johnson himself—became further convinced that unless they defeated the North Vietnamese on the battlefield, they would set in motion a series of disasters in foreign policy. Ignoring the fact that John F. Kennedy had signed an executive order one month before his assassination to have all American troops withdrawn from Vietnam after the 1964 presidential election, LBJ decided to *increase* the number of American troops in Vietnam from 16,000 under Kennedy to more than 200,000 by the end of 1966, and 550,000 by 1968. As the troop commitment escalated, anti–Vietnam War protests operated side by side with Black protests to perplex, befuddle, and enrage the Johnson administration.

In that context, Johnson and his aides had neither patience nor respect for continued Black protest. "What really bothered me," one

White House staffer remarked, "was the Negro's assertiveness. . . . Demanding rights from the entire society, they were no longer content merely to ask for help from the well-intentioned whites within it." With those simple words, the staff person conveyed the gist of how many white liberals felt about the civil rights movement: Blacks should ask for help, not demand change, and white liberals should be in charge of the response.

Others in the White House saw two problems. "White resentment is great and still growing," LBJ special counsel Harry McPherson noted, while "the Negro community is fragmented." But McPherson's solution was to convene a meeting of the Black civil rights establishment—the NAACP and the Urban League—to find a way out. "There is no longer any need to have SNCC and CORE," he wrote. "The only way to move to the next stage of progress in civil rights [is] to return the leadership of the movement, . . . to business, labor, Wilkins and Young." In short, the best way to deal with Black restlessness was to ignore the protestors who had been most radicalized, those most responsible for the grassroots activism that had shattered white indifference and helped transform places like Mississippi, Alabama, and Georgia.[9]

At the same time, Johnson and his administration became increasingly consumed by the war in Vietnam. Although Johnson knew that "victory" in Vietnam was virtually impossible, he insisted on escalating the battle, with over five hundred thousand troops now in the field. In response, the antiwar movement turned from teach-ins in 1965 to bold confrontations with the police in 1967. Violent protest replaced peaceful political rallies. The war in Vietnam destroyed the War on Poverty, with the billions that were supposed to go to help the poor funneled instead to bombs, planes, and soldiers six thousand miles away. What had seemed a moment of promise and progress in 1964–1965 had turned into complete polarization. The country was coming apart.

The story of the civil rights movement provided a perfect prism for understanding the fragmentation of the wider society. For decades the movement had oscillated between a top-down protest movement orchestrated by executives from the NAACP and the Urban League, and a "bottom-up" insurgency that began in the Black neighborhoods of Rulesville, Mississippi, and Americus, Georgia. There, grassroots activists came together in churches, lodges, women's groups, and neighborhood centers to share their grievances, strengthen their communities, and assiduously pursue small reforms—safe streets, resistance to manipulation by city officials—that might, inch by inch, lead to improvement in the conditions Blacks experienced and the aspirations they could entertain. The movement involved both elitist and grassroots perspectives, and more often than not, the two came together. Thurgood Marshall could not have imagined challenging the oppressive inequality of school segregation in Clarendon County, South Carolina, had not J. A. DeLaine, the local pastor—along with his neighbors—put their lives on the line by demanding a school bus to take their kids to the nearby Black grade school, and then sued the county for its denial of equal rights to their children. The sit-in movement started from the ground up, local college students talking themselves into taking action, finding new ways to put into action what their parents and teachers had been telling them for years.

But by 1964 the tensions between a top-down approach and grassroots activism reached a new intensity. SNCC and SCLC were at the heart of the conflict, the one planting roots in the community and generating a locally grown movement, the other—SCLC—coming in from above to seize the moment and rally national and governmental support. For a brief moment, things came together when the indigenous civil rights movement forced John F. Kennedy to take a definitive stand in favor of racial equality in June 1963.

But that was not going to last. Divisions continued to fester, culminating when SNCC demanded that LBJ and the national Democratic Party live up to its promises of supporting racial equality by seating MFDP delegates at the national Democratic convention in Atlantic City. At that point, it became increasingly clear to SNCC activists that playing by white rules was not going to bring the control over their own lives that stood at the foundation of grassroots Black activism.

Thus, even as the movement secured its greatest victories, with the Civil Rights Act of 1964, the Voting Rights Act of 1965, and the anti-poverty bills enacted in both years—everything also started to come apart. The moment of triumph simultaneously marked the beginning of the process of disintegration. Lyndon Johnson had created the Kerner Commission in 1967 to assess the state of race relations in America and the prospects for finding a solution that whites and Blacks could both sign on to. But the Commission's report—issued in early 1968—concluded that the forces of division were far stronger than those of coming together in unity. America, the Commission concluded, had become two societies, one white and one Black, with the division widening between them.[10]

The movement had come so far—yet it was not over, and there were so many more roads to travel! In some ways, the moment was a replay of the division between Booker T. Washington and W. E. B. DuBois—one willing to depend on those in power to set the rules of the game, and be responsible for deciding how and when progress might be achieved; the other insisting on being able to dictate what changes were needed in order to achieve equality.

The question was whether the country, and the Black community, were ready for a continuing struggle to find the right answer.

Chapter 13

The Struggle Continues

For millions of white Americans, the legislative victories of 1964 and 1965 signified a positive end to the struggle for racial equality. The country had finally come to grips with the legacy of slavery and Jim Crow. Now, the United States could put the shame of racial prejudice behind it and move forward to a new day, free at last from the stigma of treating one segment of the population as unequal because of their skin color.

Unfortunately, this response represented one more example of a long tradition: the idea that America was different, better, and purer than its competitors across the globe. As "the land of the free and the home of the brave," the United States boasted that it embodied the ideals celebrated in its Declaration of Independence: "All men are created equal, endowed by their Creator with certain inalienable rights, including life, liberty and the pursuit of happiness." Yes, slavery and segregation represented a blatant violation of those ideals. But now, many white Americans believed, the country had put these contradictions behind them. Black civil rights had finally been recognized. Racial discrimination had been outlawed. The problem had been solved.

Most Black Americans, on the other hand, understood that racism was so fundamental to the country's social and economic structure that it could never be eliminated overnight. The most blatant "physical" examples of racial prejudice might now be illegal; theoretically, Blacks now had the same right to vote as whites, to buy tickets for entry to the same theaters, to eat in the same restaurants. But it would take a lot more change than the enactment of new laws to eliminate a *system* of racial prejudice that was embedded in the culture, reflected in the class structure of the economy and apparent in every institution of the society.

Some of the results of the new civil rights laws were encouraging. The Civil Rights Act of 1964 had ended discrimination in restaurants, theaters, and employment opportunities for Black citizens. This was especially true among those who were middle class. Thousands of African Americans moved to the suburbs and out of urban ghettoes. Affirmative action—a policy announced by LBJ to compensate for years of employment discrimination against Blacks—opened higher-paying jobs to African Americans. During the 1960s, the number of African Americans earning more than $10,000 a year—a middle-class income in those years—more than doubled. Civil rights legislation, in combination with massive new federal aid to higher education, led to an explosion in Black college enrollments. By 1975 the number of African Americans graduating from college had increased by 500 percent. This, in turn, helped increase the number of Blacks entering the middle class. In a state like Mississippi, the Voting Rights Act exploded the number of Blacks who could cast ballots on election day, with the result that scores of Black citizens were elected to public office. By 1990, Mississippi, in the heart of the Deep South, boasted more Black mayors and city council members that any other state in America.[1]

Yet for those Black families earning less than $10,000—a majority—the gains were minimal. Unemployment for that segment of the population remained twice that of white people. High school dropout rates among Blacks continued to be more than 50 percent higher than for whites, perpetuating a trend with devastating long-term consequences. Although poverty rates had decreased briefly among American Blacks in the 1960s and 1970s, they soon rose again, so that by the end of the twentieth century, 25 percent of Black Americans fell below the poverty line. There were now two Black Americas—one where chances for advancement had increased as a result of the civil rights legislation of the 1960s, the other where conditions stayed the same as they had been, or became even worse.

One simple statistic told the whole story. Black Americans comprised 13 percent of the American population. Yet they brought home only 3 percent of the national income. How could it be possible to talk about racial equality given that figure—which was getting worse rather than better, and which underlined—powerfully—the degree to which economic and educational equality were essential to the possibility of racial equality. Ironically—and frighteningly—the connection between economic rights and political rights that had animated the Freedmen's Bureau in 1865 remained the centerpiece of American race relations more than a century and a half later.

Throughout the entire history of Black Americans after the Civil War, racial inequality and economic inequality had gone hand in hand. They were inseparable. Nothing confirmed the linkage of racial and economic issues more than the fact that the Freedmen's Bureau adopted as its *first* step to making former slaves equal citizens with whites the act of breaking up the plantations of former slaveholders into forty-acre (and a mule) parcels, to be distributed to emancipated Blacks. At the very beginning, therefore, the interconnectedness of racial justice and economic opportunity was recognized.

But it was not allowed to last. Instead, racial equality came to be defined only in political terms—the right to vote, to have access to public facilities like restaurants and buses. Occasionally, as with some New Deal policies and Lyndon Johnson's "War on Poverty," the economic policies of government worked to benefit Black Americans. But ultimately—as revealed in the dramatic statistics on unemployment, poverty, and social mobility—Black Americans were never aided, directly, by the federal government to have access to economic equality.

For a very brief period in the mid-1960s there existed a possibility that a renewed focus on the interconnection of political rights and economic opportunities could be revived. In the aftermath of the March on Washington, Martin Luther King Jr. became more radicalized. Although he had always opposed America's growing involvement in Vietnam, he now became increasingly outspoken in his antiwar position. J. Edgar Hoover and the FBI cascaded King with their threats to expose his extramarital affairs. At the same time, King became ever more willing to indict America for its economic oppression of Blacks. More and more, King was ready to critique US foreign policy, particularly the war in Vietnam. As Lyndon Johnson started to increase dramatically the presence of American troops in Vietnam, from 16,000 in 1964 to 550,000 four years later, King became ever more outspoken in his denunciation of the war effort. In a series of lectures in Canada, he brought together his new, more radical critique of both America's foreign policy and its failure to address the structural economic inequality that left more than a third of America's Black population living in poverty.

During those same years, King's growing radicalism was matched by that of Robert Kennedy (RFK). After his brother's assassination, Kennedy—who never had a good relationship with Lyndon Johnson—became still more critical of the president, both in foreign affairs and on domestic policy. Recently elected as a US senator from New York, he quickly became an outspoken critic of LBJ's Vietnam policy. He *knew* that his brother had signed an executive order one month before his assassination to withdraw all American troops from Vietnam after the 1964 presidential election. Now, LBJ had trashed that order and had gone in exactly the opposite direction. At the same time, Kennedy became further outraged at the poverty that existed in minority groups across America. He would spend hours holding a Latino baby in his arms while listening to the baby's parents tell him of their impoverishment. Cesar Chavez, a leader of the Latino farmworkers community, became a close RFK ally, joining the millions of Black Americans who saw Kennedy as a heroic ally.

By 1968, King and Kennedy were marching down parallel paths. King was organizing the Poor People's Campaign to occupy Washington, DC, and demanded a dramatically increased War on Poverty. Kennedy was delivering the same message across America, as he initiated his campaign to replace Lyndon Johnson as president. Together, each in his own way, was preaching a more radical message than the country had ever heard from nationally respected leaders. It seemed that, *finally*, there were two charismatic political leaders who wished to transform the country, eliminate poverty, and create a society whose values would come close to realizing the Founder's belief that Americans were born with certain "inalienable rights," with equality of opportunity as the birthright of every citizen.[2]

But then, this new movement *against* the Vietnam War, and *for* a revitalized war against poverty, was shattered. Martin Luther King Jr. was assassinated in Memphis, Tennessee, the morning after rallying the Black citizens of that city around his renewed war on poverty. Just two months later, Robert Kennedy was murdered in the kitchen of a Los Angeles hotel where he had just won California's Democratic primary. The crusade that had galvanized so much of the nation had suddenly crashed. All seemed lost.

In an eerie way, the story of American Blacks now free of segregation under the law was directly parallel to that of South African Blacks after racial apartheid was outlawed in that nation. While Black empowerment—like affirmative action—helped some Blacks in South Africa with the education and skills they needed to advance, nothing changed for those who were poor, uneducated, and consigned to racial ghettos and townships.[3] The same phenomenon was now occurring in America.

During most of the 1970s, 1980s, and 1990s, little progress occurred on issues relevant to the well-being and advancement of the majority of America's Black population. While the average Black family income had grown by 1965 to be 61 percent of the average white family income, that gain now disappeared, with Black family income back to only 56 percent of white family income by 1980. Instead of having Martin Luther King Jr. and Robert F. Kennedy as political leaders, the dominant political voices of the 1970s and 1980s were Richard Nixon and Ronald Reagan. Far from embracing racial equality, each of these Republicans—historically the party that had *defended* Black

Americans—came to personify a seismic shift in what the Republican Party stood for. A century earlier, Republicans had endorsed racial equality. Now, they defended states' rights, opposed federal support for desegregation, and blasted civil rights advocates as "radicals" who were "un-American."

It all started with Richard Nixon's presidential campaign of 1968. Although in the Eisenhower administration Nixon had been one of the few high-level officials to support civil rights reforms, Nixon now soared to dominance in the Republican presidential race by pursuing what became known as his "Southern strategy." Early in the 1968 Republican nomination race, Nixon reached out to South Carolina's segregationist senator, Strom Thurmond, making him a major lieutenant in the campaign. Seizing on Thurmond's support to capitalize on the country's growing uneasiness around urban violence and antiwar protests, Nixon exploited the race issue to create a political polarization unlike anything seen since the Civil War. Race riots in Detroit, New York, and Los Angeles; militant antiwar marches in Washington and New York; and the growth of "anti-establishment" movements among student groups and women—all galvanized conservative sentiments. Nixon exploited that anger, issuing scathing attacks against the forced busing of Black children to white schools, while declaring that he had a secret plan to end the war in Vietnam, and wrapping himself in the mantle of patriotism. His top priority as president, Nixon declared, would be "the restoration of law and order." Nixon promised to "be the voice of the great majority of Americans, the forgotten Americans, the non-shouters, the non-demonstrators . . . those who do not break the law, people who pay their taxes, . . . who go to their churches . . . people who love this country [and] cry out . . . 'that is enough, let's get some new leadership.'"[4]

Ever since the ascendancy of the civil rights movement in the 1950s, social activists on the left had energized American politics. Now, the politicians of the right took over—with Nixon and his "Southern strategy" in the lead. Nixon attacked the idea of using busing to promote school integration. "Freedom of choice," he insisted, was a far better strategy. He nominated conservative, pro-white Southerners to the Supreme Court (his first two nominees were denied confirmation because of flaws in their legal records), and he ordered his Justice Department to request that the federal courts slow down the process of desegregation already agreed to in thirty-three Mississippi school districts. "You know," one senior Nixon aide said, "the President really *believes* in that Southern strategy—more than he believes in anything else." Most important, it seemed that a majority of whites agreed with his stance, and resented continued Black agitation. By 1966, 85 percent of whites were certain that the pace of civil rights progress was too fast.[5]

Meanwhile, the Federal Bureau of Investigation (FBI), under the leadership of J. Edgar Hoover, infiltrated Black Power groups. In California, FBI agents triggered raids on Black Panther offices and rallies. In Chicago, federal law enforcement officials raided the apartment of Fred Hampton, a Black Panther leader, and shot him dead in his bed. In Greensboro, North Carolina, COINTEL operatives (Counter-Intelligence agents) joined a local Black Power movement and proceeded to instigate a violent attack on police that provided the justification for police to decimate the group.[6]

Although Nixon's presidency ended in disgrace with his forced resignation after the Watergate scandal, the next Republican president who was elected to office renewed and deepened Nixon's Southern strategy. Significantly, Ronald Reagan launched his 1980 presidential campaign with a rally in Philadelphia, Mississippi—the same city where Michael Schwerner, Andrew Goodman, and James Chaney were murdered by white supremacists at the beginning of Freedom Summer in 1964. His choice of venue was no accident. Preaching the political gospel of law and order, evangelical religiosity, and fervent anti-communism, Reagan presided over an administration that did nothing to advance civil rights for Black Americans. Instead, he targeted Black civil rights activists as radicals who sought to undermine the harmony symbolized by Reagan's pledge to "make America great once again." As president, Reagan attacked "welfare mothers" who allegedly were cheating the system—collecting multiple checks by using forged documents, living in posh housing, and spending the change they received from purchasing oranges at a supermarket to then buy a bottle of vodka at a liquor store (he never produced evidence of this).

In his budgets, Reagan targeted programs that benefited Blacks. He cut school lunch programs by 25 percent, and slashed training, unemployment, and labor services by 70 percent. Under the Reagan administration, Black unemployment rates rose to 15.5 percent, and for African American young people, the jobless figure grew to 45.7 percent. At the same time, Black college enrollments plummeted from 34 percent to 26 percent of the overall college population. Between 1980 and 1990, the federal share of local government expenditures fell dramatically, from just over 12 percent to just over 3 percent. In 1982 alone, Reagan cut welfare funds by $32 billion.[7]

With the election of Bill Clinton in 1992, some improvement occurred in the status of American Blacks. But that improvement turned out to be more symbolic than real. Clinton prided himself on how effective he had been in supporting Black rights in Arkansas. His rhetorical embrace of the civil rights movement, and of Black equality, often reached soaring heights. The best speech of his presidency, he believed, occurred in Selma, Alabama, at a Black church that was celebrating the victories of thirty years earlier. In a booming economy—under Clinton the country added twenty-two million new jobs—Blacks did better than they had during the 1970s and 1980s. More and more Blacks were employed in the public sector—more than half of all Black professionals, including more than seven out of ten college-educated Black women, and 60 percent of college-educated Black men. The aura surrounding issues of civil rights during the decade even led the African American novelist Toni Morrison to call Clinton "the country's first Black president."[8]

Still, during the Clinton administration the overall poverty rate in the Black community did not fall, nor did the number of high school dropouts in America's urban ghettoes diminish. In fact, two of

Clinton's most celebrated legislative achievements eventually proved devastating for millions of Blacks. The welfare reform bill he signed in 1996 resulted in ending federal government support for millions of Blacks whose healthcare, income, and child support depended on federal welfare payments. But under the Clinton legislation, no one could receive federal welfare payments for more than five years. Even more important, Clinton's crime legislation—mandating life sentences for people convicted three times for crimes they committed, no matter how minor—resulted in hundreds of thousands more Blacks ending up in prison on life sentences. The same legislation focused especially on drug-related arrests. The result was a spate of record-setting prison sentences, which ended up hurting Black offenders far more than whites, even though the incidence of using drugs was basically the same in white and Black communities. In fact, except for his early efforts to secure universal healthcare for Americans, Clinton was as much an Eisenhower Republican as a liberal Democrat. To be sure, he was pilloried by Republicans—culminating in impeachment for his personal conduct—but in truth, his politics were more moderate and conservative than they were activist and liberal.[9]

Under George W. Bush, the situation worsened. Rates of economic inequality increased dramatically. In 1979, the top 1 percent of American earners took home 9 percent of the national income. By the end of Bush's second term, the top 1 percent took home almost 40 percent. After World War II, the middle class had grown steadily. At the beginning of the war, 40 percent of Americans owned their homes. By 1960, that figure had increased to 60 percent. During the thirty years after World War II, the distance between rich and poor remained relatively stable, even decreasing for a period. But by the time George W. Bush left office in 2008, the middle class was shrinking, the gap between the rich and poor was growing, and the notion of America being a society of equal opportunity came increasingly to be a myth, not a reality.

Significantly, the situation was even worse for Black Americans. In 2006, 25 percent of all Blacks lived beneath the poverty line, versus 10 percent of whites. The median household income for Blacks was only 62 percent of that for whites, while Blacks were twice as likely to be unemployed as whites. Nearly 75 percent of whites owned their own homes, while for Blacks, that figure was only 45 percent. Even more important, white homes were worth an average of $74,900, Black homes $7,500.[10]

Then came the Great Recession of 2007–2009. Suddenly, everything started to fall apart. Banks closed, the stock market plummeted, factories shut down—the country was almost in as bad shape as during the Great Depression. But no one suffered more during this period than those Black Americans who had only recently entered the middle class. Foreclosure rates on Black mortgages skyrocketed. Savings accounts plummeted. Confidence eroded. Capital disappeared. Blacks who had made it into the middle class were always fearful that they might fall backward rather than moving ahead. Now, those fears turned into reality.[11]

Barack Obama came closer than any recent politician to recognizing the linkage between racial equality under the law and economic equality. Rooted in his experience as a community organizer in Chicago, Obama went to Harvard Law School where, with Robert Fisher, a friend and former economics professor, he wrote "Transformative Politics," a draft manuscript that called for recruiting working-class whites into a new version of the movement against poverty that Robert Kennedy and Martin Luther King Jr. had championed in 1967 and 1968 before both were assassinated. Under this plan, the movement would move from a focus on race alone, and "use class as a proxy for race." In that way, the juxtaposition of race and class inequality would be addressed.[12]

To many Americans, the election of Barack Obama as the first Black person ever to hold the highest office in the land signaled the ultimate triumph of the civil rights struggle. From any perspective, Obama's success represented an extraordinary achievement. The son of a Black African father and a white American mother, Obama had charted a dramatic path to political success. A brilliant scholar, born in Hawaii, he received his college and graduate school education in California, New York, and Massachusetts. In the midst of his graduate school years, Obama made the critical decision to become a community organizer in Chicago, learning the lessons of listening to the poor and powerless. He then took his dream of a new kind of politics to the American people, inspiring them with his idealism. He garnered 66 percent of voters under age thirty, 62 percent of Asians, 66 percent of Hispanics, 56 percent of women, and 95 percent of African Americans. Those making less than $15,000 per year doubled in their electoral turnout, while 69 percent of first-time voters cast their ballots for Obama. He had persuaded an enthusiastic majority that he represented a different breed of American leader, dedicated to a new and different kind of bipartisan politics and committed to realizing the nation's highest ideals.[13]

But it was not to be. Republican leaders in Congress declared from day one that they would oppose even the most moderate items in Obama's legislative agenda. With solid Democratic support, Obama secured passage of a major deficit reduction package that helped leverage the country out of depression. He then succeeded in enacting, with no votes to spare, the country's first national healthcare bill, giving every citizen the right to purchase medical insurance, often with a government subsidy, and including coverage of preexisting conditions. Through executive actions, he created major changes in the country's policy toward climate change, environmental protection, development of national parks, and workplace safety. Obama even negotiated a treaty that prevented Iran from developing nuclear weapons.

But what Obama could not control was the degree to which rampant inequality and persistent racism remained alive and well in America. Some people insisted that the real issue was not race, but economic ambition and talent. Black people, they said, were simply less able than others. Some of the most powerful people in the land even insisted that racism had long since been eliminated. Indeed, the Chief Justice of the United States, John Roberts, wrote in the 2013 *Shelby* decision that racial prejudice no longer was imbedded in American society. Hence the provisions of the Voting Rights Act of 1965 imposing restrictions on states with a history of Black voter disenfranchisement no longer applied. Since the racism that had prompted enactment of those restriction had disappeared, he said, federal supervision of voter registration policy in Southern states was no longer needed. As a result, North Carolina and all other Southern states could now pass legislation specifically designed to erode Black political power and to undercut fundamental rights of citizenship. No official act or court decision spoke more powerfully to the degree to which important white leaders had put blinders on with regard to the persistence of racism as a fundamental feature of American life.

In the next few years, events occurred throughout the country which made it even more difficult to pretend that America had put racism behind it. In 2015, a Black teenager named Trayvon Martin was killed in a Florida suburb by a white man who perceived Martin as a threatening presence in the neighborhood where both men lived. George Zimmerman, the white man, regularly patrolled his suburb on a voluntary basis, evidently moved by a suspicion that "outsiders" might threaten the neighborhood's safety. Instinctively, Zimmerman appears to have taken Martin's skin color as a warning sign. He called the police to notify them of his concern. They told him they would follow up, and that he should do nothing further. But Zimmerman ignored their instructions. He continued to pursue Martin, then confronted him. When Martin resisted, challenging Zimmerman's right to pursue him, the white man took out his gun and shot him. Subsequently, a jury acquitted Zimmerman of assault and second-degree murder. The jurors used as their rationale Florida's "stand your ground" law, which allows individuals facing a situation they deem to be threatening to "stand your ground" and fire a weapon in self-defense. To most observers, the verdict seemed to sanction a crime that occurred only because the victim was Black.

A few months later, Michael Brown, a Black man in Missouri, was chased down by police after an alleged attempt to rob a convenience store. Brown turned around, raised his hands in the air, and prepared to surrender to police. Yet even as he raised his hands—captured on video—the officers fired their weapons, killing him instantly. His body lay in the street for more than an hour before doctors confirmed his death and a funeral director took him away.[14]

The run of police-induced homicides did not stop. Eric Garner was a Staten Island resident, known to his neighbors as someone who illegally sold cigarettes, some of them stolen, to neighbors on the street. He had no record of violent crimes. The police knew of his illegal activity, and seized him one day. Wrestling him to the ground, one officer choked him. Garner screamed "I can't breathe," but the officer did nothing. Garner then suffocated. No police were convicted of a crime. None was even put on trial.

It was like an epidemic. A seven-year-old, carrying a toy gun in a Cleveland housing project, was shot to death by police who never even confronted the child. In Minnesota, a police officer shot Philando Castile, a Black man with no weapon, sitting in a car with his girlfriend and her child, on the grounds that he appeared to be reaching for something in his pocket. Alton Sterling was shot and killed by police outside a Baton Rouge convenience store where he was selling music and movies on discs. Samuel DuBose was pulled over by officers in Cincinnati for not having a license plate. He was shot as he tried to drive away. The frequency of such shootings seemed to increase, not decrease. The impact of the killings became ever more explosive with the increased presence of cell phone cameras and audio recordings.[15]

By the second decade of the twenty-first century, the reality of persistent racism could no longer be ignored, whatever the wishes of many whites. Belatedly—but with increasing frequency—people began to read and talk about the "prison-industrial complex," the spread of mass incarceration among young Black people doomed to spend much of the rest of their lives in prison.

The statistics on the mass imprisonment of young African Americans from 1980 to 2010 were staggering. First of all, the overall prison population skyrocketed, increasing more than 400 percent—from

500,000 in 1980 to 2.3 million in 2008. The United States had six times as many people imprisoned—as a portion of their population—as Australia, eight times more than Germany, ten times more than Sweden, and twenty-five times more than India. While citizens of the United States comprised only 5 percent of the world's population, they represented 25 percent of the world's prisoners. In Missouri, Blacks were 11.2 percent of the population, but 41.2 percent of those in jail. In at least twenty states, the percentage of Blacks who were incarcerated was more than five times their proportion of the population. The amount of money government agencies spent on this imprisonment also skyrocketed—nearly 800 percent—from $6.7 billion in 1985 to $52 billion in 2013.[16]

But the incarceration figures represented just the tip of the iceberg. Due to the Clinton crime legislation, it turned out that a huge percentage of the increases of those imprisoned came from people arrested for *nonviolent* drug offences. The number of people in jail for arrests related to drugs exploded from forty-one thousand in 1980 to nearly five hundred thousand in 2013—more than a twelve-fold increase. Even more telling, nearly 80 percent of all drug-related arrests had to do with *possession only*—no use of guns, no crime or violence.

The real secret of the mass incarceration epidemic, however, was the degree to which, as Michelle Alexander has written, it became a modern-day version of Jim Crow. Although the arrest figures allegedly had nothing to do with race, in fact they provided the vehicle for infusing racism into whole segments of American society.

The racial figures on drug-related offenses were stunning. Although surveys showed that Blacks used drugs at approximately the same rate as whites, *Black men were five and a half times more likely to be incarcerated* than white men! Most of the imprisoned were arrested for using crack cocaine—a less expensive form of cocaine more likely to be found in poor neighborhoods than in affluent suburbs. Although Blacks comprised only 13 percent of the population, they constituted 59 percent of those in state prisons for drug offenses. The situation was even worse in federal prisons. There, in 2002, Blacks made up 80 percent of those convicted under federal law—this despite that fact that two-thirds of crack cocaine users in the United States were white or Hispanic. Although whites comprised 78 percent of the overall population, they constituted just 35 percent of all prisoners; and even though five times as many whites used drugs as Blacks, African Americans were sent to prison for drug use at ten times the rate of whites. They also received longer jail sentences. Blacks served almost as much time for a drug offense (58.7 months) as did whites for a violent crime (61.7 months).[17]

Nor did the dilemma stop there. In many states, a person convicted of a felony automatically lost the right to vote. Inevitably—and especially given the statistics listed above—this took a greater toll on Blacks than on whites. Indeed, Blacks were three times more likely to be disenfranchised for time served in jail than whites. More than 13 percent of African American men have been denied the right to vote because of a prior felony conviction. In Florida the figure was 23 percent of age-eligible African Americans—even though they had completed their time in jail. Of even greater concern, the population of the disenfranchised has been more concentrated in Southern states like Louisiana, Florida, Mississippi, Alabama, and Texas than in Northern states like Maine, Massachusetts, and Minnesota.[18]

The story could go on and on. Racial profiling existed everywhere. Black students at elite universities like Duke, Emory, or Princeton are customarily stopped and questioned by police multiple times. Blacks and Hispanics who are "pulled over" for a possible traffic violation are three times more likely to be searched by police than whites, and four times more likely to be subjected to some form of physical intimidation.

Perhaps most disturbing—and most confirming of the degree to which racism has remained a central reality of our society—the right of African Americans to vote has now come under renewed and vicious attack. Within six weeks after Justice John Roberts invalidated *the* key enforcement provision of the 1965 Voting Rights Act in 2011, several Southern states acted to limit, curtail, and make more difficult the right of Blacks and Hispanics to cast ballots. In North Carolina, the state legislature reduced the number of days set aside for early voting, limited same-day registration, and passed a voter ID law requiring a form of state photographic identification for a person to be able to enter a voting booth. The voter ID most likely to be used for that purpose was a state driver's license. But in North Carolina, six hundred thousand Blacks and Hispanics did not have driver's licenses. Moreover, getting to a Department of Motor Vehicle office for an average citizen working a forty-hour week was not easy to arrange. While states like Oregon enacted universal suffrage laws, encouraging every citizen to vote, other states did all they could to limit voting, and to make casting ballots more difficult for minorities. Perhaps the most outrageous example of such behavior occurred in Alabama. First, it passed a law requiring each voter to show a state-certified photo ID. Then, it shut down all driver's license offices in *every county in the state that was more than 75 percent Black.* The voter ID requirement, historian Carol Anderson has pointed out, would eliminate more than six million Black voters, and three million Latinos (potentially 25 percent of Black voters, and 16 percent of Latinos, while only 8 percent of whites lacked a voter ID). In North Carolina, the Mecklenburg County election board—Republican dominated—eliminated eighteen polling sites in a county with 15 percent of the Black voters in the state, leaving 750,000 eligible voters with only four sites for early voting. Following a similar pattern, 43 percent of the Southern counties previously covered by the Voting rights Act closed 868 polling places.[19]

Understandably, the optimism that had existed in the mid-1960s among activists in the civil rights movement could no longer be sustained. Yes, the Civil Rights Act of 1964 barring economic discrimination against Blacks had made a difference. The fivefold increase in college enrollments, the government's support for affirmative action, the growth of a Black middle class—all critically affected the life chances of Blacks. So did the Voting Rights Act. In places like Mississippi, the percentage of Blacks who were registered to vote went from 6.7 percent in 1964 to 60 percent four years later. Throughout the

South, the number of Blacks elected to public office skyrocketed—from 33 in 1941 to 195 in 1965, to 764 in 1970, to 1,909 in 1980. Blacks from North *and* South now served in Congress.[20]

But developments after 1970 did not sustain this sense of optimism. By 1990, Blacks in the bottom 20 percent of the African American population were poorer in relation to whites than at any time since the 1950s. By the early twenty-first century (2006), the median Black household income was 62 percent of white median income. Blacks were twice as likely to be unemployed. One-quarter of Blacks lived below the poverty line versus one-tenth of whites. In 2013, only 9.9 percent of white households in the country brought home less than $10,000 per year, but 32.9 percent of Blacks fell into that category. While 74 percent of whites owned their own homes, only 45 percent of Blacks did. The infant mortality rate among Blacks remained two and a half times higher than the infant mortality rate among whites. The number of Black households without male wage-earners had increased from 22 percent in 1960 to more than 50 percent by 2010. Meanwhile, the number of factory jobs in Northern, Midwestern, and Western cities plummeted in the 1960s and 1970s, replaced by only a tiny percentage of service jobs.[21]

In the meantime, sensationalized media coverage of two events in the 1990s highlighted the degree to which the Kerner Commission's finding that there were now two Americas—one Black, the other white—had become more and more entrenched. Both took place in California. The first involved the arrest and beating of Rodney King, a Black motorist in Los Angeles. Stopped by police for speeding, King protested. Quickly, police threw him to the ground, then mercilessly pummeled him with their batons and fists. Only on this occasion, a bystander with a camera videotaped the entire episode, then made the film available to media outlets everywhere. Although everyone who saw the beating was scandalized, an all-white jury acquitted the officers responsible for the beating, concluding that they had done nothing criminal in hammering King as he lay helpless on the street.

The second episode involved the trial of former football star and media personality O. J. Simpson. The former wife of Simpson, a beautiful blonde, had been brutally slain—along with a male friend—at her home in Los Angeles. On a previous occasion, Simpson had beaten her and she had called 911. Now, police zeroed in on Simpson as a suspect in her murder. He had flown to Chicago shortly after the killing. But DNA tests linked blood in Simpson's car and on his gloves to the body of his former wife. Each day, the country witnessed the trial of Simpson on television. Soon, they learned not only about the blood in Simpson's car, but also about the careless ways the police had handled the evidence. One officer in particular frequently used the "N" word, and was a prime witness against Simpson. When the predominantly Black jury delivered its verdict the next day, it found Simpson innocent on all counts.

Most revealingly, the country's response to the verdict confirmed the extent to which the Kerner Commission's conclusion about there now being "two Americas" was on target. White Americans, by a three to one margin, said that they believed Simpson was guilty of murder. By contrast, Black Americans, by the same three to one margin, said that they believed Simpson to be innocent.

In short, most of the optimism about racial equality that came out of movement's victories in the 1960s had now been dashed. In 1969, almost 80 percent of Blacks in America believed that their status had improved significantly over the past five years. By 1984, that figure had fallen to 37 percent. In 2007, only 20 percent of Black Americans believed that positive change was happening. Surveying the changes that had and had not happened over the previous century and a half, historian Ira Berlin concluded that "the inner city [had become] what the plantation had been in the seventeenth and eighteenth centuries and what the sharecropper plot had been in the late nineteenth." Yes, important and dramatic changes had taken place. But racism remained a pervasive presence in the "land of the free and the home of the brave."[22]

Reflections

How might an observer from another planet assess the history of race in America since the end of the Civil War? Such an observer might well conclude that despite extraordinary reforms, propelled largely by Black activists, fundamental divisions between white and Black Americans remained. Systemic racism—a combination of economic inequality and unequal access to political power—continued to divide American society along the color line.

To be sure, dramatic reforms had taken place after the Civil War ended slavery. But once the federal government abandoned the Freedmen's Bureau proposal to break up the plantations of white Southerners into forty-acre-and-a-mule packages to be distributed to millions of former slaves, it became ever more difficult to create the framework within which equal economic opportunity could exist for Blacks. To be sure, the policies of some Reconstruction state governments—then of the Virginia Readjuster movement and the biracial Populist government of the 1890s—raised hopes for the possibility of economic freedom and political independence. But then the era of *Plessy* and of Jim Crow descended, stifling for decades the possibility of securing change.

Black protest never ceased—whether it be the "accommodationist" approach of Booker T. Washington, or the more militant demands of W. E. B. Du Bois and the NAACP. International conflicts, like World War I and the struggle "to make the world safe for democracy" offered further hope for change, but instead produced repression of Black aspirations through multiple race riots. The New Deal, and liberal racial policies initiated by people like Eleanor Roosevelt and Harold Ickes, represented further positive changes, including, informally, a "Black Cabinet" in Washington, DC, to advocate for racial equality.

Then came World War II, which helped to shatter the status quo. Millions of Black Americans enlisted in the army. Other millions migrated to the North and West of the country. Black employment in war industries skyrocketed. The positive treatment of Black soldiers in Asia and Europe helped spawn a new sense of possibility for racial change at home. Membership in the NAACP rose tenfold, from fifty thousand to five hundred thousand. The pressure from Black activists forced President Harry Truman to establish a national Civil Rights Commission. And the NAACP made the critical decision to ask the Supreme Court to reverse the *Plessy* decision of 1896 and to desegregate all American schools in the *Brown* decision of 1954.

The galvanized Black protest movement now seized control of the national political agenda. From the Montgomery Bus Boycott of 1955–1956, to the Greensboro sit-ins of 1960 and the founding of SNCC two months later, the demonstrations of Black young people in Birmingham in April 1963, the March on Washington of August 1963, and Freedom Summer in 1964, the civil rights movement captured the attention of the world. Finally, after decades of failing to address America's sanction of racism and segregation, the president and Congress agreed to abolish segregation in all public facilities and hiring procedures, and to guarantee Black citizens' voting rights.

On the surface, the battle for racial equality seemed to have been won. Black Americans had secured recognition as equal citizens. But then there was the other side of the equation. What about jobs, income, access to the best schools, the ability to own a home anywhere in the country?

In the end, the murders of Trayvon Martin, Breonna Taylor, George Floyd, and countless others simply highlighted the *systemic* nature of America's race problem. The battle against racial discrimination was not over. The intersection of the problems of race and class simply highlighted how deep-rooted and fundamental the nation's struggle with racism has always been. Yes, with each generation, new forms of activism have come alive. The Black freedom struggle has never stopped. The basic reason for that is how central the issue of race has been to the entire social, economic, and political structure of America. But until *economic* progress goes hand in hand with equal political rights, racial discrimination will continue to be a dominant reality in America.

Perhaps—just perhaps—progress in combating racism can still occur. But that will happen only if—and when—the nation acts, not only to end racial prejudice, under the law, but to reduce the economic and social inequality that sustains and reinforces that racism.

Notes

CHAPTER 1

1. Galloway's story is a centerpiece of David Cecelski, *The Waterman's Song: Slavery and Freedom in Maritime North Carolina* (Chapel Hill: University of North Carolina Press, 2003), see especially 180–183. On the relation between slavery and democracy, see Edmund S. Morgan, *American Slavery, American Freedom* (New York: W. W. Norton, 1975). For a concise history of slavery, see Peter Kolchin, *American Slavery: 1619–1877* (New York: Hill and Wang, 2003). See also Eugene Genovese, *Roll Jordan Roll: The World the Slaves Made* (New York: Pantheon, 1974); and Steven Hahn, *A Nation under Our Feet* (Cambridge, MA: Harvard University Press, 2003).
2. Cecelski, *Waterman's Song*, 180–181.
3. Eric Foner, *Reconstruction: America's Unfinished Revolution* (New York: Harper Collins, 2002), 8–10, 77; Hahn, *Nation under Our Feet*, 7.
4. David Blight, *Race and Reunion: The Civil War in American Memory* (Cambridge, MA: Harvard University Press, 2001), 31.
5. See Genovese, *Roll Jordan Roll*; Hahn, *Nation under Our Feet*; Kolchin, *American Slavery*; John Blassingame, *The Slave Community* (New York: Oxford University Press, 1975); and James Horton and Lois Horton, *Hard Road to Freedom: The Story of African America* (New Brunswick, NJ: Rutgers University Press, 2001), 250, 326–327.
6. Hahn, *Nation under Our Feet*, 28–35. See also Blassingame, *Slave Community*; Theodore Rosengarten, *All God's Dangers: The Life of Nate Shaw* (New York: Knopf, 1975); and Leon Litwack, *Trouble in Mind* (New York: Knopf, 1998), 5.
7. Foner, *Reconstruction*, 8–10, 77; Hahn, *Nation under Our Feet*, 7.
8. Cecelski, *Waterman's Song*, 180–183.
9. Foner, *Reconstruction*, 73; Cecelski, *Waterman's Song*, 187, 192; Carol Anderson, *White Rage: The Unspoken Truth of Our Racial Divide* (New

York: Bloomsbury, 2017), 29. See also Horton and Horton, *Hard Road to Freedom*.

10. Laura F. Edwards, "The Politics of Marriage and Households in North Carolina during Reconstruction," in *Jumpin' Jim Crow*, ed. Jane Dailey, Glenda Gilmore, and Bryant Simon (Princeton, NJ: Princeton University Press, 2000), 14; Litwack, *Trouble in Mind*, 53; Foner, *Reconstruction*, 9, 92, 97; Hasan Kwame Jeffries, *Bloody Lowndes: Civil Rights and Black Power in Alabama's Black Belt* (New York: New York University Press, 2009), 11.
11. Foner, *Reconstruction*, 73, 79; Tera Hunter, *To "Joy My Freedom"* (Cambridge, MA: Harvard University Press, 1997), 3.
12. Foner, *Reconstruction*, 28–67.
13. Foner, *Reconstruction*, 67; Cecelski, *Waterman's Song*, 192; Hahn, *Nation under Our Feet*, 146–147; Adam Fairclough, *Better Day Coming: Blacks and Equality, 1890–2000* (New York: Viking, 2001), 2.
14. Hahn, *Nation under Our Feet*, 7, 78, 86, 113, 147; Litwack, *Trouble in Mind*, 331; Foner, *Reconstruction*, 3–10.
15. Horton and Horton, *Hard Road to Freedom*, 184; Foner, *Reconstruction*, 105; W. E. B. Du Bois, *The Souls of Black Folks* (Chicago: A. C. McClurg, 1903), 23–41. William A. Darity and A. Kirsten Mullen, *From Here to Equality: Reparations for Black Americans in the Twenty-First Century* (Chapel Hill: UNC Press, 2022), 9, 130, 156–160. Darity and Mullen make a powerful case for reparations being paid to descendants of former slaves, pointing out that from the beginning, the Freedmen's Bureau and political leaders like Thaddeus Stevens insisted that political equality and economic equality existed side by side and needed to be addressed together, but that never happened.
16. Foner, *Reconstruction*, 159–160, 234–236; Jeffries, *Bloody Lowndes*, 13.
17. Foner, *Reconstruction*, 160, 164.
18. Hahn, *Nation under Our Feet*, 171; Litwack, *Trouble in Mind*, 117, 131; Howard Rabinowitz, *The First New South, 1865–1920* (Arlington Heights, IL: Harlan Davidson), 13–17.
19. Litwack, *Trouble in Mind*, 131, 134; Jeffries, *Bloody Lowndes*, 10.
20. Foner, *Reconstruction*, 236; Fairclough, *Better Day Coming*, 2–4.
21. Fairclough, *Better Day Coming*, 3–4; Horton and Horton, *Hard Road to Freedom*, 190–220; Foner, *Reconstruction*, 274–281.
22. Foner, *Reconstruction*, 279.
23. Foner, *Reconstruction*, 355; Hahn, *Nation under Our Feet*, 204, 219; Rabinowitz, *First New South*, 90–96; Jeffries, *Bloody Lowndes*, 14.
24. Foner, *Reconstruction*, 281, 289, 355, 370.

25. Hahn, *Nation under Our Feet*, 2–5, 9, 281–289; Foner, *Reconstruction*, 281; the quotation is from a Black description of election day in 1868 in Alabama.
26. Earl Lewis, *In Their Own Interests: Race, Class and Power in Twentieth Century Norfolk, Virginia* (Berkeley: University of California Press, 1991), 8–11, 16; Edward L. Ayers, *The Promise of the New South: Life after Reconstruction* (New York: Oxford University Press, 1992), vii.
27. Howard Rabinowitz, *Race Relations in the Urban South, 1865–1890* (New York: Oxford University Press, 1978), 187; W. E. B. DuBois, *Souls of Black Folk* (New York: Harper and Row, 1903), 174. [AU: Are there 2 different *Souls* books cited, with different publishers, or should this be a shortened citation here?] Readers should note that there are two Rabinowitz books cited in this chapter, *The First New South, 1865–1920* and *Race Relations in the Urban South, 1865–1890*. The different titles are delineated in the notes.
28. Rabinowitz, *Race Relations in the Urban South*, 145–148.
29. Ayers, *Promise of the New South*, 132 ff.
30. Rabinowitz, *Race Relations in the Urban South*, 186–188.
31. Ibid.
32. Rabinowitz, *Race Relations*, 186; Fairclough, *Better Day Coming*, 281; W. E. B. DuBois, *Souls of Black Folk*.
33. Grace Elizabeth Hale, *Making Whiteness: The Culture of Segregation in the South* (New York: Pantheon, 1998), 13–14; Hahn, *Nation under Our Feet*, 50, 113; Litwack, *Trouble in Mind*, 434; Lewis, *In Their Own Interests*, 72; Cecelski, *Waterman's Song*, 208; Rabinowitz, *Race Relations in the Urban South*, 197–201; Ayers, *Promise of the New South*, 70.
34. Horton and Horton, *Hard Road to Freedom*, 134–135; Rabinowitz, *Race Relations in the Urban South*.
35. Litwack, *Trouble in Mind*, 9, 46, 54, 62; Jeffries, *Bloody Lowndes*, 21.
36. Horton and Horton, *Hard Road to Freedom*, 146.
37. Litwack, *Trouble in Mind*, 98; Hahn, *Nation under Our Feet*, 220.
38. Lewis, *In Their Own Interests*, 19, 23, 72; Fairclough, *Better Day Coming*, 17; Rabinowitz, *First New South*, 135–145; Rabinowitz, *Race Relations in the Urban South*, 75–90; Hunter, *To "Joy My Freedom,"* vii, 33, 60–66.
39. Hunter, *To "Joy My Freedom,"* 33, 61–65.
40. Ibid., 33, 61–65.
41. Ibid., 61–65; Litwack, *Trouble in Mind*, 171.
42. Rabinowitz, *Race Relations in the Urban South*, 285; Foner, *Reconstruction*, 442, 539–541, 577.

CHAPTER 2

1. Glenda Gilmore, *Gender and Jim Crow: Women and the Politics of White Supremacy in North Carolina, 1896–1920* (Chapel Hill: University of North Carolina Press, 1997), 69; Steven Hahn, *A Nation without Borders: The United States and Its World of Civil Wars, 1896–1920* (New York: Penguin, 2017), 309.
2. Milan Kundera, *The Book of Laughter* (New York: Penguin, 1980), 22.
3. "Colored Troops during the War of the Rebellion," *Richmond Planet*, November 16, 1895; "The Live in Our Memory," *Southwest Christian Advocate*, June 1, 1899.
4. James Scott, *Weapons of the Weak* (New Haven, CT: Yale University Press, 1987), 240.
5. Charles Jones, interview by Kara Miles, June 16, 1993, Charlotte, NC, Behind the Veil (BTV) Collection, John Hope Franklin Center (JHF), Duke University Library; John Cooper, Barbara Cooper, and Edgar Hunt, interview by Paul Ortiz, July 6, 1995, Memphis, TN, Behind the Veil Collection (BTV Collection), John Hope Franklin Collection, JHF Center, Duke University. All future citations of interviews are from this collection unless otherwise noted.
6. Cleaster Mitchell, interview by Paul Ortiz, July 16, 1995, Blackton, AR.
7. David Matthews, interview by Paul Ortiz, August 5, 1995; Toni Morrison, *Sula* (New York: Penguin, 2003), 167; Merlin Jones, interview by Paul Ortiz, August 11, 1994, Indianola, MS.
8. Cleaster Mitchell, interview; W. E. B. Du Bois, *Souls of Black Folk*, 140–151.
9. Leon Litwack, *Trouble in Mind* (New York: Knopf, 1998), 62; Cleaster Mitchell, interview; David Matthews, interview.
10. Litwack, *Trouble in Mind*, 98, 218.
11. C. Vann Woodward, *Origins of the New South, 1877–1913* (Baton Rouge: Louisiana State University Press, 1951, 1971), 56–57; Edward L. Ayers, *The Promise of the New South: Life after Reconstruction* (New York: Oxford University Press, 1992), 38–47; Howard Rabinowitz, *The First New South, 1865–1920* (Arlington Heights, IL: Harlan Davidson), 96.
12. Rabinowitz, *First New South*, 94–96, 165–169; Howard Rabinowitz, *Race Relations in the Urban South, 1865–1890* (New York: Oxford University Press, 1978), 45–47.
13. Ibid.
14. Rabinowitz, 285; Ayers, *Promise of the New South*, 39–40.

15. Ayers, *Promise of the New South*, 15–17, 71; Rabinowitz, *First New South*, 150–155; Theodore Rosengarten, *All God's Dangers* (New York: Knopf, 1974); Marsha Darling, "The Growth and Decline of the African-American Family Farm, Warren County, N.C., 1910–1960" (Ph.D. dissertation, Duke University, 1982).
16. Litwack, *Trouble in Mind*, 117; Rabinowitz, *First New South*, 17; Tera Hunter, *To "Joy My Freedom"* (Cambridge, MA: Harvard University Press, 1997), iv, 3.
17. Hunter, *To "Joy My Freedom,"* viii, 3.
18. Ibid., 30–33, 60–65, 87–90.
19. Ibid., 90–97.
20. Ibid., 85–87; Earl Lewis, *In Their Own Interests: Race, Class and Power in Twentieth Century Norfolk, Virginia* (Berkeley: University of California Press, 1991), 16–17. Richard Wright, *Black Boy* (New York: Harper Brothers, 1945).
21. Rabinowitz, *Race Relations in the Urban South*; David Morehead, interview by William Chafe, Chafe papers, Duke University. Morehead's mother chased down and berated a local white storeowner who had mistreated her son.
22. Litwack, *Trouble in Mind*, 442.
23. Cleaster Mitchell, interview by Ortiz; David Morehead, interview by Chafe; Hunter, *To "Joy My Freedom,"* 106.
24. Hunter, *To "Joy My Freedom,"* 123–125, 175–184; Ayers, *Promise of the New South,* 75.
25. Maurice Lucas, interview by Mausiki Scales, August 7, 1995, Renova, MS.
26. Rabinowitz, *Race Relations in the Urban South*, 143–149; Ayers, *Promise of the New South*, 25.
27. For a discussion on historians' views on when and how segregation evolved, see Ayers, *Promise of the New South*, 17–33, 137–146; Adam Fairclough, *Better Day Coming: Blacks and Equality, 1890–2000* (New York: Viking, 2001), 16–17; Rabinowitz, *First New South*, 85–93, 132–135.
28. Litwack, *Trouble in Mind*, 218; Rabinowitz, *First New South*, 145–147; Rabinowitz, *Race Relations in the Urban South*, 187–195; Ayers, *Promise of the New South*, 137–142, DuBois, *Souls of Black Folk*, 75.
29. DuBois, quoted in Liteack, Litwack, *Trouble in Mind*, 150.
30. Litwack, *Trouble in Mind*, 158, 329, 335; Ayers, *Promise of the New South*, 210, 431; Grace Elizabeth Hale, *Making Whiteness* (New York: Pantheon Press, 1998).
31. Ayers, *Promise of the New South*, 16–17, 430; Rabinowitz, *Race Relations in the Urban South*, 234–240.

32. Rabinowitz, *Race Relations in the Urban South*, 188; Ayers, *Promise of the New South*, 138, 346; Litwack, *Trouble in Mind*, 138, 310; Grace Elizabeth Hale, *Making Whiteness: The Culture of Segregation in the South, 1890–1940* (New York: Pantheon, 1998), 5, 21, 45. Richard Wright, *Black Boy* (New York: Harper and Row, 1945), 45.
33. Litwack, *Trouble in Mind*, 153, 284, 309; Wright, *Black Boy*, 147.
34. Litwack, *Trouble in Mind*, 284; Wright, *Black Boy*, 145–149; Ralph Thompson, interview by Paul Ortiz. For an elaboration of these forms of social control, see William H. Chafe, *Women and Equality* (New York: Oxford University Press, 1977), 43–78.
35. Booker T. Federick, interview by Mausiki Scales, August 2, 1995, Itta Bena, MS; Litwack, *Trouble in Mind*, 240.
36. Roosevelt Williams, interview by Paul Ortiz, June 24, 1993, Birmingham, AL; Wright, *Black Boy*, 183–186.
37. Litwack, *Trouble in Mind*, 3, 7, 9.
38. Litwack, *Trouble in Mind*, 431; Hale, *Making Whiteness*, 15–20; Ayers, *Promise of the New South*, 369–370. Du Bois's analogy played on this "two-ness": "It is a peculiar sensation, this double consciousness, this sense of always looking at one's self through the eyes of others, of measuring one's soul by the tape of a world that looks on in amused contempt and pity. One ever feels his two-ness—an American, a Negro; two souls, two thoughts, two unreconciled strivings; two warring ideals in one dark body, whose dogged strength alone keeps it from being torn asunder." Du Bois, *Souls of Black Folk*, 18–19.
39. Hale, *Making Whiteness*, 20.
40. See Woodward, *Origins of the New South*; Rabinowitz, *Race Relations in the Urban South*; Fairclough, *Better Day Coming*; Ayers, *Promise of the New South*; Rabinowitz, *First New South*; and Gilmore, *Gender and Jim Crow*.
41. Rabinowitz, *First New South*, 97–100; Ayers, *Promise of the New South*, 47; Jane Dailey, "The Limits of Liberalism in the New South: The Politics of Race, Sex and Patronage in Virginia, 1789–1883," in *Jumpin' Jim Crow*, ed. Jane Dailey, Glenda Elizabeth Gilmore, and Bryant Simon (Princeton, NJ: Princeton University Press, 2000), 88–114.
42. For an overview of the farmers' movements, see Lawrence Goodwyn, *Democratic Promise* (New York: Oxford University Press, 1976), and Woodward, *Origins of the New South*. See also Fairclough, *Better Day Coming*, 7–8; Ayers, *Promise of the New South*, 210–262.
43. Ayers, *Promise of the New South*, 273–275.
44. Ibid., 150–154; Rabinowitz, *Race Relations in the Urban South*, 289ff.
45. Ayers, *Promise of the New South*, 147; Sitkoff, 6–7.

46. Ayers, *Promise of the New South*, 148; Hahn, *Nation without Borders*, 441; Fairclough, *Better Day Coming*, 6. When the Mississippi constitution of 1890 went into effect, the number of Black voters in the state declined from 190,000 to 8,000. In Louisiana, there were 130,000 registered Black voters in 1896, 1,342 eight years later.
47. Quoted in Ayers, *Promise of the New South*, 140–155, 327.
48. Ibid., 327, 435.
49. Fairclough, *Better Day Coming*, 14; Litwack, *Trouble in Mind*, 105–108, 243–244; Ayers, *Promise of the New South*, 326–327.
50. Cecelski, *Waterman's Song*, 181; Gilmore, *Gender and Jim Crow*, 6–9.
51. Gilmore, *Gender and Jim Crow*, 11–17.
52. Ibid., 62.
53. Ibid., 72–75.
54. Ibid., 76–80; Fairclough, *Better Day Coming*, 7–9; Ayers, *Promise of the New South*, 290–293, 296–297.
55. Gilmore, *Gender and Jim Crow*, 101–103.
56. Ibid., 83–89.
57. Ibid., 88–91.
58. Ibid., 90–92.
59. Ibid., 106–108; Ayers, *Promise of the New South*, 301–302; Fairclough, *Better Day Coming*, 9.
60. Gilmore, *Gender and Jim Crow*, 107–108; Ayers, *Promise of the New South*, 299–304.
61. Gilmore, *Gender and Jim Crow*, 107–109; Ayers, *Promise of the New South*, 301–302.
62. Gilmore, 110–120; Fairclough, *Better Day Coming*, 9–10; Ayers, *Promise of the New South*, 303–304.
63. Gilmore, *Gender and Jim Crow*, 66, 125; Ayers, *Promise of the New South*, 299–300; Hahn, *Nation without Borders*, 441.

CHAPTER 3

1. For an overview of these years, see Rayford Logan, *The Negro in American Life and Thought: The Nadir* (New York: Dial Press, 1954); W. E. B. Du Bois, *The Souls of Black Folk* (Chicago: A. C. McClurg, 1903); David Levering Lewis, *W. E. B. Du Bois: Biography of a Race, 1868–1919* (New York: Owl Books, 1998).
2. Sydney Nathans, *To Free a Family: The Journey of Mary Walker* (Cambridge, MA: Harvard University Press, 2012), 268–270. See also Tera Hunter, *Bound in Wedlock* (Cambridge, MA: Harvard University Press, 2019).

3. "North Carolina Freedmen's Convention, 1866," *Raleigh News and Observer*, October 6, 1866; Ann Pointer, interview by Paul Ortiz, July 22, 1994, Tuskegee, AL.
4. Willie Tims, interview by Paul Ortiz, July 21, 1995, Magnolia, AR.
5. Olivia Cherry, interview by Blair Murphy, August 10, 1995, Hampton, VA; Willie Tims, interview by Paul Ortiz. See also Brenda Armstrong, interview by Theodore Segal, March 3, 2017.
6. Susie Weatherby, interview by Sonya Ramsey and Leslie Brown, June 20, 1993, Halifax County, NC; Ann Pointer, interview by Paul Ortiz, July 22, 1994, Tuskegee, AL.
7. Carol Stack, *All Our Kin* (New York: Harper and Row, 1974); Celestyne Porter, interview by Kisha Turner, August 2, 1995, Matthews County, VA. See also Charles Becton, interview by Theodore Segal, April 19, 2017.
8. Malvin Moore, interview by Charles Houston, June 7, 1994, Pine Bluff, AR; David Matthews, interview by Paul Ortiz, August 5, 1995, Le Flore County, MS; Leonora Bradley, interview by Michelle Mitchell, June 29, 1994.
9. Celestyne Porter, interview, August 2, 1995; Leslie Brown, *Upbuilding Black Durham: Gender, Class and Black Community Development in the Urban South* (Chapel Hill: University of North Carolina Press, 2008).
10. Pauli Murray, *Proud Shoes: The Story of an American Family* (New York: Beacon Press, 1973); see also Pauli Murray, *The Autobiography of a Black Activist, Feminist, Lawyer, Priest and Poet* (Knoxville: University of Tennessee Press, 1989).
11. William Turner, interview by Theodore Segal, March 17, 2017.
12. Du Bois, *Souls of Black Folk*, 140–152.
13. Albert Raboteau, *Canaan Land: A Religious History of African Americans* (New York: Oxford University Press, 1999); Du Bois, *Souls of Black Folk*, 74–81.
14. Leslie Brown, *Upbuilding Black Durham: Gender, Class and Black Community Development in the Jim Crow South* (Chapel Hill: University of North Carolina Press, 2017).
15. "An Address to the White People of North Carolina," Bishop Hood.
16. Timothy B. Tyson and David Cecelski, eds., *Democracy Betrayed: The Wilmington Race Riot* (Chapel Hill: University of North Carolina Press, 1998).
17. Tolbert Chism, interview by Paul Ortiz, July 15, 1995, Youngstown, OH; Anthony Farmer, interview by Sonya Ramsey, June 25, 1993, Danville, VA; William Davis, interview by Doris Dixon and Stacey Scales, August 8, 1995, LeFlore County, MS.

18. Emma Bell, interview by Chris Stewart, July 29, 1993, James City, NC; Theresa Lyons, interview by Leslie Brown, August 16, 1995, Durham, NC; Cleaster Mitchell, interview by Paul Ortiz, July 16, 1995, Blackton, AR.
19. Leamon Dillahunt, interview by Sonya Ramsey, August 7, 1993, New Bern, NC; Wilhemina Baldwin, interview by Paul Ortiz, July 19, 1994, Anderson, SC; Cleaster Mitchell, interview by Ortiz.
20. Theresa Lyon, Anthony Farmer, and Cleaster Mitchell, interviews.
21. Susie Weatherbee and Cleaster Mitchell, interviews.
22. Susie Weatherbee and Cleaster Mitchell, interviews; Zora Neale Hurston, *Their Eyes Were Watching God* (New York: J. B. Lippincott, 1937).
23. Celestyne Porter and Ann Pointer, interviews, July 22, 1994.
24. Booker Federic, interview by Stacey Scales, August 2, 1995, Itta Bena, MS.
25. Celestyne Porter, interview; Dora Dennis, interview by Paul Ortiz, July 19, 1995, Forrest City, AR; Benjamin Nays and Joseph Nicholson, *The Negro's Church* (New York: Institute of Social and Political Research, 1933).
26. Lillian Fenner, interview by Chris Stewart, June 16, 1993, Enfield, NC; Gwendolyne Patterson, interview by Jeanne Lucas, February 10, 2005.
27. Price Davis, interview by Sonya Ramsey, June 16, 1993, Charlotte, NC; Herbert Cappie, interview by Michele Mitchell, July 2, 1994, New Orleans, LA.
28. Gwendolyne Patterson, interview by Jeanne Lucas; Walter Cavers, interview by Karen Ferguson, June 17, 1993, Charlotte, NC; James Hall, interview by Gregory Hunter, July 6, 1994, Sylvester, GA.
29. James Hall, interview by Gregory Hunter, June 17, 1994.

CHAPTER 4

1. Frederick Douglass, *Narrative of the Life of Frederick Douglass* (New York: Dover Publications, 1995), 48–58; see also *The Life and Times of Frederick Douglass* (New York: Random House, 1993).
2. Douglass, *Life and Times of Frederick Douglass*.
3. David Cecelski, *The Waterman's Song: Slavery and Freedom in Maritime North Carolina* (Chapel Hill: University of North Carolina Press, 2003), 181–200.
4. William Childs, interview by Rhonda Mawhood, July 12, 1993, Wilmington, NC.

5. Cleaster Mitchell, interview by Paul Ortiz, July 16, 1995, Brinkley, AR; Celestyne Porter, interview by Kisha Turner, August 2, 1995, Virginia Beach, VA .
6. Ann Pointer, interview by Paul Ortiz, July 22, 1994, Tuskegee, AL; Brenda Armstrong, interview by Theodore Segal, March 3, 2017; Jeanne L., interview by Gerrelyn Patterson, February 10, 2005; Minnie Forte, interview by Gerrelyn Patterson, February 10, 2005.
7. Celestyne Porter, interview; Minnie Forte, interview; essays on Cornelia Bower, Lucey Laney, and Emma J. Wilson, all from *Wikipedia.*
8. Nancy Ann Zrinyl Long, *Mary McLeod Bethune: Her Life and Legacy* (Florida Historical Society, 2019); Aubrey McClusky, *Mary McLeod Bethune: Building a Better World* (Bloomington: Indiana University Press, 1999).
9. Suzie Weatherbee, interview by Sonya Ramsey.
10. Teresa Lyons, interview by Leslie Brown; Ann Pointer, interview; Anne Moody, *Coming of Age in Mississippi* (New York: Doubleday, 1968)
11. James Anderson, *The Education of Blacks in the South: 1860–1935* (Chapel Hill: University of North Carolina Press, 1988),
12. Douglass, *Narrative of the Life.*
13. Anderson, *Education of Blacks in the South.*
14. William E. King, "Charles McIver Fights for the Tarheel Negro's Right to an Education," *North Carolina Historical Review* (July 1964): 360–369
15. Heather Paterson, "James Edward Shephard (1875–1947)," Blackpast.org, July 2, 2008, https://www.blackpast.org/african-american-history/shepard-james-edward-1875-1947/.
16. On Washington and Du Bois, see Louis Harlan, *Booker T. Washington: The Wizard of Tuskegee* (New York: Oxford University Press, 1983); David Levering Lewis, *W.E.B. Du Bois: A Biography* (New York: Holt and Company, 2009); and William H. Chafe, "W. E. B. Du Bois: An Intellectual Biography" (senior thesis, Harvard College, 1962).
17. Harlan, *Booker T. Washington.*
18. Ibid.
19. Lewis, *W. E. B. Du Bois*; Chafe, "W. E. B. Du Bois."
20. Chafe, "W. E. B. Du Bois."
21. Ironically, Du Bois's faith in the idea of the "talented tenth" reflected some of the same flaws as the "Best Man" ideas of Blacks in North Carolina in the 1890s. Just as some Blacks thought that the "best white men" could be depended on to develop a political perspective similar to that of the "best black men," Du Bois hoped that the "talented tenth"

of white people would share the same vision as the "talented tenth" of Black people. Neither set of assumptions proved to be valid.

22. See the discussion of Durham in Chapter 3.
23. Booker Federick, interview by Junius Scales, August 2, 1995, Itta Bena, MS.
24. Booker Federick, interview.
25. "Florida, Duval County Folklore: Negro Songs," box A878, folder "Florida Folklore Lifestyle," WPA Manuscript, Library of Congress.
26. "The Life of a Ship Loader or Puller: Captain's Gun," box 2, file folder 6, Stetson Kennedy Collection, Bureau of Florida Folklife Programs, Florida Folklife Archive, Department of State, Tallahassee, Florida.
27. John Hope Franklin, *Mirror to America: The Autobiography of John Hope Franklin* (New York: Simon and Schuster, 2006).
28. Brown, *Upbuilding Black Durham.*
29. Ibid.; Christina Greene, *Our Separate Ways* (Chapel Hill: University of North Carolina Press, 1989). Greene and Brown were graduate students in the Duke Oral History Program.
30. York Garrett, interview by Kara Miles, June 3, 1993, Durham, NC.

CHAPTER 5

1. *News and Observer* (Raleigh), January 2, 1902; *Morning Post* (Raleigh), January 2, 1902.
2. *Birmingham Wide Awake*, April 14, 1906; National Association of Colored Men, "Address to the United States, 1896," in *A Documentary History of the Negro People in the United States*, ed. Herbert Aptheker, vol. 2, *From the Reconstruction Era to 1910* (New York: Citadel Press, 1964), 766.
3. "W. J. Campbell," *The Indianapolis Freeman*, March 1, 1902.
4. Ibid.
5. Money Allan Kirby, interview by Stacey Scales, July 13, 1995, Magnolia, AR.
6. Editorial, *Southern Christian Recorder*, February 1988; *Gazette* (Raleigh), March 2, 1892; Charles Hunter Papers, Duke University.
7. "The Wilds of Arkansas," *New York Age*, November 28, 1891.
8. "Persistence and Sacrifice" (master's thesis on the Jeanes schools by Joanne Abel, Duke University, 2013).
9. "Cullings for Afro-Americans," *Birmingham Wide Awake*, April 14, 1906.
10. NCP, *Florida Metropolis*, November 11, 1919, November 13, 1919.
11. "The Bloody South," *Indianapolis Freeman*, July 9, 1904; *Houston Daily Post*, March 8, 1904. See also August Meier and Elliott Rudwick,

"The Boycott Movement against Jim Crow Streetcars in the South, 1900–1906," *Journal of American History* LV (March 1969): 756–775; and Jennifer Roback, "The Political Economy of Segregation: The Case of Segregated Streetcars," *Journal of Economic History* XLVI (December 1986): 893–917.

12. John E. Hartridge to William H. Tucker, May 28, 1905, box 41, folder 1845, George Baldwin Papers; "Negroes Continue to Boycott Street Cars," *Pensacola Journal*, May 20, 1905.
13. "Negroes Continue to Boycott Street Cars," *Pensacola Journal*, May 20, 1905.
14. "Race Gleanings," *Wide Awake, I*, December 7, 1905.
15. *Montgomery Advertiser*, September 12, 1912; "Forced to Give Up Seat to White Woman," *Atlanta Constitution*, July 1917; "Negroes Stone Motor 'Jim Crow,' Law on East End Car," *Statesman* (Austin), March 1920.
16. "New Method Adopted for Securing Labor," *Montgomery Advertiser*, April 6, 1912.
17. *Indianapolis Freeman*, March 8, 1902; Charles Hunter Papers.
18. E. Merton Coulter, *James Monroe Smith: Georgia Planter, Before Death and After* (Atlanta: University of Georgia Press, 1961), 41, 49
19. "Mr. Flanagan Talks of Black Belt Problem," *Montgomery Advertiser*, January 31, 1911.
20. "Great God! What Is This? How Long, O Lord?," *Southern Ploughman*, December 16, 1911; "What Lynching Means in the South," *News and Observer* (Raleigh), February 5, 1922.
21. "Meant Business," *Richmond Planet*, June 1, 1895; "Sympathy for the Oppressed," *Richmond Planet*, September 7, 1895.
22. *Richmond Planet*, November 2, 1895, and May 15, 1897.
23. "Killed in Race War," *Tuskegee Institute News Clipping File*, reel 1, frame 11; "A Clash of Races," *Jasper News*, April 4, 1902.
24. Raymond Gavins, "North Carolina Black Folklore and Song in the Age of Segregation: Toward Another Meaning of Survival," *North Carolina Historical Review* LXVI (October 1989): 412–442; Philip S. Foner, ed., *Paul Robeson Speaks: Writing, Speeches, Interviews, 1918–1974* (New York: Citadel Press Book, 1978), 215–216. Gavins notes that "[o]rdinary men and women have played a crucial role in finding ways to preserve black self-esteem and solidarity. But historians generally ignore them or obscure their point of view." Gavins, 415.
25. James Weldon Johnson, ed., *The Book of American Negro Spirituals* (New York: Viking Press, 1925), 32.

26. "Alachua County Work Songs, box A878, folder, "Florida Folklore, Songs, Ballads & Rhymes," WPA Manuscript, Library of Congress; "I'm Goin to Georgy," file folder 13: "Black Songs," Stetson Kennedy Collection, Bureau of Florida Folklife Programs, Florida Folklife Archives, Florida State Archives, Department of State, Tallahassee, Florida; Foner, *Paul Robeson Speaks*, 216.
27. James Eaves, interview by Alex Byrd, July 26, 1995, White Plains, KY.
28. "Lexington Conference," *Southwestern Christian Advocate*, February 7, 1895.
29. *News and Observer* (Raleigh), August 27, August 29, September 30, 1903.
30. "Cullings for Afro-Americans," *Birmingham Wide Awake*, May 6, 1906.
31. Peter Wood, *The Black Majority* (New York: Knopf, 1975), 285.
32. Henry Hooten, interview by Paul Otiz, July 11, 1994, Tuskegee, AL.

CHAPTER 6

1. David Levering Lewis, *W.E.B. Du Bois: Biography of a Race, 1868–1919* (New York: Henry Holt, 1993), 578.
2. "Negroes Not Pleased When Board Rejects," *State* (Columbia, SC), August 9, 1917; "Negro Registration Exceeds That of the Whites in Many Sections of the South," *New York Age*, June 14, 1917; "Sent Colored Citizens Instead," *Afro-American*, May 23, 1919; "Jacksonville Has Big Registration," *Associated Press*, June 5, 1917.
3. John Hope Franklin estimated that "[a]pproximately 31 percent of the Negroes who registered [for the draft] were accepted, while 26 percent of the whites who registered were accepted. This was due not to the superior physical and mental qualifications of Negroes, but to the inclination of some draft boards to discriminate against Negroes in the matter of exemptions." John Hope Franklin, *From Slaver to Freedom* (New York: Knopf, 1947), 457.
4. General Pershing, the Commander of American Expeditionary Forces in Europe, observed, "In modern warfare the organization of services of supply has acquired an importance it never had before," *New York Times*, October 29, 1921; W. E. B. Du Bois, "An Essay Toward a History of the Black Man in the Great War," *The Crisis* (June 1919), 65.
5. "Soldiers Experience Overseas," NCP, *Florida Metropolis*, April 4, 1919.
6. Du Bois, "Soldiers," *The Crisis* (November 1918), 8.
7. Emmett Scott, *The American Negro in the World War* (Washington, DC: The Negro Historical Publishing Company, 1919), 135–139.

8. Ibid., 231–238; Du Bois, "The Black Man in the Revolution of 1914–1918," *The Crisis* (March 1919), 22. Eighty-nine enlisted soldiers from the 371st were awarded the *Croix de Guerre*.
9. "Soldier's Letter to Mother," NCP, *Florida Metropolis*, November 28, 1918.
10. "'Yellow-Faced Coon' Says Tampa Paper," *Afro-American* (Baltimore), June 6, 1919. See also "Georgia to Deny Soldiers a Vote," *Chicago Defender*, August 28, 1920.
11. Ira Berlin, *The Making of Africa-America* (New York: Penguin Books, 1910), 154; Wikipedia, "Great Migration (African American)," August 26, 2019.
12. Paul Ortiz, *Emancipation Betrayed* (Berkeley: University of California Press, 2005), 134.
13. "Rich Whites, No Friends: Urban League Secretary Says Capital Always Exploited Colored Labor," *Afro-American*, April 11, 1919.
14. For details on the confrontation, see "Colored Citizens Resent School Board Methods," in *Norfolk Journal and Guide*, November 30, 1918; "Slapping Teacher Arouses Wilson," *Afro-American*, May 3, 1918; "Eleven Techers Out Their Jobs at Wilson," *Greensboro News,* April 12, 1918; Matthew Davis, interview by Paul Ortiz, July 5, 1995, Memphis, TN .
15. "Jacksonville Has Big Registration," *Associated Press*, June 5, 1919.
16. "White Assailant of Negro Gets Beating," *Birmingham Reporter*, April 6, 1918; "Reverend Dr. Bray Still Getting Endorsements," and "Endorsed by the African American Episcopal Ministers Union," *Birmingham Reporter*, April 20, 1919. See also "Offensiveness of Birmingham Conductors," *Birmingham Reporter*, March 30, 1918.
17. James Weldon Johnson, *Along This Way* (New York: Viking Press, 1933), 315.
18. Cameron McWhirter, *Red Summer: The Summer of 1919 and the Awakening of Black America* (New York: Macmillan, 2012); Elliott Rudwick, *Race Riot in East St. Louis* (Bloomington: University of Illinois Press, 1964); William Tuttle, *Race Riot: Chicago in the Red Summer of 1919* (Bloomington: University of Illinois Press, 1964).
19. On Tulsa, see Scott Ellsworth, *Death in a Promised Land: The Tulsa Race Riot of 1921* (Baton Rouge: Louisiana State University Press, 1982); Ellsworth, *The Ground Breaking: The Tulsa Race Riot and the American Search for Justice* (New York: Penguin Press, 2021). See Rudwick, *Race Riot in East St. Louis*; Tuttle, *Race Riot*, on the Chicago Race Riot; and Ortiz, *Emancipation Betrayed*, on Florida's race riots.
20. Rudwick, *Race Riot in East St. Louis*, 13–14.

21. Josh Gregory, *World War I* (New York: Scholastic Library Publishing, 2012), 47.
22. Ortiz, *Emancipation Betrayed*, 214.
23. Rudwick, *Race Riot in East St. Louis*, 13–14; Gregory, *World War I*,47.
24. Rudwick, *Race Riot in East St. Louis*, 19.
25. *Afro-American*, August 2, 1918.
26. Tuttle, *Race Riot in East St. Louis*, 13.
27. Ellsworth, *Death in a Promised Land*; Rudwick, *Race Riot in East St. Louis*, 19.

CHAPTER 7

1. Theodore Rosengarten, *All God's Dangers: The Life of Nate Shaw* (New York: Knopf, 1974); James Hall, interview by Gregory Hunter, June 17, 1994, Sylvester, GA.
2. Harvard Sitkoff, *A New Deal for Blacks* (New York: Oxford University Press, 1981), 8.
3. See Joanne Abels, "Persistence and Sacrifice" (master's thesis on the Jeanes schools, Duke University, 2013).
4. W. E. B. Du Bois, editorial in the NAACP magazine, *The Crisis* (June 1919), 65.
5. Robert Durden, *The Dukes of Durham, 1865–1929* (Durham, NC: Duke University Press, 1987); John Egerton, *Speak Now against the Day* (Chapel Hill: University of North Carolina Press, 1996), 19; York Garrett, interview by Kara Miles, June 3, 1993, Pineland, SC.
6. Egerton, *Speak Now against the Day*, 50.
7. Ibid., 50–60; and Howard Fitts, interview by Paul Ortiz, June 8, 1994, Durham, NC; and Money Allen Kirby, interview by Paul Ortiz and Stacey Scales, July 13, 1995, Wilmington, NC.
8. Egerton, *Speak Now against the Day*, 19, 50.
9. See Howard Fitts and Money Allen Kirby, interviews by Ortiz.
10. The rapid decline in cotton juice prices from World War I coincided with a diminishing market during the 1920s, and then the horrific onset of the Great Depression.
11. Blanche Davis, interview by Tywanna Whorley and Stacey Scales, June 28, 1994 in Birmingham, AL; and Stephen Best, interview by Sonya Ramsey on August 7, 1993 in New Bern, NC.
12. Arnette Davis, interview, August 8, 1995.
13. Blanche Davis, Stephen Best, Josephine McCray, and Arnette Davis, interviews.

14. Blanche Davis, interview.
15. Sitkoff, *New Deal for Blacks*, 32, 211; William Earl Davis, interview by Doris Dixon and Stacey Scales on August 8, 1995, in Indianola, MS.
16. Thomas Sugrue, *Sweet Land of Liberty: The Forgotten Struggle for Civil Rights* (New York: Random House, 2008), 462; Blanche Davis, interview.
17. Sitkoff, *New Deal for Blacks*, 32, 211.
18. Ibid., 32–40.
19. Ibid., 40.
20. Ibid., 38.
21. Sugrue, *Sweet Land of Liberty*, 20, 52; Sitkoff, *New Deal for Blacks*, 30, 40.
22. Sitkoff, *New Deal for Blacks*, 38, 40.
23. Egerton, *Speak Now against the Day*, 89–95; Sugrue, *Sweet Land of Liberty*, 51; Sitkoff, *New Deal for Blacks*, 50–53.
24. Egerton, *Speak Now against the Day*, 95–102; Sitkoff, *New Deal for Blacks*, 55–57.
25. Sitkoff, *New Deal for Blacks*, 50–59.
26. See ibid. on Parren, Ickes, and Foreman.
27. On Eleanor Roosevelt and Mme. Souvestre, see David Michaelis, *Eleanor Roosevelt* (New York: Simon and Schuster, 2020); and William Chafe, "Eleanor Roosevelt," in *Notable American Women* (Cambridge, MA: Harvard University Press, 2004).
28. Egerton, *Speak Now against the Day*, 187–197.
29. Chafe, "Eleanor Roosevelt."
30. Sugrue, *Sweet Land of Liberty*, 33, 51.
31. Chafe, "Eleanor Roosevelt."
32. Cleaster Mitchell, interview.
33. Egerton, *Speak Now against the Day*, 186–202.
34. Geoffrey Ward, 1, 10–14.

CHAPTER 8

1. See August Meier and Elliott Rudwick, *Black Detroit and the Rise of the* UAEW (New York: Oxford University Press, 1965); Robert H. Zieger, *The CIO: 1935–1955* (Chapel Hill: University of North Carolina Press, 1995); Walter Galenson, *The CIO Challenge to the AFL: A History of the American Labor Movement* (Cambridge, MA: Harvard University Press, 1994); William E. Leuchtenburg, *FDR and the New Deal* (New York: Harper and Row, 1964); Sydney Fine, *Sit-Down: The General Motors Strike of 1936–1927* (Ann Arbor: University of Michigan Press, 1969).

2. Thomas Sugrue, *Sweet Land of Liberty: The Forgotten Struggle for Civil Rights* (New York: Random House, 2008), 47.
3. John Egerton, *Speak Now against the Day: The Generation before the Civil Rights Movement in the South* (New York: Knopf, 1994), 214–217.
4. Ibid.; and Cornelius L. Bynum, *A. Philip Randolph and the Struggle for Civil Rights* (Urbana: University of Chicago Press, 2010).
5. "Women Workers in Ten Production Areas," *Women's Bureau Bulletin* No. 206 (Washington, DC, 1946), 3–4, 7; "Report of Conference on Women in War Industries," folder entitled "Conferences, Women's Bureau, General, 1943," WBA, Accession No. 58A-850, container 3.
6. Sugrue, *Sweet Land of Liberty*, 77; Ira Berlin, *The Making of Africa-America* (New York: Penguin Book, 2010), 154–155, 165–167, 187–189.
7. Charles Lewis, interview by Doris Dixon, June 29, 1995. Memphis, TN; Florence Borders, interview by Kate Ellis and Michelle Michell, July 5, 1994, New Iberia, LA.
8. Florence Borders, interview; Charles Lewis, interview.
9. Geoffrey Ward and Ken Burns, *The War: An Intimate History* (New York: Knopf, 2007), 48–50
10. Charles Lewis, interview; William Zapherin, interview by Felix Armfeld, June 30, 1994, Loreauville, LA.
11. Edran Auguster, interview by Michele Mitchell, July 19, 1994, New Iberia, LA.
12. Lovie Mae Griffin, interview by Laurie Green, August 15, 1995, Memphis, TN; Howard Fitts interview by Paul Ortiz.
13. Howard Fitts, interview; Charles Lewis, interview.
14. Howard Fitts, interview; Charles Lewis, interview.
15. Howard Fitts, interview; Jason Sokol, *There Goes My Everything: White Southerners in the Age of Civil Rights, 1945–1975* (New York: Knopf, 2007), 19.
16. William Chafe, *The Unfinished Journey: America Since World War II* (New York: Oxford University Press, 2022), 16–18.
17. Ibid., 15–16.
18. Barbara Ransby, *Ella Baker and the Black Freedom Movement* (Chapel Hill: University of North Carolina Press, 2003); Robert Korstad, *Civil Rights Unionism* (Chapel Hill: University of North Carolina Press, 1999), 188, 255–259; Ward, *Defending White Democracy*, 38.
19. Sugrue, *Sweet Land of Liberty*, 74.
20. Egerton, *Speak Now against the Day*, 305–320.
21. Ibid., 242, 254–256, 265, 271, 274, 278–282.
22. Harvey Johnson, interview by Blair Murphy.

23. Dominic Capeci, *Race Relations in Wartime Detroit: The Sojourner Truth Housing Controversy of 1942* (Philadelphia:Temple University Press, 1984).
24. Harvard Sitkoff, "The Detroit Race Riot, 1943," *Michigan History* 53 (May 1969): 183–206; Domenic Capeci Jr. and Martha Wilkerson, *Layered Violence: The Detroit Rioters of 1943* (Jackson: University of Mississippi Press, 1991).
25. Howard Fitts interview; Charles Lewis interview; William Chism interview, with Paul Ortiz, July 15, 1995, Youngstown, OH.
26. Emmett Cheri, interview by Kate Ellis, June 23, 1994, New Orleans, LA; Clarence Marable, interview by Paul Ortiz, July 14, 1994, Tuskegee, AL; Charles Lewis, interview.
27. Cheri interview.
28. Korstad, *Civil Rights Unionism*, 306–310; Chafe, *Civilities*, 15–56.
29. Ward, 42, 67, 93; Egerton, 363; Gail Williams O'Brien, *The Color of the Law: Race, Violence and Justice in the ZPost World War II South* (Nashville: Tennessee Historical Society, 1999); Chafe, *Unfinished Journey*, 80–82.
30. Charles Lewis interview; Howard Fitts interview; William Chism interview.

CHAPTER 9

1. John Egerton, *Speak Now against the Day: The Generation before the Civil Rights Movement in the South* (Chapel Hill: University of North Carolina Press, 1995), 9–12.
2. For an overview of Truman and civil rights, see William Berman, *The Politics of Civil Rights in the Truman Administration* (Columbus: Ohio State University Press, 1970); Steven Lawson, *Black Ballots: Voting Rights in the South, 1944–69* (New York: Columbia University Press, 1976); Michael Gardner, *Harry Truman and Civil Rights: Moral Courage and Political Risks* (Carbondale: Southern Illinois University Press, 2012); and Robert Shogan, *Harry Truman and the Struggle for Racial Justice* (Boston: Barnes and Noble, 2013). See also Egerton, *Speak Now against the Day*, 411. The best single-volume biography of Truman is Alonzo L. Hamby, *Man of the People: A Life of Harry S. Truman* (New York: Oxford University Press, 1995), see especially 272, 364–366, 433–435.
3. Hamby, *Man of the People*, 365, 443; Egerton, *Speak Now against the Day*, 353–365, 393.
4. Hamby, *Man of the People*, 366, 433; Egerton, *Speak Now against the Day*, 415. The Supreme Court case was *Shelley v. Kraemer.*
5. Egerton, *Speak Now against the Day*, 517–518.

6. Ibid., 412–414 .
7. "Civil Rights in America: Racial Voting Rights," *A National Historic Landmark Theme Study*, 25–30.
8. Melvyn Dubofsky, *The State and Labor in Modern America* (Chapel Hill: University of North Carolina Press, 1994); Robert Korstad, *Civil Rights Unionism* (Chapel Hill: University of North Carolina Press, 1999), 307, 405.
9. Korstad, *Civil Rights Unionism*, 124–125, 234–238, 265–275, 335–336.
10. Thomas Sugrue, *Sweet Land of Liberty: The Forgotten Struggle for Civil Rights* (New York: Random House, 2008), 102–106.
11. Gober was a student at Albany State College when she became involved with SNCC through the recruitment efforts of Cordell Reagan and Charles Sherrod. She soon became a freedom singer. For more information, see Clayborne Carson, *In Struggle: SNCC and the Black Awakening in the 1960s* (Cambridge, MA: Harvard University Press, 1981); and Charles Cobb, *On the Road to Freedom* (Chapel Hill: Algonquin Books, 2008).
12. For a full accounting of Ella Baker's pivotal role in creating and sustaining the civil rights movement, see Barbara Ransby, *Ella Baker and the Black Freedom Movement* (Chapel Hill: University of North Carolina Press, 2003); Ella Baker, interview by William Chafe, Duke University, Chafe papers.
13. Richard Kluger, *Simple Justice: The History of Brown v Board of Education and Black America's Struggle for Equality* (New York: Knopf, 1976), 1–10.
14. Carson, *In Struggle*, 26, 46.
15. Kluger, *Simple Justice*, chap. 13.
16. Kluger, *Simple Justice,* chap. 14–17.
17. Ibid., chap. 18; and James Patterson, *Brown v. Board of Education* (Boston: Barnes and Noble, 2001).
18. Kluger, *Simple Justice*, chap. 19; Patterson, *Brown v. Board of Education.*
19. Kluger, *Simple Justice*, chap. 22–24; Patterson, *Brown v. Board of Education*; Ed Cray, *Chief Justice* (New York: Simon and Schuster, 2008); Bob Woodward and Scott Armstrong, *The Brethren: Inside the Supreme Court* (New York: Simon and Schuster, 2005); Jim Newton, *Justice for All: Earl Warren and the Nation He Made* (New York: Penguin, 2007).
20. Egerton, *Speak Now against the Day*, 338; Jason Sokol, *There Goes My Everything: White Southerners in the Age of Civil Rights, 1945–75* (New York: Random House, 2007), 50.
21. For a detailed discussion of the response to *Brown*, see Kluger, *Simple Justice.*

22. On Eisenhower's response to *Brown* and to Faubus, see Kluger, *Simple Justice*.
23. Egerton, *Speak Now against the Day*, 609.
24. "The Segregation Problem. . . . A Summary of Statements," *Daily News* (Greensboro), April 1–30, July 13, 1955; statement by Luther Hodges, July 17, 19, 1955; statements by Luther Hodges, July 17, 19, 1955, all in the Luther Hodges Papers, North Carolina Historical Society.
25. For a full discussion of Frankfurter's role, see Kluger, *Simple Justice*, 679–691, 698–700.
26. See Timothy Tyson, *The Blood of Emmett Till* (New York: Simon and Schuster, 201). Tyson interviewed the woman who denied she had ever accused Till of inappropriate advances toward her. Tyson won the Robert F. Kennedy Book Award for his work.
27. Danielle McGuire, *At the Dark End of the Street: A New History of the Civil Rights Movement from Rosa Parks to the Rise of Black Power* (Boston: Barnes and Noble, 2010), 3–23, 58–65.
28. Ibid., 93–131, 212–245.
29. McGuire, *At the Dark End of the Street.*
30. Laurie Dixie, interview by Paul Ortiz, August 9, 1994, Tallahassee, FL.

CHAPTER 10

1. *Record* (Greensboro), February 2–9, 1960; *News and Observer* (Raleigh), February 3–9; *New York Times*, February 2, 1960; Miles Wolff, *Lunch at the Five and Ten* (New York: Stein and Day, 1970) provides a chronological narrative of the sit-ins.
2. Ezell Blair Jr., Mr. and Mrs. Ezell Blair Sr., David Richmond, Joseph McNeill, Franklin McCain, Vance Chavis, Nell Coley, interviews by William Chafe, Chafe Papers, Duke University.
3. Vance Chavis, interview. On the Pearsall Plan, see statement by Luther Hodges, July 17, 19[AU: Missing complete year, please correct], in the Luther Hodges papers, North Carolina State Archives, and the Greensboro *Daily News*, July 13, 18, 19, and 20, 1955. In a letter to Hodges on July 19, 1955, Eugene Hood, a leader of North Carolina's White Citizens Council, praised him for attacking the NAACP.
4. Ezell Blair Jr. and Franklin McCain, interviews.
5. Nell Coley, interview.
6. Cleveland Sellers, interview.
7. Barbara Ransby, *Ella Baker and the Black Freedom Movement* (Chapel Hill: University of North Carolina Press, 2003); Ella Baker, interview.

8. Ransby, *Ella Baker and the Black Freedom Movement*; Clayborne Carson, *In Struggle: SNCC and the Black Awakening of the 1960s* (Boston: Barnes and Noble, 1981); Robert Moses, interview by William Chafe.
9. Robert Moses, interview.
10. Carson, *In Struggle*, 31–38.
11. Ibid., 31–38, 43–45.
12. Howard Zinn, *SNCC: The New Abolitionists* (Boston: Haymarket Books, 1964), 108–109.
13. On Robert F. Kennedy and civil rights, see Patricia Sullivan, *Justice Rising: America in Black and White* (Cambridge, MA: Harvard University Press, 1971); Gordon Mantler, *Power to the Poor* (Chapel Hill: University of North Carolina Press, 2013); and Larry Tye, *Bobby Kennedy: The Making of a Liberal Icon* (New York: Random House, 2017).
14. Carson, *In Struggle*, 73–74, 123–126.
15. Taylor Branch, *Parting the Waters: America in the King Years* (New York: Simon and Schuster, 1988), 524–528; "Albany Movement Formed," *SNCC Digital Gateway*, Duke University Archives.
16. Branch, *Parting the Waters*, 526–530.
17. "Albany Movement Formed," *SNCC Digital Gateway*.
18. Branch, *Parting the Waters*, 570–573, 683–684, 793–802; for a detailed discussion of the complexities surrounding the Birmingham campaign, see Dianne McWhorter, *Carry Me Home: Birmingham, Alabama: The Climactic Battle of the Civil Rights Revolution* (New York: Simon and Schuster, 2002).
19. Branch, *Parting the Waters*, 775–788.
20. Jason Sokol, *There Goes My Everything: White Southerners in the Age of Civil Rights, 1945–1975* (New York: Knopf, 2007), 105; Branch, *Parting the Waters*, 602, 737–746, 875.
21. Branch, *Parting the Waters*, 822–824.
22. Ibid., 208–210.

CHAPTER 11

1. For a historians' summary of the March, see Thomas Sugrue, *Sweet Land of Liberty: The Forgotten Struggle for Civil Rights* (New York: Random House, 2008), 287, 326; see also *New York Times*, August 29–30, 1963.
2. See Barbara Ransby, *Ella Baker and the Black Freedom Movement* (Chapel Hill: University of North Carolina Press, 2003), 4, 10, 35, 139, 170–195, 209–238.

3. On SCLC, see Adam Fairclough, *To Redeem the Soul of America: The Southern Christian Leadership Conference and Martin Luther King, Jr.* (Athens: University of Georgia Press, 1987); David Garrow, *Bearing the Cross: Martin Luther King, Jr. and the Southern Christian Leadership Conference*. On SNCC, see Clayborne Carson, *In Struggle: SNCC and the Black Awakening of the 1960s* (Cambridge: Harvard University Press, 1981). See also Courtland Cox, Robert Moses, Charles Cobb, and Fannie Lou Hamer, interviews with William Chafe, Chafe Papers, Duke University.
4. Clayborne Carson, *In Struggle*, 73–74; Sugrue, *Sweet Land of Liberty*, 357.
5. William H. Chafe, *Never Stop Running: Allard Lowenstein and the Struggle to Save American Liberalism* (New York: Basic Books, 1993), 166–210; Carson, *In Struggle*, 96–132.
6. Carson, *In Struggle*, 111–129.
7. Ibid., 119–129.
8. Ibid., 141–149; Laura Visser-Maessen, *Robert Parris Moses: A Life in Civil Rights and Leadership at the Grass Roots* (Chapel Hill: University of North Carolina Press, 2016).
9. Visser-Maessen, *Robert Parris Moses*; Carson, *In Struggle*, 149–151, 173, 232–233.
10. Carson, *In Struggle*, 149–151, 173, 232–233; Robert Caro, *The Passage of Power: The Years of Lyndon Johnson* (New York: Knopf, 2012).
11. Robert Dallek, *Flawed Giant: Lyndon Johnson and His Times* (New York: Oxford University Press, 1998), 162–165, especially 163; Carson, *In Struggle*, 191–211.
12. Dallek, *Flawed Giant*, 212–219, 222.
13. John Dittmer, *Local People: The Struggle for Civil Rights in Mississippi* (Champaign: University of Illinois Press, 1995), 205; Michael Paul Sistrom, "The Authors of Liberation: The Mississippi Freedom Democrats and the Redefinition of Politics" (Ph.D. dissertation, University of North Carolina, 2002), 124, 135, 154, 169, 175–176, 184–186; Arnold A. Offner, *Hubert Humphrey: The Conscience of the Country* (New Haven, CT: Yale University Press, 2018), 298–302; Carson, *In Struggle*, 157–162.
14. See Hasan Jeffries, *Bloody Lowndes: Civil Rights in Alabama's Black Belt* (New York: New York University Press, 2010); Carson, *In Struggle*, 215–242.
15. Carson, *In Struggle*, 149–151, 232–233.
16. Ibid., 201; Visser-Maessen, *Robert Parris Moses*.

17. Karlyn Forner, *Why the Vote Wasn't Enough for Selma* (Durham, NC: Duke University Press, 2017), 152–191; Taylor Branch, *Pillar of Fire* (New York: Simon and Schuster, 1998).
18. Courtland Cox and Charlie Cobb, interviews by William Chafe, Chafe papers.
19. Peniel Joseph, *Dark Days, Bright Nights: From Black Power to Barack Obama* (New York: Basic Books, 2013), 2–13, 35–106. In early 2023, speculation increased that the FBI and other federal agents were part of the conspiracy to murder Malcolm.

CHAPTER 12

1. For a discussion of SCLC and SNCC during this period, see David Garrow, *Bearing the Cross: Martin Luther King, Jr. and the Southern Christian Leadership Conference* (New York: William Morrow and Companu, 2004); and Clayborne Carson, *In Struggle: SNCC and the Black Awakening of the 1960s* (Cambridge: Harvard University Press, 1995).
2. Memorandum from a white Northern volunteer from New York who joined the Northern Student Movement on a ten-day trip to Montgomery to lay the groundwork for lodging and food supplies for the march from Selma.
3. Clayborne Carson, *In Struggle*: *SNCC and the Black Awakening in the 1960s* (Cambridge, MA: Harvard University Press, 1981), 127–129, 209–211, 215–228, 233–242.
4. Carol Anderson, *White Rage*: *TheUnspoken Truth of our Racial Divide* (New York: Bloomsbury Press, 2017), 104.
5. On Black migration to the North, see Isabel Wilkerson, *The Warmth of Other Suns: The Epic Story of the Great Migration* (New York: Vintage Books, 2011); and Nicholas Lemann, *The Promised Land: The Great Migration* (New York: Vintage Books, 1992).
6. Carol Anderson, *White Rage*, 101, 118–120; Thomas Sugrue, *Sweet Land of Liberty: The Forgotten Struggle for Civil Rights* (New York: Random House, 2008), 526–528.
7. Sugrue, *Sweet Land of Liberty*, 505, 440–409.
8. For a discussion of white response to these developments, see Alan B. Murray, *Coming Apart: The State of White America, 1960–2010* (New York: Crown Forum, 2012).
9. Sugrue, *Sweet Land of Liberty*, 539.
10. Steven M. Gillon, *Separate and Unequal: The Kerner Commission and the Unraveling of American Liberalism* (New York: Basic Books, 2018).

CHAPTER 13

1. John Dittmer, *Local People: The Struggle for Civil Rights in Mississippi* (Chicago: University of Illinois Press, 1994); *New York Times,* May 18, 1981.
2. For an analysis of King's and Kennedy's commitment to economic change for the poor, see Gordon Mantler, *Power to the Poor: Black-Brown Coalition and the Fight for Economic Justice, 1960–1974* (Chapel Hill: University of North Carolina Press, 2013). For a compelling assessment of how economic inequality has continued to obstruct the achievement of racial equality, see William A. Darity, Jr. and A. Kirsten Mullen, *From Here to Equality: Reparations for Black Americans in the Twenty-First Century* (Chapel Hill: UNC Press, 2022).
3. Lindsay Mishie Eads, *The End of Apartheid in South Africa* (Capetown: APC-CIO, LLC, 1999).
4. Angie Maxwell and Todd Shields, *The Long Southern Strategy* (New York: Oxford University Press, 1999).
5. Carol Anderson, *White Rage: The Unspoken Truth of Our Racial Divide* (New York: Bloomsbury, 2017) 104.
6. Prince Williams, "The FBI and the Killing of Fred Hampton, *Harvard Political Review* (October 15, 2021); Chafe, *Civilities*, 247.
7. Carol Anderson, *White Rage*, 101, 118–120; Thomas Sugrue, *Sweet Land of Liberty: The Forgotten Struggle for Civil Rights* (New York: Random House, 2008), 526–528.
8. Sugrue, *Sweet Land of Liberty*, 440–490, 505.
9. Chafe, *Bill and Hillary*, 259–267.
10. Sugrue, *Sweet Land of Liberty*, 539.
11. Berlin, *Making of Africa-America*, 202.
12. Timothy Shenk, "A Lost Manuscript Shows the Fire Barack Obama Couldn't Reveal on the Campaign Trail," *New York Times*, October 7, 2022.
13. C. Anderson, *White Rage*, 138–140.
14. Devon Johnson and Amy Farrell, eds., *Deadly Injustices: Trayvon Martin, Race and the Criminal Justice System* (New York: New York University Press, 2015); and Jim Salter and the Associated Press, *Deadly Force, Fatal Confrontations with the Police.*
15. www.pewresearch.org, "Incarceration Gap Widens between Whites and Blacks."
16. C. Anderson, *White Rage*, 135; Michelle Alexander, *The New Jim Crow* (New York: New Press, 2012), 2–4, 7–9, 11–12, 185–187.

17. Alexander, *New Jim Crow*, 185–187.
18. Ibid., 158–161.
19. C. Anderson, *White Rage*, 165–168.
20. Sugrue, *Sweet Land of Liberty*, 501–505; C. Anderson, *White Rage*, 108.
21. Sugrue, *Sweet Land of Liberty*, 194, 195, 514–520; C. Anderson, *White Rage*, 97, 122.
22. Ira Berlin, *The Making of Africa-America* (New York: Penguin Books, 1910), 196; Sugrue, *Sweet Land of Liberty*, 535.

Index

For the benefit of digital users, indexed terms that span two pages (e.g., 52–53) may, on occasion, appear on only one of those pages.